LAW AS A MORAL IDEA

Law as a Moral Idea

N.E. SIMMONDS

OXFORD
UNIVERSITY PRESS

OXFORD
UNIVERSITY PRESS

Great Clarendon Street, Oxford OX2 6DP

Oxford University Press is a department of the University of Oxford.
It furthers the University's objective of excellence in research, scholarship,
and education by publishing worldwide in

Oxford   New York

Auckland   Cape Town   Dar es Salaam   Hong Kong   Karachi
Kuala Lumpur   Madrid   Melbourne   Mexico City   Nairobi
New Delhi   Shanghai   Taipei   Toronto

With offices in

Argentina   Austria   Brazil   Chile   Czech Republic   France   Greece
Guatemala   Hungary   Italy   Japan   Poland   Portugal   Singapore
South Korea   Switzerland   Thailand   Turkey   Ukraine   Vietnam

Oxford is a registered trade mark of Oxford University Press
in the UK and in certain other countries

Published in the United States
by Oxford University Press Inc., New York

British Library Cataloguing in Publication Data

Data available

Library of Congress Cataloging in Publication Data

Data available

Typeset by Newgen Imaging Systems (P) Ltd., Chennai, India
Printed in Great Britain
on acid-free paper by
Biddles Ltd., King's Lynn

ISBN 978–0–19–927646–2

1 3 5 7 9 10 8 6 4 2

Preface

The completion of this book was made possible by the award of a Leverhulme Research Fellowship for one term in the spring of 2006. I am most grateful to the Leverhulme Trustees for their invaluable support.

The chapters that follow incorporate substantial extracts from four recent essays. I am grateful to the editors of the *University of Toronto Law Journal*, the *Canadian Journal of Law and Jurisprudence*, the *Cambridge Law Journal*, and *Current Legal Problems*, for permission to reuse material in this way.

A number of people have been kind enough to comment on parts of the book, or on the essays that preceded it. My partner June Chappell cast a lawyerly eye over most of the typescript, spotting numerous anomalies and infelicities that I would certainly have missed. I am also indebted to Trevor Allan, Mátyás Bódig, Raymond Plant, Jerry Postema, Amanda Perreau-Saussine and Veronica Rodriguez-Blanco. A more intelligent author could perhaps have accommodated their various criticisms and insights, to the considerable improvement of the book's argument. This author, however, has had to rest content with the imperfect pages that now lie before the reader.

N.E. Simmonds

Contents

Table of Contents

1

Jurisprudence and the Nature of Law

Jurisprudence has a dual status. On the one hand, it is a tradition of philosophical inquiry that is centrally concerned with the nature of law and justice. On the other, it is an integral part of developed legal systems, shaping the forms of doctrinal reasoning that characterize such systems and articulating the presuppositions on which those forms of reasoning rest. Understanding how this dual status is possible (how jurisprudence can be both a reflection upon law's nature and itself a part of the phenomenon of governance by law) requires us to understand the nature of law. Consequently, jurisprudence can fully understand its own status only when it has solved its central problem, by answering the question 'what is law?' Jurisprudence reveals the reflexivity of legal thought: the sense in which law is always 'in quest of itself'.[1]

It is perhaps not hard to understand how justice comes to be a subject for philosophy, but the idea of philosophical reflection upon the nature of law may seem less familiar. We think of justice as an ideal standard against which human actions and institutions are to be measured. Such an ideal, we assume, must be distinct from the settled practices on which it is called to adjudicate. Consequently, we find it hard to form a clear conception of the way in which knowledge of that ideal standard might be attained. Plato's image of the philosopher seeking to escape from the cave of conventional understandings may be misleading as well as mysterious, but it is in some respects an appropriate expression of our sense that justice is an ideal that is independent of convention, and our consequent puzzlement as to how we might discover the content of that ideal. It is precisely this sense of puzzlement about what would count as an answer to our question, and how any such answer might be arrived at, that is the hallmark of philosophical inquiry.

We are inclined to think of law in a very different way. For is not law itself a human institution rather than an ideal standard against which our institutions are judged? Is the content of the law not encoded in books, statutes and precedents? Is the existence of law not manifest in the daily actions of judges, lawmakers and policemen? Law seems to be an observable social phenomenon,

---

[1] Lon Fuller, *The Law in Quest of Itself* (Chicago: Foundation Press, 1940).

available for study by social scientists and historians, and by traditional doctrinal legal scholars. How then can the philosopher hope to add to our knowledge of law's nature something that is not obtainable in these more familiar ways? When a philosophical inquiry into justice is proposed, we may have difficulty in imagining the form that such an inquiry would take; but, if the proposed inquiry concerns the nature of *law*, we have difficulty in seeing how any more could be required than the ordinary methods of careful observation and description. When we investigate the ideas of justice, or of reason, we may be anxious to avoid reducing such ideas to the local and variable features of human practice (though unsure *how* to do so). But can there be a problem in treating law as local, variable and dependent upon practice? Is not law precisely a matter of human convention? How can there be any desire, other than a wholly foolish and self-deceiving one, to present the idea of law as an ideal that transcends such variable arrangements?

One large part of the problem of law's nature stems from the fact that law is invoked as a justification for the ordering of sanctions against individual citizens. Judges sentence defendants to prison, or order them to pay damages, because they have broken the law and because the law prescribes that sanction as a consequence of the breach. What must law be that it can, seemingly, possess the power to justify such coercive measures? For an older tradition of philosophical thought about law, preceding the rise of modern analytical jurisprudence, this question provided the core of the inquiry: it was assumed that an understanding of law's nature as a distinctive form of human institution would reveal the basis of its justificatory power. Consequently, the accounts of law's nature that were offered formed an integral part of broader moral and political philosophies, exploring the nature of the human condition and the character and legitimacy of political communities. Some such theories portrayed law as wholly a product of deliberate enactment, beneficially imposing upon us a framework of rules that can rescue us from the mutually destructive anarchy of the state of nature, and binding for that reason. Other theories viewed law as a system of principles, only partly reflected and realized in deliberate enactment, embodying the set of conditions for jointly possible freedoms, or the attainment of the common good. The assumption was that law's binding or justificatory force was intrinsic to its nature, not a result of the variable features of this or that particular legal rule or legal system.

Thus, when Hobbes sets out to explain the nature of law in general, 'as Plato, Aristotle, Cicero and divers others have done',[2] he distinguishes such an account from a description of the content of the law of particular countries. The *content* of the law might be local and variable, he assumes, but its binding

---

[2] Thomas Hobbes, *Leviathan* (1651) Chapter 26.

force is not contingent upon such particular circumstances, being grounded in the very nature of law as such. Similarly, when Kant sets out the conditions which give to the law its binding force, he regards these conditions as 'the basis for any possible giving of positive laws':[3] without such a basis we have, not law, but a simulacrum thereof.

In recent decades it has been assumed that an account of law's nature can and should be separated from any inquiry into law's justificatory force. It is taken as more or less obvious that a theory of the nature of law calls for careful description and conceptual clarification, rather than moral inquiry into questions of legitimacy and justificatory force. The two different types of inquiry are sometimes assigned to quite distinct branches of jurisprudence. On the one hand is 'analytical' jurisprudence, which tries to 'clarify' concepts, including the concept of 'law'. On the other hand is 'normative' jurisprudence which addresses some of the traditional evaluative issues of political philosophy, such as the question of what justice requires, whether there is an obligation to obey the law, the justification of punishment, and so forth. Attention to this distinction between the analytical and the normative enterprises, it is thought, can dissolve many of the traditional problems addressed by the philosophy of law. Thus careful analysis has been undertaken to show that, when judges 'justify' their decisions by reference to the law, the 'justification' involved need not be regarded as any more than a purely technical one: simply a matter of subsuming situations under rules, without regard to the question of whether the application of those rules in that way is morally appropriate or permissible. Similarly, when we speak of laws as conferring rights and imposing duties, we may simply be expressing conclusions about the applicability of the rules without any presupposition as to their morally binding force or the justice that might or might not underpin them. According to a somewhat different view, analysis of the concept of law demonstrates that it is part of law's nature to *claim* justificatory authority; but substantive normative inquiry reveals that law does not in fact possess authority in the way or to the extent that it claims. On either view, the moral justification of the sanction is contingent upon the law's content, and upon all of the circumstances: it is not intrinsic to the character of law itself.

This book is in part an effort to push jurisprudence back towards those more unified models of inquiry that preceded the emergence of so-called 'analytical' jurisprudence as a distinct enterprise, and to re-establish connections with an older tradition of debate in the philosophy of law. This does not imply a rejection of 'analysis', understood as the attempt carefully to distinguish ideas and arguments: anyone who is seriously concerned with any intellectual

---

[3] Immanuel Kant, *Metaphysics of Morals* (1797), translated by Mary J Gregor, *Practical Philosophy: The Cambridge Edition of the Works of Immanuel Kant* (Cambridge: Cambridge University Press, 1996) 6:229.

problem values analysis in that sense. But what it does imply is a rejection of the idea that an 'analysis' of the nature of law can be detached from our moral understanding. 'Law', I will be arguing, is a moral idea; and an inquiry into law's nature therefore requires us to draw upon our moral understanding.

Of course, any effort to reorient inquiry must begin from where the discipline currently stands. Consequently, the main focus of this book will be upon contemporary legal theory, and in particular upon the work of HLA Hart, who played such a large part in establishing the basic categories and assumptions in terms of which jurisprudential debate is now generally constructed. By teasing out and revealing the blind spots within Hart's position, I hope to make a reconsideration of older approaches seem both more pertinent and more inviting. But references to the great works composing the tradition of philosophical thought about law will be few and brief in character. My object is not to change the subject by 'changing the subject', so to speak, but to undermine a current orthodoxy by direct opposition.

While analytical jurisprudence, with its distinctive assumptions, is a relatively recent feature of the intellectual landscape, the nature of law has long represented an intractable philosophical puzzle. The Greek historian Xenophon for example, writing in the fourth century BC, gives us an imaginary dialogue between Pericles and Alcibiades which addresses one aspect of the enigma.[4] Alcibiades begins, seemingly innocently, by asking Pericles what a law is. Pericles tells him that whatever the ruling power enacts is a law, and adds that this is true even if the ruling power is a despot. Alcibiades then asks what force is, for he understands that force is the negation of law, and he takes it that the despot rules by force rather than by persuasion. Seeking to defend the idea that force is indeed the negation of law, Pericles retracts his earlier statement that the decrees of a despot are law, for he concedes that they are based upon force. But Alcibiades then points out that, even where the majority rules, they rule by force rather than by persuasion. His implicit suggestion seems to be that, either law is not simply the enactments of the ruling powers, or the antithesis between law and force is bogus, for law itself seems ultimately to be grounded in force. Pericles reacts with irritation, and describes Alcibiades as engaging in 'clever quibbling'. Most people will at first react in pretty much the same way, feeling confident that a little clear thinking should be enough to dispel the puzzle, while being unwilling to invest time and energy on such an issue. Yet, if they reflect further, they may begin to suspect that Alcibiades has not only identified a genuine problem but a problem that is only one of many interconnected problems concerning the nature of law.

---

[4] The dialogue is conveniently set out in Stanley Paulson's introduction to Hans Kelsen, *Introduction to the Problems of Legal Theory* (1934), translated by BL Paulson and SL Paulson (Oxford: Clarendon Press, 1992) xxii.

We contrast the inquiry into the nature of justice with inquiry into the nature of law because we take justice to be an ideal standard, while law is an observable social phenomenon. Yet is the contrast really so clear? In many contexts, the notions of law and legality can themselves play the role of ideals to which our fallible practices should aspire, and by reference to which they can be criticized. We criticize individuals and governments that act unjustly, but we also criticize those that depart from standards of legality; and sometimes duly enacted laws may themselves be criticized by reference to the idea of 'the rule of law', as when they confer very extensive and uncontrolled discretion upon officials, or when they create very vaguely defined criminal offences. For, like Pericles and Alcibiades, we regard governance by law as itself a moral ideal, representing the very antithesis of force and arbitrary power, even while we are uneasily aware that legal systems can sometimes appear to be no more than complex institutional systems wherein the rule of force is made more perfect, and power more encompassing and systematic.

Is it possible, then, that the idea of law itself represents a moral ideal distinct from that of justice? Perhaps social practices count as instances of law only when they partially embody an idea that they can never fully realize. Perhaps we can never grasp the nature of law by careful description of established practice if our description does not take account of this relationship to the ideal. These are possibilities that we will consider more carefully in the chapters to follow, but they are possibilities that many contemporary legal theorists would reject as sources of confusion rather than insight. They insist that 'law' is not an intrinsically moral idea. Jurisprudential inquiry, according to these theorists, reveals law to be no more than a specific technique of governance that may be employed for good purposes or bad.[5] Law may be employed to do justice and serve the common good, but may equally become an instrument of exploitation and injustice. Consequently, it is argued, the value of law is always contingent upon circumstances, and especially upon the just or unjust content of the law. To treat law as *intrinsically* valuable is to sanctify the products of political power without regard to justice; or it is to treat the term 'law' as an honorific label that is to be applied only to just institutions, thereby obscuring the distinctive character of law as a form of governance. To insist that the essential nature of law has to be understood as a manifestation of certain moral ideals

---

[5] Summarizing the position of one such theorist, Andrei Marmor writes 'essentially, what Hart is saying is that law is a tool, and tools can be used for good or bad purposes alike.' Andrei Marmor, *Positive Law and Objective Values* (Oxford: Clarendon Press, 2001) 159. Such characterizations of Hart's position should not be taken as suggesting that, in Hart's view, law is to be judged simply in terms of its causal efficacy in advancing this or that state of affairs. Hart could acknowledge that, in appropriate circumstances, law may express or articulate general moral commitments. But any such expression of value is not intrinsic to the nature of law as such, according to Hart: it is contingent and dependent upon all of the circumstances.

simply confuses the factual domain of actually existing institutions and practices with the ideal domain of standards against which those institutions and practices must be measured.

Theorists who endorse these currently familiar views see jurisprudence as a clarificatory enterprise that aims to explicate, and perhaps regiment, the categories in terms of which we understand the phenomena of law. The enterprise is to be distinguished from any moral inquiry wherein we might deepen our understanding of values such as justice; and it is to be distinguished also from the practical concerns of judges and lawyers who seek to follow and apply the law. Our theoretical reflections upon the nature of law must not (we are told) be confused with ethical questions concerning what ought to be done, nor with disputes concerning the content and meaning of laws within this or that legal order. We must not confuse clarificatory conceptual or descriptive endeavours with ethical engagements; nor system-specific attempts to state the law of a particular jurisdiction with the abstract and universal inquiry into the nature of law as a distinctive type of human institution. To think otherwise is simply to confuse questions concerning the existing *nature* of law with questions concerning what law *ought to be*; or it is to confuse questions concerning the nature of *law* with questions concerning the content of *the law* within this or that system.

In this book we will reject each of these currently orthodox claims. It will be suggested that 'law' is an intrinsically moral idea, and that inquiry into the nature of law is ultimately a form of moral inquiry; and it will be argued that system-specific debates about law's content can never wholly be separated from the philosophical inquiry into the nature of law as such.

Practice and Value

Since its infancy, philosophy has concerned itself with the central values governing our moral and intellectual life. In deciding what we ought to do or to think, we appeal to ideas such as reason, truth, legality and justice. But what is the status of these ideas? How are they related to the familiar facts of power and unreflective conformity that seem to underpin the workings of most human institutions?

The ideas of reason and justice, and other fundamental values, present themselves as standards that are *normative* for us, governing what we *ought* to do, regardless of what current practices and institutions might require of us. It is this apparent independence from practice that leads philosophers to portray such values as located in a realm quite separate and remote from the actions and understandings composing ordinary life: on the one hand we have the realm of belief, of practice, of appearances; on the other, the realm of knowledge, of value, of reality. We must escape from the cave of conventional understandings before we can hope to grasp the true nature of justice, reason and the good. Worldly experience may equip us to understand and address the demands of our fellow men, but our knowledge of the moral and intellectual standards to which we are all ultimately answerable must come from elsewhere.

This trajectory of thought within philosophy has always been resisted by those who see it as ultimately serving to encourage scepticism. If we assume that knowledge is to be found only in a realm quite distinct from that of our conventional beliefs, we are likely to end by concluding that knowledge is unattainable. If values are wholly separate from the practices with which we are familiar, they perhaps represent an unknowable divinity with little bearing on the sub-lunar world.

In the end, no light is cast by postulating a transcendent realm and locating fundamental values within it. How, in the first place, could we ever come to know the contents of such a realm, escape from the cave not really being an option? And what bearing could such unfathomable values have upon our conduct? We might at first assume that only by treating values as transcendent can we take seriously the idea that they are normative for us, standing in judgment on all of our actions and decisions. Yet we could equally say that the pervasive relevance of such values indicates a need to understand them as somehow grounded in what we do, part of the humanly constituted world of language, thought and culture. If the most fundamental values can be understood only by the philosopher who has escaped from the cave of conventional understandings, the knowledge that he possesses will be of little relevance to those who are still the denizens of that cave. We will suspect him of seeking to impose upon us with his talk of reason and goodness. Perhaps we will be led to conclude that all such talk does no more than cloak a battle of subjectivities.

To be something other than an idle fiction, our grasp of value must be implicit in our understanding of the commonplace world, rather than requiring us to gain intellectual access to some other world. Settled understandings may be imperfect and open to criticism, but they cannot be rejected in their totality as wholly erroneous. The difficulty for philosophy is to capture this quotidian groundedness of value without stripping values of their critical and normative force, and reducing them to a placid reflection of 'what we do around here'.

Men and women create their moral identities and values as by-products of interaction and mutual acknowledgment, just as they create culture, language and the structures of thought. The relationships in which we associate together can embody values that structure our choices and decisions. They are (as Michael Oakeshott puts it) 'invented *ambulando* in the course of living and imposing conditions upon conduct'. Having once appeared, a form of human association is 'glimpsed, sketched in a practice, unreflectively and intermittently enjoyed, half-understood, left indistinct: and the task of reflection is ... to endow this somewhat vague relationship with a coherent character by distinguishing its conditions as exactly as may be'.[6]

Jurisprudence is, at its best, an integral part of this process of deepening by reflection our grasp of the values implicit in our forms of association. It seeks to endow with coherence a form of association that is partially glimpsed and unreflectively understood in our ordinary juridical ideas and practices. The form of association in question is one that we know as 'the rule of law'. The historical existence of law perhaps *begins* with an array of established practices that are 'half understood' and 'indistinct'; but it may then attain a degree of reflective self-awareness whereby the participants deepen their understanding of the values served by their practice, and strive to crystallize and refine the practice so as to serve those values more fully.

If we are inclined to think of our fundamental values as quite distinct from the facts of human practice, the entanglement of law with practice may seem to deepen the mystery of its nature rather than to dissolve it: law might seem to be puzzlingly located between the ideas of 'fact' and 'norm';[7] or it might seem to embody an impossible 'incarnation' of value within reality.[8] Responses to this discovery can vary. Some will conclude that traditional understandings of law should be rejected as metaphysical (in a pre-Kantian and, it is assumed, unacceptable way) and replaced by an austerely reductivist account that suppresses law's normative character. Others may view the nature of law more positively, as a fertile indicator of the path whereon we might 'de-sublimate' our ideas of reason and value.[9]

More commonly, however, assumptions about the independence of value from practice will predispose us towards certain categories of solution to the problem of law's nature and the status of jurisprudence. Perhaps, for example, (since law is to some considerable extent a matter of practice and observable fact) we will conclude that law's value is derivative rather than fundamental; contingent rather than intrinsic and necessary. When judges 'justify' their judgment by reference to the law, perhaps they assume that the law serves a deeper value, such as justice, and view the justification as dependent upon

---

    [6] Michael Oakeshott, *On History and Other Essays* (Oxford: Blackwell, 1983) 120–121.

    [7] Jurgen Habermas, *Between Facts and Norms* (Cambridge, Mass: MIT Press, 1996).

    [8] Alf Ross, *Towards a Realistic Jurisprudence* (Copenhagen: E Munksgaard, 1946) 11, 20.

    [9] Habermas turns to legal theory in his later work precisely because an understanding of law's nature points us to the 'de-sublimation' of reason and normativity that has always been central to his thought.

that contingency. Or perhaps they 'justify' their decision only in a somewhat special and technical sense, showing that the legal rules are applicable to the case, without addressing the question of whether the enforcement of those rules is itself morally permissible. And perhaps understanding that this is so is a matter of careful description and conceptual analysis, quite distinct from the separate enterprise of evaluation and prescription.

If, on the other hand, we are inclined to believe that value must somehow be immanent within our practices, we will be more receptive to the thought that an understanding of those practices requires a grasp of the values that they express and embody. Such a thought might even be taken as implicit in the assumption that law has a unified nature which is there to be discovered. As Gustav Radbruch observes, 'we speak of the essence of a thing when we think of value as the principle of its being.'[10] Legal theorists who reject the possibility that values are immanent within our legal practices nevertheless see themselves as inquiring into the general nature of a distinctive type of human institution. Yet why should they assume that the diverse phenomena referred to as 'law' all share something in common, some set of characteristics that can helpfully be identified and articulated by the theorist? Why might there not be a disorderly chaos of overlapping and cross-cutting analogies and resemblances underlying our characterizations of different phenomena as instances of law? Why should the phenomena of law not be linked by a great multiplicity of 'family resemblances' possessing no core set of elements that could be articulated as a systematic theory?[11] Once we have set our moral understanding on one side as irrelevant to a descriptive grasp of human practices, it becomes hard to see why the theorist should assume that law has a unitary nature that is there to be discovered and articulated in the form of a theory.

The *idea* of law occupies a prominent place within the moral and political values of our civilization. We need clearly to comprehend that idea if we are to adopt an intelligent stance towards those values. Also, the *practices* that we regard as embodying (albeit imperfectly) the idea of law must be understood through their relationship to those values. For it is central to the practices of law that they invoke the 'idea' of law as their guiding ideal, and as the source of their power to justify the ordering of sanctions. We must render that invocation, and that proffered justification, fully intelligible before we can hope to attain an understanding of legal institutions that is at all adequate, even on a purely descriptive plane.

---

[10] Gustav Radbruch, in *The Legal Philosophies of Lask, Radbruch and Dabin*, translated by Kurt Wilk (Cambridge, Mass: Harvard University Press, 1950) 51.

[11] Ludwig Wittgenstein, *Philosophical Investigations*, translated by GEM Anscombe (2nd edition, Oxford: Blackwell, 1958) paragraph 67.

The Ideality of Law

In contrasting the inquiry into the nature of justice with the inquiry into the nature of law, we spoke of law as an observable social phenomenon. In one respect this is obviously true: in many contexts, to speak of the existence of law is to speak of the existence of practices such as the enactment of laws by legislatures, the interpretation and application of law by courts, the enforcement of law by policemen and other officials. Yet, without disputing these obvious facts, we may doubt whether they really serve to dissolve the mystery of law's nature, reducing our task to one of careful description and classification. Even though law is closely bound up with the existence of such practices, we should not assume that law can unproblematically be *equated* with those practices. For the concept of 'law' is not one that simply *describes* a distinctive type of practice: the concept also has a role *within* the relevant practices. Legislatures, for example, do not make demands or issue threats: they claim to enact laws, and they view the enactment of law as significantly different from the issuing of an order. In particular, the fact that their enactments are laws is seen as giving those enactments a claim to be followed and obeyed: it is because the enactments of the legislature are law that they are regarded by judges and citizens as imposing obligations and conferring rights. Courts do not punish defendants because they have disobeyed the powers-that-be, nor because they have broken rules that the courts support and consider to be just: they punish defendants because they have broken *the law*. The status of the rules as law is central to the justification of the judgment. Yet (we may ask) what must law be, that we ascribe to it this power to justify coercion?

If the justificatory force of law remains obscure and contested, the sources of law are equally dark. Legislatures claim to have the power to enact laws, not in virtue of their control over the resources of violence such as police forces and armies, but in virtue of more fundamental constitutional laws which confer upon them the *authority* to make law. Such authority-conferring constitutional laws cannot themselves be equated with the orders of the powerful. What then can they be? What exactly qualifies such fundamental constitutional rules as law?

If we ask how the lawmaker comes to have the authority to create law, two tempting possibilities seem to present themselves. On the one hand, we might seek to derive the lawmaker's authority from a deeper set of norms: those of morality. Perhaps the lawmaking power is a matter of the lawmaker's *legitimacy*, in the sense of his moral claim to be obeyed, or the moral permissibility of his actions in enforcing commands against the non-compliant. The most fundamental constitutional laws are perhaps widely endorsed moral conclusions about legitimacy. On the other hand, we might seek to show that the law-making power is nothing more than an unmysterious state of affairs constituted by the lawmaker's control of coercive mechanisms, or by the disposition of some large segment of the population to do as he says. In this way, we are led back to the question addressed by Xenophon: is law simply the body of orders issued by the powerful, or is it the embodiment of a moral ideal that can be contrasted with governance by force?

Analyses that reduce law directly to the facts of power come at too high a price, being unable to explain and accommodate the language of rights and obligations by which most (if not all) regimes articulate law's demands. But theories that ground legal validity in moral legitimacy do not constitute the only alternative to such reductive analyses.

Legal theorists sometimes say that law 'governs its own creation'. But they clarify this thought in different ways. Some see the enacted laws as authorized by other rules that are themselves simply *accepted* without being enacted. They then face the question of what makes these accepted rules *law*. Their response is to reject the question as either meaningless or irrelevant to the issue in hand. Legal justificatory argument (they tell us) is a matter of tracing relations of subsumability and derivability between rules, all of which can be derived from a basic accepted 'rule of recognition'. It makes no sense to ask how that basic rule derives its legality, for it is the ultimate basis of legality. If we ask, on the other hand, what makes the system as a whole law, we ask a general classificatory or conceptual question that is not connected to the structure of legal justification. With a little tidying up, a certain imposition of categories and distinctions, the intractable problems can be made to dissolve. Or so we are told.

But suppose that we do not think of our values as so distinct from the practices that they govern. We might, for example, think of some of our practices as *expressing* and *embodying* ideals, so that it is our familiarity with the practice that gives us access to an understanding of the ideal. We may then be inclined to say that our practices count as law in so far as they approximate to a certain ideal that they themselves suggest. Perhaps legal justificatory argument relates rules and decisions to that ideal, and it is the ideal that transmits to those rules and decisions what justificatory power they possess. Here law 'governs its own creation', but not in the sense that the creation of law is made possible by higher legal rules: rather, the *idea* of law governs its own realization. Law, we may say, is the process of its own becoming.

When lawyers try to discover the content of the law, they will of course consult sources such as statutes and cases. But this is not to say that the law can be *equated* with the totality of statutes and cases. You and I might possess the same knowledge of a particular statute or case (or of the totality of statutes and cases) and yet may disagree about the law that results from that statute or case. Nor need such disagreement concern the way in which agreed general rules should be applied to particular instances: lawyers can disagree about the general rules that result from enactments or decisions, as well as about the application of those rules. A body of law is not a long list of enacted rules but a *system* of rules and general organizing ideas (doctrines and categories) where each innovation must be fitted to the system as a whole. A complex inheritance of legal concepts (property and obligation; contract and tort; public and private; etc.) plays a vital part in this task. The enactments of authority must be integrated within this inheritance before we can clearly discern their law-making effect.

Lawyers sometimes like to express this point in a way that is calculated to heighten the sense of mystery. Thus, Philip Allott tells us that 'Legislative texts and reported cases are not themselves the law. They do not even contain the law. The law is somewhere else and something else.'[12] Being told that the law is 'somewhere else and something else' does not advance our understanding very much; but it does serve to remind us of the sense in which law can be thought of as an abstract ideal rather than a readily available assemblage of discrete rules printed in books. Indeed, the law that is found in books might be said to be either the raw materials from which the law's true content is to be constructed (if the books are law reports or collections of statutes) or a multiplicity of rival attempts to state the law, all of the attempts being imperfect approximations (if the books are treatises).

To dispel the sense of irreducible mystery, it might be useful for us to have before our minds an example of the way in which these various features of law can be connected together in a philosophical theory. Let us therefore consider, by way of illustration, the position developed by Kant in the 'Doctrine of Right' of his *Metaphysics of Morals*. Distinguishing between natural laws 'that can be recognised as obligatory by reason even without external lawgiving' and positive laws 'that do not bind without external lawgiving', Kant observes that it is possible to conceive of a system containing only positive laws, but 'a natural law would still have to precede it, which would establish the authority of the lawgiver'. In this way he rejects the idea that positive law could be, as it were, self-grounding, or grounded in the fact of power alone: enactments can constitute law only in virtue of some deeper and inherently obligatory principles (natural laws) that lend their binding force to the enactments. On this basis, Kant proposes that 'the basis for any possible giving of positive laws' lies in 'the sum of the conditions under which the choice of one can be united with the choice of another'.[13] Positive enactments (in this view) derive their legal

    [12] Philip Allott, *The Health of Nations: Society and Law Beyond the State* (Cambridge: Cambridge University Press, 2002) 43.   [13] Above n 3, 6:229–230.

authority from the way in which they serve to realize the conditions for jointly possible freedoms. But this is not to say that those conditions are fully ascertainable independently of positive enactment, so that the lawmaker's decrees must at every point reflect a pre-established content if they are to be law. Rather, freedoms can co-exist within a political community only if authority posits certain common bounds to freedom: the exercise of legislative choice is therefore amongst the conditions for jointly possible freedom. Since the set of conditions for jointly possible freedoms will constitute a *system* of principles, each individual positive enactment will have legal effect only as a contribution to that system. The legal effect of such enactments will therefore be a function of the contribution that they make to that set of conditions, in common with all other such enactments.

Kant's theory ingeniously connects the *posited* yet *systematic* character of law with the fact that law is invoked as a justification for coercion. If we ask 'what must law be, that it can justify coercion?' we may conclude with Kant that law (*Recht*) is the set of conditions for jointly possible freedoms. This explains both the need for, and the basis of, sovereign legislative authority: the enactments of the powerful become law in so far as they realize a set of conditions within which freedoms are jointly possible, and the realization of such a set of conditions requires legislative choice. But it also explains why laws must of necessity form a system that is a product of intellectual reconstruction, rather than a straightforward collection of diverse, and potentially conflicting, enacted materials.

We may now be able to see why the nature of law presents philosophical problems every bit as genuine and intractable as those presented by the nature of justice. The institutions in which law is embodied are certainly variable human arrangements rather than abstract standards by which such arrangements are judged, but features internal to those institutions suggest that the law itself is a more elusive idea. The institutions of law centre, for example, upon a concern for legality; and this involves a practice whereby acts can be regarded as creating law only if the acts are themselves authorized and empowered by law. But what then can be the status of the fundamental laws that authorize the supreme law-making power? How can law be a product of human acts if those acts can produce law only when legally authorized so to do? Similarly, the institutions of law include practices whereby enacted rules are interpreted, and conclusions are reached about the legal effect of those enactments. Lawyers emphasize the need to treat each such enactment as part of a *system* of rules, and they may disagree with each other about what the law is, even though they are agreed on what the published and printed enactments say. Thus it would seem that 'the law' is something other than the simple aggregate of enacted and printed provisions.

The rules enacted by the powerful therefore seem to become law only by their absorption into a system and a body of ideas that transcends the totality of enacted rules. Law seems to be not the builder's yard full of materials but the edifice that results when they are put together in the best way, and that is an edifice that is always an ideal to be achieved rather than a given.

Reductivism and Idealism

While the institutions of law are clearly a matter of human practice, it is far from clear exactly how the idea of law that orders those institutions and underpins our juridical discourse is to be related to the various observable features of that practice. Just as a notional point in space may give coherence to a geometrical drawing without itself forming a part of the drawing, so the idea of law seems to give coherence to our practices without itself being reducible to any particular practice or to the totality of such. The law within a jurisdiction is not the aggregate of statutes and decisions, for example. When lawyers disagree about the content of the law, they may all be fully familiar with each of the enactments and precedents that are in intellectual play: their disagreement concerns the law that *results* from those materials. The law is always, as Philip Allott reminds us, 'somewhere else and something else'.

Moreover, the law (an entity that now begins, perhaps, to seem more elusive) is invoked in judicial judgments as a justification for imposing sanctions. What must law be that it can possess this justificatory power? On the one hand, it strikes us as obvious that law is simply 'what we do around here'; yet, at the same time, we feel that it must be more than that if it is to justify the state's use of force. Indeed (for we must allow for the possibility of moral error in our assumption that such force is justified) it must be more than this if it is *intelligibly to be invoked* as a justification.

Idealistic theories of law (we may take Kant's 'Doctrine of Right' as an example) probably strike most modern legal theorists as wild flights of fancy rather than sober attempts to arrive at a careful account of law's nature. Indeed, it is sometimes assumed that the subject matter of Kant's theory is *justice* rather than *law* (the German word *Recht* is treated as creating the room for such an ambiguity), presumably on the basis that a claim that *law* represents the set of conditions for jointly possible freedoms is too weird and preposterous to be ascribed to a writer of genius.[14] Or it might even be suggested that such works are really discussions of moral and political ideals, but conducted (for some

---

[14] See e.g. John Ladd's translation: Kant, *The Metaphysical Elements of Justice* (Indianapolis and New York: Bobbs-Merrill, 1965).

mysterious and undisclosed reason) under the convention that they must be framed as concerned with the nature of law.[15]

Yet theories such as Kant's exerted a powerful influence upon the development of modern legal thought, and formed the background against which much of the twentieth century jurisprudential debate emerged. When Oliver Wendell Holmes denounced the idea that law is a 'brooding omnipresence in the sky', and announced an intention to regard law as 'prophecies of what the courts will do', he might well have been reacting against the outlook of a form of German jurisprudence strongly influenced by Kant.[16] Such a jurisprudence had provided a theoretical underpinning for doctrinal systematization, suggesting that the conditions of jointly possible freedom formed the guiding ideal implicit within such systematization. Even in the traditionally unsystematic body of English law, such ideas were to exert their influence. In describing the common law as a 'wilderness of single instances',[17] Tennyson was articulating a not uncommon Victorian perception of the unsatisfactory state of English law. Jurists and students were increasingly looking to German jurisprudence as the model to be copied, and this in turn was to make it a model to attack and react against.[18]

Sometimes, the most anti-idealist and reductivist positions within jurisprudence have sprung, not from an inability to take idealism seriously, but from a full appreciation of the extent to which our ordinary practice and discourse could be said to harbour an immanent ideal of law: a dim suggestion of a form divine contained within the commonplace features of our institutions. After all, Holmes would scarcely have considered it necessary to fight for a 'realistic' picture of law if he had not believed that our ordinary legal thinking had a strong tendency to generate abstract (and, to his mind, misleading) ideals. Similarly Alf Ross, in proposing an equally reductivist view, took himself to be overcoming unacceptable metaphysical commitments implicit in our ordinary legal practice and juridical thinking. Thus he claimed that the concept of law contains a basic conflation of the categories of 'reality' and 'validity', a 'belief in an incarnation of the valid, the metaphysical, the ideal in the realm of the actual, the physical, the real'.[19] Legal realists who insisted on treating propositions of law as predictions of future judicial decisions took for granted the impossibility of equating law with the totality of enacted rules: statutes and past judicial pronouncements were therefore said to be 'sources of law',

---

[15] Tony Honoré, *Making Law Bind* (Oxford: Clarendon Press, 1987) 32.

[16] See Matthias Reimann, 'The Common Law and German Legal Science' in Robert W Gordon (ed), *The Legacy of Oliver Wendell Holmes, Jr.* (Edinburgh: Edinburgh University Press, 1992) 92.

[17] Tennyson, 'Aylmer's Field'.

[18] See Simmonds, 'Rights at the Cutting Edge' in M Kramer, NE Simmonds and H Steiner, *A Debate Over Rights* (Oxford: Clarendon Press, 1998); and Simmonds, *Central Issues in Jurisprudence* (2nd edition, London: Sweet and Maxwell, 2002) 271–275.   [19] Above n 8, 11, 20.

rather than the law itself.[20] Their realism consisted, not in a denial of the idealism implicit in ordinary legal thought, but in the belief that such idealism is
grounded in illusions and therefore needs to be overcome by a revision of our
thought and practice.

For theorists who adopt such views, the attempt to rid our legal thinking of
any commitment to an immanence or incarnation of value becomes central to
their project. The theory that results will be one that tries to *revise* our understanding of law by proposing a set of concepts in terms of which the phenomena may be understood, and from which all traces of value have been purged.
Such theories may be characterized as 'reductivist' in that they seek to reduce
the seemingly idealistic and normative categories of our ordinary thought
to straightforwardly descriptive terms, reconstructing them in such a way as to
eliminate their entanglement with values so that they refer exclusively to
value-neutral facts such as the issuing of orders and the application of sanctions. Thus we may be urged to think of law as simply a set of predictions of
how courts are likely to decide cases, or a set of commands issued by those who
successfully wield coercive power.

HLA Hart's principal contribution to legal theory is best understood as
pointing out the inadequacies of such reductivist theories of law while demonstrating that an idealistic account of law's nature need not be the only alternative. By treating propositions of law as predictive or descriptive statements
(concerning the likelihood of suffering sanctions, the likely reactions of courts,
or the fact that certain decrees have been issued) reductivist theories are unable
to account for the sense that such propositions of law bear within legal discourse. A proposition to the effect that the defendant has a legal duty, for
example, might be invoked as a *reason* for ordering a sanction against him,
rather than as a *prediction* that such a sanction would probably be incurred.
The 'framework of legal thought' that Hart undertook to elucidate[21] is *normative* in character: that is, it is concerned with the existence and content of
prescriptions that purport to guide and regulate conduct. To understand such
a normative form of discourse, we must locate it within the 'internal point of
view' of the participants (particularly officials), who regard the laws as standards that ought to be complied with. In suggesting that the primary sense of
propositions of law must be located within the 'internal point of view', however, Hart is not suggesting that propositions of law are essentially moral in
character. For, in believing that the laws 'ought' to be followed, participants
who adopt the internal point of view need not regard the law as morally binding: the 'ought' need not be a moral 'ought', but might be grounded in

    [20] See John Chipman Gray, *The Nature and Sources of Law*, s.276 (1909, reprinted Boston, Mass:
Beacon Press, 1963) Chapters 8 and 9.
    [21] HLA Hart, *The Concept of Law* (2nd edition, Oxford: Clarendon Press, 1994) Preface.

prudential self-interest (for example). In this way, Hart hopes to show that the *normative*, action-guiding aspect of law (with its associated vocabulary of rights and duties) cannot be analysed reductively as purely descriptive in character, but that this need not propel us into an idealized account of law's nature as essentially moral.

We saw above that the normative character of legal concepts is not the only feature driving the tendency towards idealism in legal thought. Lawyers, judges and legal scholars will disagree about the content of the law even though they are fully and equally familiar with all of the extant official materials such as statutes and cases. The law therefore seems to be something more than the totality of established materials: it is a system to be built, primarily from such materials, and thus it is always an ideal of contestable content rather than a readily available and fully articulated given.

Hart's theory invites us to view the idealistic appearance of law as a kind of illusion that extends the notion of governance by rules beyond the limits that are integral to it in the circumstances of the real world.[22] The illusion arises if we assume that *every* dispute must be resolvable by reference to the rules, and that *every* act must stand in some determinate relationship to the rules (as prohibited, or permitted; as authorized or unauthorized; as valid or invalid). When questions arise that are not resolvable by reference to the established legal materials of statutes and cases, we will then assume that they are nevertheless resolvable by reference to 'the law', if only we could discover the law's true content: a content that is immanent within, but not exhausted by, the aggregate of enactments and decisions.

In fact, Hart argues, every system of rules will leave some situations unregulated, as a consequence of what Hart (following Friedrich Waismann) calls 'the open texture of language'.[23] Each rule will have a core of settled meaning: a range of plain cases where the rule seems to require no interpretation, for its applicability (or inapplicability) appears to be obvious. But there will also be cases where people will disagree about the applicability or otherwise of the rule. In these latter situations ('penumbral' situations) the decision to apply the rule or not cannot, in the nature of the case, be determined by the rule

---

[22] Hart places much of his emphasis upon the way in which certain features of legal thought can generate scepticism about the existence of law as something that is at least partially independent of, and binding upon, the behaviour of judges. My discussion of Hart's arguments as a response to idealism may therefore strike some readers as misplaced. However, Hart's position seems to be that scepticism is fuelled by the assumptions of an overly demanding and idealistic account of what law must be, if it is to be a reality that binds judges. The sceptic, in other words, is a disappointed idealist. See Hart, 'The Nightmare and the Noble Dream' in *Essays in Jurisprudence and Philosophy* (Oxford: Clarendon Press, 1983).

[23] Hart, above n 21, 128–136; Friedrich Waismann, 'Verifiability' (1945) *Proceedings of the Aristotelian Society*, supplementary volume 19, 119. An edited version of Waismann's essay is printed in AGN Flew (ed), *Logic and Language* (Oxford: Blackwell, 1978).

itself, since the whole point is that the rule is indeterminate in application with respect to the penumbral case. They must therefore be resolved by the judge taking account of extra-legal considerations of justice or social policy as a basis for deciding whether the rule ought to be applied or not. The law empowers judges to give authoritative binding decisions on such issues, thereby resolving the penumbral uncertainty.

In addition to the indeterminacies inherent in language, Hart points to a further feature of legal thought that can easily become a source of idealist and formalist illusions. For, particularly when dealing with the rules established in caselaw, judges will frequently modify the rules as expressed in earlier decisions: they might, for example, add to the rule's formulation an exception that has the effect of taking the present case outside the scope of the rule, even though the rule as originally established contained no such exception. This practice, when combined with the assumption that judges must and do apply the law, can fuel a conception of law as 'somewhere else and something else': as a system of principles that is only partially and imperfectly captured by the articulated rules, so that the stated rules may be modified to make them more accurately reflect the true law. Here too, the idealist path is portrayed by Hart as grounded in error: in this case, the erroneous assumption that rules must bind 'as fetters' if they are to bind at all. In fact, he tells us, rules can be binding and yet be subject to unstated exceptions that are incapable of exhaustive statement: '[a] rule that ends with the word "unless . . . " is still a rule.'[24]

Hart's suggestion is that, by accepting the existence of penumbral cases and the possibility of open-ended rules subject to unstated exceptions, we can resist the temptation to project the idea of law beyond the commonplace surface of statutes and judicial decisions, and can overcome any dependence upon a conception of law as a system that is only partly represented by the ascertainable rules and decisions. The law can be regarded as fully ascertainable (we can establish what the rules are) but partially indeterminate (the rules do not yield all the answers), rather than fully determinate (the rules yield all the answers) but only imperfectly ascertainable (we cannot be sure what they are). The sublimation of law is overcome, and a naturalistic account is enabled to accommodate all of the relevant phenomena. Or so Hart would have us believe.

Problems lie beneath the apparently cool and reasonable surface, however. Take, for example, the idea that rules may be binding even though they are subject to exceptions which cannot be exhaustively stated, and which it might be impossible to anticipate in advance of the situations that cause them to seem appropriate. Is this really so? How can judges be bound by rules that they

---

[24] Hart, above n 21, 139.

are also empowered to modify (even if the power of modification is authorized by the rule itself, in the word 'unless . . . ')? Joseph Raz has suggested that such a power of modification is compatible with being bound provided that it is a *limited* power. In principle he is correct; but his attempts to give content to the relevant limitations are less successful. In an early attempt, he suggested that the relevant power was limited in so far as it could only be exercised for certain sorts of reasons.[25] The problem here is that any account of the relevant reasons that is sufficiently broad to cover the various grounds on which judges can and do modify the stated rules will encompass all of the reasons on which a court may legitimately act quite apart from the binding force of rules. In a later version of the same argument,[26] Raz claims that the power to alter rules is limited by constraints on the *form* that the alteration can take: it must consist in the addition of a new exception to the rule, so that the rule-plus-exception would justify earlier cases as successfully as the original rule-without-exception did. This version of the argument, however, fails to explain the way in which judges can fundamentally reformulate rules in a way that cannot be analysed as the addition of an exception.[27]

Furthermore, while Hart's theory generally sustains the normative character of law without collapsing law directly into the facts of power, some such collapse is admitted to occur at the margins. For example, when penumbral cases arise in relation to ordinary rules of law, such as the rules of private law, the courts may be regarded as empowered by law to resolve the uncertainty in an authoritative manner. But this seems to produce a circularity when the rules in question are themselves the fundamental constitutional rules that confer law-making authority. Hart's solution is to say that, in such cases, the courts 'get their authority to decide them accepted after the questions have arisen and the decision has been given'. He adds that 'here all that succeeds is success'.[28]

Hart emphasizes that the points at which legality becomes indistinguishable from the successful exercise of power are marginal to law as a whole: 'at the fringe of these very fundamental things', he tells us, we should welcome the sceptical thought that law is simply what the officials succeed in doing.[29] But we should not be blind 'to the fact that what makes possible these striking developments by courts of the most fundamental rules is, in great measure, the prestige gathered by courts from their unquestionably rule-governed operations over the vast central areas of the law.'[30] The import of this last observation seems, however, less than clear. Its tone implies that Hart sees the point

---

[25] Joseph Raz, *Practical Reason and Norms* (London: Hutchinson, 1990, first issued 1975) 140.

[26] Joseph Raz, *The Authority of Law* (Oxford: Clarendon Press, 1979) 186–188.

[27] Simmonds, 'Bluntness and *Bricolage*' in H Gross and R Harrison (eds), *Jurisprudence: Cambridge Essays* (Oxford: Clarendon Press, 1992) 1 at 8–11.   [28] Hart, above n 21, 153.

[29] Ibid, 154.   [30] Ibid.

as demonstrating the restricted significance of the sceptic's view. Yet the substance of the observation suggests quite the opposite. Courts are said to acquire 'prestige' from the way in which, across much of the law, they decide cases by reference to established rules. This 'prestige' is said to make possible the success of the courts in determining fundamental constitutional issues that are *not* governed by any established rules. Far from restricting the significance of the sceptic's insight (if such it be) Hart's remark seems to extend and reinforce it. At the foundations of the law, it seems, not only does legality boil down to 'success', but the success in question is facilitated by the mistaken belief that the fundamental and penumbral case is to be decided in precisely the same way as a straightforward case devoid of penumbral indeterminacies.

We should not allow ourselves to be too easily persuaded by Hart's analysis of the distinction between core and penumbral cases. The analysis enables us to identify the law with the totality of enacted or established rules, and so avoids any supposed need to project the idea of law beyond those rules. Such a need only seems to arise if we seek a concept of law that tallies with the practice whereby lawyers will disagree about what the law's content might be, while nevertheless agreeing about what the published legal materials such as statutes and cases actually say. But we can treat such disagreements, says Hart, as disagreements generated by the law's partial indeterminacy in penumbral cases, or as disagreements about how the rule should be modified by qualifying exceptions. Lawyers in such situations are not in reality disagreeing about what the law *is*, but about the considerations of justice and policy on the basis of which the court should exercise its power to resolve the specific indeterminacy by a law-creating decision. These debates might take the form of a debate concerning the law's existing content, but the form is misleading and a more accurate view is revealed by the proposed analysis.

Hart's analysis treats the surface appearance of legal argument as misleading: its true significance is revealed only by legal theory. His view will be found compelling by those who see it as an imperative for legal theory to depict law as a matter of commonplace practice that can be understood without necessary reference to any moral ideal. But, if we have no such specific philosophical agenda to motivate us, we might do better by approaching the ordinary assumptions of judges and lawyers in a sympathetic fashion, trying sensitively to reconstruct the idea of law that seems to be implicit in their forms of speech and argument. Since the aim of philosophy is to introduce clarity in place of mystery, the philosopher can sometimes expel the *numina* from the world prematurely, by an act of truncation rather than a sustained attempt at elucidation. A reduced and impoverished intellectual landscape can appear very satisfactory to theorists of this disposition. Their endeavours are, however, rarely successful in the long term, for what has been exorcized from the formal reception rooms often continues to haunt the corridors and vacant spaces of the philosopher's construction. In the end, the ghosts can exact a heavy price. It is better to begin by considering whether the seemingly numinous might not in fact be a genuine manifestation of the ideal rather than a mere apparition. In this way we may discover that the ideal is relatively unmysterious and that it is possible to attain an improved understanding by bringing phenomena clearly into focus, rather than by regimenting our categories so as to exclude their problematic features from view. In this way we may hope for a jurisprudence that enriches our perception of the world and respects its complexity, rather than a jurisprudence that takes clarity of thought to require the austerity of a desert.

The Fragmentation of Inquiry: Hart

An understanding of law's nature is hard to attain because, on the face of things, law seems to possess characteristics that cannot be combined within a single entity: law is an established social institution, but also a guiding ideal for such institutions; an apparatus of organized force, but also the antithesis of force; a product of authority, but also the source of any such authority. It is this quality that has led some theorists to conclude that traditional ideas of law embody a belief in the 'incarnation' of the ideal within the realm of the actual, or a belief that law is a 'brooding omnipresence in the sky'. Rejecting such beliefs as clearly unacceptable, theorists who adopt this line seek to propose a revised and philosophically acceptable conception of law that is 'realistic' in character, in the sense that it seeks to shed from the notion of law any element of the ideal.

Others take the view that a hard-headed and unmysterious grasp of law can be attained without any need to *revise* our ordinary understanding, since an entanglement with the ideal is not intrinsic to that ordinary understanding but is rather the product of defective theoretical analysis. Our ordinary notion of law, they argue, does not embody a strange incarnation of the ideal within the realm of actuality, and any appearance to the contrary can be dispelled by careful conceptual analysis. In the absence of such analysis, we are liable to be misled by the shared vocabulary of law and morals ('right', 'duty', 'ought' and so forth); or we will extend the idea of governance by rules beyond its inherent limits, postulating thereby an ideal realm where law transcends the workaday reality of statutes and law reports. The first step towards an adequate analysis, they suggest, is to see that the question 'what is law?' is misleading, for there are in fact several different issues here, which need to be separated. In particular, questions about the nature of law as a distinct type of social institution need to be distinguished from questions about the content of law within a particular jurisdiction; and both of these questions need to be distinguished from inquiry into the political value that we call 'the rule of law'.

For Hart, general philosophical inquiry into law's nature concerns the central characteristics of law as a type of social institution, a type of institution that includes a distinctive form of discourse: the discourse of legal 'validity', legal rights and duties, powers and jurisdictions. Hart's object is to reveal, within a single integrated theory, the nature and basis of this discourse (the 'framework of legal thought') and the most distinctive features of law as a type of social structure.

Hart considers the most distinctive feature of law as a type of social institution to be the acceptance of a 'rule of recognition': that is, a rule providing criteria by which other rules of the system may be identified, perhaps by reference to their source of enactment. A rule of recognition exists only in so far as people (most importantly, the officials of the system) take 'the internal point of view' towards the rule: that is to say, they must regard the rule as a common standard that ought to be complied with. The existence of such a rule of recognition explains the distinctive discourse of law, a discourse which can otherwise seem intensely problematic. For propositions of law (propositions about the existence of legal rights and duties, for example) are not descriptive statements about acts performed or likely to be performed: they do not describe the issuing of commands, nor do they predict the application of sanctions. Propositions of law seem to *prescribe* conduct: they tell us what *ought* to be done, rather than what has been or will be done. Yet, at the same time, these prescriptions should not (in Hart's view) be equated with either moral or prudential prescriptions. In fact, the acceptance of a basic rule of recognition creates a distinct form of prescriptive discourse with its own array of concepts. Thus, legal validity is neither a matter of the law's efficacy nor its moral bindingness, but is a distinct concept that only has application within the context of a rule of recognition: propositions about the validity of rules draw conclusions about the applicability of the rule of recognition. Legal reasoning of the type whereby judges and scholars seek to identify, expound and apply the laws of a particular system is essentially a matter of rule-application, informed by moral or social policy judgements in those cases (penumbral cases) where the rules do not provide a determinate answer. Lawyers within a particular system, who seek to ascertain and apply the existing law, are therefore not addressing a general philosophical question about law's nature, but applying the rule of recognition and the rules flowing from it. The general philosophical inquiry into law's nature is an inquiry constructed from the external viewpoint of a detached observer, and it seeks to *take account of* the internal point of view of the participants, but not to *adopt* that viewpoint or try to resolve the substantive questions of law raised within it.

Hart's approach, therefore, suggests that there is a general philosophical question concerning the distinctive nature of law as a type of social institution, but that this question is quite distinct from the questions about the content of the law that might be addressed by judges and lawyers within particular systems. The latter questions are not philosophical in nature at all: they do not concern the nature of law as such, but simply seek to apply the rules accepted within that system.

On this account, there is no particular reason why a judge would of necessity have to consider the philosophical question concerning law's nature. As Joseph Raz puts it:

> There is no denying that questions about the nature of law can arise in courts, and can feature in judicial decisions. But so can just about any other issue, from astrophysics to biology, sociology, and the rest.

After mentioning some cases where Kelsen's jurisprudential ideas were discussed and formed the basis for the decisions, Raz adds that '[s]uch judicial use of jurisprudential ideas may sometimes be in place, but it is analogous to the judicial use of ideas from biology'.[31]

It might at first seem plausible to say that inquiry into the general nature of a type of institution should be distinguished from the practical questions that arise in the course of operating and sustaining that institution. In the case of law, however, the suggestion is misleading. Jurisprudence is not a detached reflection upon practices that run smoothly according to a discrete set of rules, for the task of reflection (wherein we seek to endow our form of association with a coherent and transparently understood character) is one that only arises in response to fractures and discontinuities. The reflective posture of philosophy is not a free-floating attitude that we may adopt or renounce just as we please.[32] The social and historical existence of law is a matter of actions and practices structured by a great many interlocking understandings and expectations. Although we may work within these understandings quite unproblematically most of the time, on occasion we are led to ask how they can all be fitted together into a single intelligible picture of law's nature. Most commonly this occurs because reflection has been forced upon us by unexpected problems, or by the disruption of a familiar background. In seeking to reveal a coherent idea of law that makes sense of our various juridical practices, jurisprudence takes as its goal the resolutions of tensions and antinomies, and the clarification of guiding ideals.

[31] Joseph Raz, 'Two Views of the Nature of the Theory of Law' in J Coleman (ed) *Hart's Postscript* (Oxford: Oxford University Press, 2001) 32–33.
[32] Dworkin, by contrast, describes an 'interpretive attitude' that he seems to regard as free-floating. See my remarks on this in Simmonds, 'Imperial Visions and Mundane Practices' (1987) CLJ 465 at 483–486.

This is reflected in the fact that jurisprudence has often been regarded as appropriately occupying a fundamental role within legal education and legal scholarship. Hart's depiction of a clear difference between jurisprudential reflection and doctrinal legal thought has encouraged a tendency to treat jurisprudence as more peripheral. It is significant, however, that Hart wrote in what was a period of relatively settled legal development. Things do not always go so smoothly; and, when lawyers face new problems for which their existing conceptions do not equip them, they turn to jurisprudential reflection in the hope of finding an answer.

In the basically agrarian society of mid-eighteenth century England, for example, it was possible for Blackstone to present an overview of English law as protecting a limited array of fundamental natural rights: the law was assumed to be capable of systematic study precisely in so far as it reflected and embodied such a system of rights.[33] With the rise of new forms of industrial and commercial activity, however, there came to be a host of new ways in which people's interests could come into conflict: forms of damage that were not anticipated by the limited catalogue of legal wrongs that Blackstone knew and expounded. The attempt to address this succession of new problems through the traditional fabric of common law ideas led to a sense that the law was lacking in deep guiding principles: a series of ad hoc solutions generated the worry that the law was a 'wilderness of single instances'. One response to this situation was to draw upon ideas found in German jurisprudence and heavily influenced by Kant. These ideas invited legal scholars to treat each legal right as a complex juridical entity from which diverse consequences could be inferred: rights formed fertile nodal points that enabled new solutions and protections to be deduced from existing legal standards.[34] Later theorists, such as Hohfeld,[35] were to attack and reject such conceptions of rights, suggesting (in effect) that they confused the internal complexity of a concept with the ambiguity of a word as between wholly distinct concepts.[36]

A Kantian conception of law as a body of complex and mutually compatible rights is quite different from a conception of law as an assemblage of discrete and potentially conflicting rules. Yet precisely such a contrast in basic conceptions of law's nature was implicit within the different forms of legal

[33] Sir William Blackstone, *Commentaries on the Laws of England* (1765). See also Simmonds, 'Reason, History and Privilege: Blackstone's Debt to Natural Law' (1988) *Savigny-Zeitschrift für Rechtsgeschichte: Germanistische Abteilung* 200.

[34] See e.g. Lord Lindley's judgment in *Quinn v. Leathem* [1901] AC 495; discussed in Simmonds, *Central Issues in Jurisprudence*, above n 18, 271–283.

[35] WN Hohfeld, *Fundamental Legal Conceptions as Applied in Judicial Reasoning* (New Haven, Conn: Yale University Press, 1923).

[36] See Simmonds, 'Rights at the Cutting Edge', above n 18; Simmonds, *Central Issues in Jurisprudence*, above n 18, Chapter 8.

reasoning that emerged as a response to the traditional common law's new problems. In such contexts, the resolution of legal problems in a principled manner seems to require that we choose between rival conceptions of law: the philosophical issue of the nature of law cannot then be presented as a detached and distinct intellectual enterprise quite separate from the development of doctrinal argument.

Hart's view that jurisprudential inquiry is distinct from doctrinal thought leaves us puzzled as to the relationship between his own claims about the nature of law, and those implicit theories about law's nature that are to be found within the body of doctrinal argument. A tempting option would be for Hart to treat such theories, when they clash with his own theory, as simply false. But one can scarcely purport to be offering a theory that is disengaged from the practice of doctrinal argument if one simultaneously treats that theory as intervening in the relevant practice by revealing the falsity of certain contested positions adopted within the practice. The other option is to treat some of the theoretical assumptions made within the practice as not being what they seem: not really claims about the nature of law, for example, but proposals about how best to resolve penumbral uncertainties in the law. But such a solution will strike us as arbitrary and contrived if we believe that we can make better sense of the practices of legal argument by abandoning Hart's theory.

The Fragmentation of Inquiry: Dworkin

An interesting variant of the general attempt to separate questions has recently been offered by Ronald Dworkin, and it takes a course that is both more radical and in some respects precisely opposite to that adopted by Hart. Dworkin distinguishes between a 'sociological' concept of law, a 'doctrinal' concept, and an 'aspirational' concept.[37] By the 'aspirational' concept, Dworkin refers to the political ideal normally known as 'the rule of law', and he follows most other legal theorists in distinguishing this value from the idea of law as a distinct type of social institution, or a body of prescriptions and doctrines. The distinction tends to be asserted without argument (Dworkin is no exception here) and taken for granted as more or less obvious. Perhaps this is because it is assumed that the same concept cannot refer both to an extant social institution and to a guiding political ideal. Whatever the reason, in the next chapter we will argue that the distinction, and the assumption on which it rests, should both be rejected. We will examine the arguments of Joseph Raz, who

---

[37] He also mentions a 'taxonomic' concept, but this will not concern us here: Ronald Dworkin, *Justice in Robes* (Cambridge, Mass: Harvard University Press, 2006) 1–5.

mounts an express defence of the distinction, and we will find that those arguments are flawed. For the moment, we will set the issue on one side.

According to Dworkin, inquiry into the nature of law in the 'doctrinal'
sense concerns the criteria underpinning our claims about what the law within
a particular jurisdiction permits or requires or creates. The inquiry focuses
upon the question of whether moral criteria are amongst the truth conditions
of doctrinal propositions of law. In particular, it asks 'whether moral tests ...
are among the tests that judges and others should use' in deciding whether
propositions attempting to state the law are true. The 'sociological' concept,
by contrast, concerns a distinctive type of institutional social structure. If our
concern is with the sociological concept of law we might (for example) ask
whether law exists in societies that lack specialized institutions of coercive
enforcement.

Dworkin is emphatic that the sociological and doctrinal concepts of law do
indeed represent different concepts of law, and not simply different ways in
which a single concept can be used, for 'they collect different instances': '[t]he
doctrinal concept collects valid normative claims or propositions, and the
sociological concept collects institutions or patterns of behaviour'.[38] In relation to the doctrinal concept, Dworkin suggests that '[i]t is obviously an issue
of capital practical importance whether moral tests ... are among the tests
that judges and others should use' in deciding upon the truth of propositions
of law.[39] Whereas Hart would see this as a question to be resolved by consulting the individual rule of recognition of each legal system, Dworkin sees it as
raising a general philosophical question concerning the idea of legality and its
relationship to other values, such as justice.

By contrast with the doctrinal concept, Dworkin holds that questions
concerning the sociological concept of law acquire importance only in specific
contexts, and their importance is then relative to the context. Thus, we might
need 'to stipulate a precise definition of what kind of social structure counts as a
legal system' to facilitate some piece of empirical research, 'or to emphasize the
moral importance of certain practices or constraints'.[40] But there is no 'natural
distinction of social kinds that marks off legal structures as having, just in
themselves, some essential nature that these distinctions try to capture.'[41] We
share a 'rough sociological concept of law', but its bounds are not precise; and,
for that reason, we would think it silly to argue about the precise applicability of
the concept to particular instances. When scholars need to specify a more exact
definition for their own purposes, 'there is enough leeway in our rough understanding to allow them to stipulate more refined definitions without outraging
ordinary usage'.[42] This 'leeway' is not, however, unlimited; and the doctrinal

---

[38] Ibid, 263.   [39] Ibid, 2.   [40] Ibid, 3.   [41] Ibid.   [42] Ibid.

concept features among the boundaries of the sociological concept, in so far as 'nothing is a legal system in the sociological sense unless it makes sense to ask what rights and duties the system recognizes'.[43]

Dworkin's view therefore seems to be that there is no general philosophical question to be asked about the nature of law as a distinct type of social structure. The types of question that we might face about the applicability of the sociological concept of law will be genuine rather than spurious only when they derive their significance from some specific context. For the purposes of some particular moral or empirical inquiry, we might need to decide (for example) whether a system of rules not backed by organized sanctions should be regarded as 'law'. But, outside some such context, the question lacks substance. Our settled semantic intuitions about the applicability of the word 'law' do not dictate an answer, and 'law' is not the concept of a natural kind with boundaries that we might seek to determine independently of those semantic intuitions.

There is no need for me to dispute Dworkin's claim that the 'sociological' and 'doctrinal' concepts of law are distinguishable. Indeed, I have already acknowledged a distinction of sorts, for it was pointed out earlier that, in some contexts, to speak of the existence of law is to speak of the existence of certain observable social practices; while, in other contexts, statements about the law refer to abstract standards, precepts and entitlements.[44] But Dworkin underestimates the intimate connections between these two 'concepts' of law, and fails to see how these connections undermine his refusal to admit any general philosophical question concerning the 'sociological' concept. This in turn means that he fails to grasp the reflexive character of legal thought: he fails to see how legal thought can be itself a matter of deepening by reflection our understanding of the distinctive form of association that we call the rule of law.

Dworkin invites us to imagine a community (perhaps on a distant planet) where, as he puts it, '*ex post facto* legislation was the norm rather than a rare exception'. '[W]e would think it silly', he tells us, 'to argue about whether they *really* had a legal system' since '[w]e normally think it unnecessary to ask for a more precise definition of "legal system" than our rough working ideas provide'.[45] At the same time we would concede that, in the context of a specific moral or empirical inquiry, scholars or social scientists might consider it

---

[43] Ibid, 4.

[44] This entails a distinction between two different concepts of law only if we regard concepts as distinguished by the 'instances' that they 'collect'. Such a distinction between concepts is nevertheless compatible with the concepts being structured by a single idea, to which the relevant sets of instances are related in different ways. In this book I argue that observable social practices and normative propositions count as law in virtue of their relationship to an abstract archetype, the idea of law.

[45] Dworkin, above n 37, 3.

desirable to propose such a refined definition: but the merits of any such proposal would always be relative to the particular research project.

The argument seems to proceed from two main ideas: (i) we have no settled semantic intuitions in relation to such examples (more refined definitions, whatever their content, would not outrage ordinary usage); (ii) law is not a 'natural kind' with an 'essential nature'. The conclusion is then drawn that any meaningful discussion of whether or not such an instance should be regarded as an instance of law would be relative to some particular research project: consequently, there is no possibility of a *general* philosophical inquiry into the sociological concept of law.

What this argument neglects is that our concepts are systematically interconnected in such a way as both to invite a general philosophical attempt at clarification and to constrain the possible outcomes of such reflection. Dworkin himself acknowledges a certain interconnectedness of concepts when he tells us that the 'doctrinal' concept of law 'figures among the boundaries of the sociological concept in this way: nothing is a legal system in the sociological sense unless it makes sense to ask what rights and duties the system recognizes'.[46] But he fails to see how this element of connectedness is but one aspect of a very complex web of connections.

As a preliminary, we should be alert to a degree of vagueness in Dworkin's example. For what exactly does he mean when he speaks of *ex post facto* legislation as being 'the norm rather than the exception'? Lon Fuller once invited us to imagine a system consisting *entirely* of *wholly* retrospective enactments, in the sense that all of the enactments did nothing but criminalize acts that had already been performed.[47] Fuller concluded that such a system would not be a system of law, for conduct within the system could not be guided by rules. Whatever we think of Fuller's conclusion, the example is at least clear. But Dworkin's example is less clear. Retrospective enactments might be 'the norm rather than the exception' in the straightforward sense that most enactments are purely retrospective, while a (perhaps large) minority of enactments are purely prospective or both prospective and retrospective in effect. In such a system, there would be norms to guide conduct (provided by the prospective enactments), so that the point of Fuller's argument is obscured.

Let us, however, set this point on one side for the moment, in order to concentrate upon the relationship between Dworkin's example of retrospective enactments and his account of how the doctrinal concept figures in the boundaries of the sociological concept. An obvious question arises here: does it make sense 'to ask what rights and duties the system recognizes' if the system consists of retrospective enactments?

---

[46] Ibid, 4.

[47] Lon Fuller, *The Morality of Law* (revised edition, New Haven, Conn: Yale University Press, 1969).

Dworkin thinks that nothing prevents us from applying the sociological concept of law to the retrospective system if we wish, and that it would be silly to deliberate on the issue as a general matter. He must therefore think that retrospectivity is not at all inconsistent with the conferment of rights and duties. But this is surely a debatable issue, and (since Dworkin recognizes the doctrinal concept as amongst the boundaries of the sociological) we would expect him to acknowledge that the example of the retrospective system raises a general and meaningful question about the limits of the sociological concept.

There are various ways in which legal theorists and philosophers have tried to elucidate the concept of a legal duty or a legal right. Theorists such as Austin,[48] for example, argued that propositions about legal duties are statements about the probability of suffering a sanction in certain circumstances. Others have argued that a duty is a pattern of conduct the opposite of which forms the conditional clause of a prescription directing judges to apply a sanction.[49] Another view holds that propositions about duty express conclusions about the applicability of rules, saying in effect that a certain action is demandable or due under the rules. Yet another view holds that a duty is a distinct type of reason for action.[50]

We cannot decide whether a system of retrospective enactments is capable of conferring rights and duties without choosing between these different analyses; and any such choice will have further consequences, precisely in so far as our concepts are systematically interconnected. This explains how there can be a general philosophical inquiry even into the sociological concept of law. Dworkin assumes that the relatively sparse nature of our strongly held and firmly settled semantic intuitions, combined with the fact that law is not a 'natural kind', renders any such inquiry empty and silly. This assumption, however, is clearly misguided. When we are confronted by the example of a system of retrospective enactments, it might be the case that we have no strong semantic intuition about the applicability or otherwise of the concept of 'law'. But an appreciation of the interconnectedness in our concepts will lead us to see that decisions on this borderline can be better or worse, more or less satisfactory, even though they find no direct endorsement within settled semantic usage or in the boundaries of a natural kind. Philosophical explication of a

---

[48] John Austin, *The Province of Jurisprudence Determined* (1832) edited and introduced by HLA Hart (London: Weidenfeld and Nicolson, 1955) 18.

[49] Hans Kelsen, *Introduction to the Problems of Legal Theory* (1934) translated by BL and SL Paulson (Oxford: Clarendon Press, 1992) 26–28; Hans Kelsen, *General Theory of Law and State* (Cambridge, Mass: Harvard University Press, 1945) 58–59; Hans Kelsen, *The Pure Theory of Law*, translated by Max Knight (Berkeley and Los Angeles: University of California Press, 1967) 114–117.

[50] See Hart's discussion of the views of Raz, in HLA Hart, *Essays on Bentham* (Oxford: Clarendon Press, 1982) 267.

concept such as the concept of 'law' (even 'law' in a sociological sense) tends to necessitate analyses of a multiplicity of related concepts. The decisions that we take about each of these concepts will have implications for our analysis of its neighbours. At some point, our theory might perhaps appeal to firmly settled semantic intuitions, but this is not essential; nor need such intuitions ever be regarded as wholly beyond challenge. Everything turns on the clarificatory power, plausibility and intellectual fertility of the analysis as a whole.

There is, however, one sense in which discussion of the boundaries of the sociological concept of law might be 'silly' if it is conducted outside any context that gives it substance; and it is at this point that the difference between Dworkin's example of a retrospective system, and Fuller's example, comes to be of great relevance. Fuller's example, it will be recalled, is a system consisting entirely of wholly retrospective enactments. Dworkin's example, by contrast, is a system where retrospective enactments are (in some sense) 'the norm rather than the exception'. We might therefore agree with Fuller that a purely retrospective system would not be law, while hesitating over Dworkin's example: after all, in Dworkin's example, it might still be perfectly possible for people to regulate their conduct by reference to enacted prospective rules. If prospectivity is a feature grounded in the essential nature of law, it need not be exhibited by every individual law: perhaps the situation is that a system will count as law only if it achieves an adequate degree of prospectivity overall. The status of such a system as law becomes, therefore, a question of degree. Perhaps it is true that discussion of such questions of degree, outside any particular context, is pointless and even foolish. But this establishes nothing about the possibility or otherwise of general philosophical inquiry into the nature of law in the 'sociological' sense, for such an inquiry could aim to identify the criteria that are relevant to a system's status as law while conceding that the applicability of the concept in particular cases will turn upon a context-sensitive question of degree.

Any account of the nature of law as a distinct type of social institution will tend to suggest a more general view of the human condition, and of law as a distinct type of response to that condition. This is because any such account will need to select, from the great diversity of features associated with the institution of law, those that should be treated as central and important. Hart's theory, for example, emphasizes the character of law as a body of rules ascertainable by publicly available tests such as the source of enactment of the rule: the rule of recognition, that Hart sees as a 'step from the pre-legal to the legal world', is portrayed by him as a remedy for the problems of *uncertainty* that would obtain in a society of any complexity that lacked such a rule.[51] A somewhat different approach, associated with Bentham and his disciples,

---

[51] Hart, above n 21, 94.

emphasizes the role of sanctions in law, and relates this emphasis to the role of sanctions in addressing structural features of human interaction in which individual interests can diverge from the collective interest in such a way as to make it difficult to maintain institutions or arrangements (such as a system of property rights) that are in fact beneficial for virtually everyone.

It is because any account of law's nature is likely to imply a more general picture of the human condition (and because of their appreciation of the interconnectedness of concepts) that sociologists and anthropologists do not treat the concept of 'law' as an otherwise empty classificatory box that is to be filled by their own stipulation. The appropriateness of a social scientist's use of the concept, therefore, is not judged simply in terms of its serviceability as a convenient label for the particular set of phenomena that the scientist wishes to highlight. When, for example, Max Gluckman chose to describe Barotse practices of dispute-resolution as 'law', and as a 'judicial process' involving its own 'jurisprudence',[52] his decision could be judged on grounds other than the issues of clarity and lack of ambiguity that would be appropriate to pure stipulation. His choice of framing concept deliberately equated Barotse institutions with the institutions of Roman law or the common law, and invited contrasts and comparisons that might not otherwise seem apposite. Debate about the appropriateness of such a choice can never be disentangled from an understanding of what it is that makes the institutions of law intelligible as a response to general (though perhaps not universal) problems of the human situation.

Detached or Engaged Inquiry?

It might be suggested, however, that questions about the general nature of law as a type of social institution will nevertheless lack determinate answers, in spite of what has been said about the interconnectedness of concepts, and about the contrasts and comparisons that are implied by any use of the concept of 'law'. For the institutions that inform our grasp of the concept of law (institutions such as punishment, adjudication, and the notions of 'duty' and 'right') have a long and complex history that is unlikely to contain at its heart some simple core or essence. As Nietzsche famously observed 'only that which has no history is definable'.[53] Long-standing practices (Nietzsche's example is

[52] See Max Gluckman, *The Judicial Process among the Barotse* (2nd edition, Manchester: Manchester University Press, 1967); Max Gluckman, *The Ideas in Barotse Jurisprudence* (2nd edition, Manchester: Manchester University Press, 1972).

[53] Friedrich Nietzsche, *The Genealogy of Morals* (1887) second essay, section 13 (various editions and translations).

the practice of punishment) have, he tells us, a certain continuity which survives changes in the *meaning* that is attached to the practice by its participants. These various layers of semiotic complexity come to be preserved in the practice that we inherit, making the familiar features of the practice suggestive of quite different meanings or rationales.

Of course, not everything that forms part of the history of punishment would itself be subsumed under the concept of 'punishment'.[54] The bloodfeud, for example, probably contributed to the emergence both of institutionalized punishment and the institutions of civil liability (monetary compensation for civil wrong having sprung from the idea that one must 'buy off the spear or bear it'). Yet we would not regard the blood feud as itself a practice of punishment: after all, the feud extended to the alleged wrongdoer's kin, without any suggestion that they shared in responsibility for the wrong (unless responsibility is simply *equated* with liability to the sanction), while 'punishment' might be thought to be conceptually tied to notions of responsibility for wrong. It is features such as this that tempt the philosopher to offer a general disengaged analysis of the concept of punishment, an analysis that is supposed to be quite distinct from any proposed *justification* for punishment. For it is assumed that some general criteria must govern our decisions on what does and does not count as an instance of punishment (informing our sense, for example, that the bloodfeud is not a form of punishment) and those criteria must be capable of explication and perhaps systematization. Nietzsche might have suggested, however, that any such attempt at general disengaged analysis will fracture upon the different strands of meaning within the historical practice, so that we cannot really produce an informative and coherent account of what 'punishment' essentially is without choosing between the various attempted *justifications* of punishment that have historically been offered.[55]

There is in fact a deep philosophical question here concerning the very possibility of an understanding of human practices and relationships that is detached from our moral and evaluative understanding. Any understanding of human society that we have available to us may be dependent on our education into practices and structures of meaning that are inhabited before they are reflected on, and the requirements of which are independent of the choices of

---

[54] It would therefore be a mistake to suggest, as Dworkin seems to, that the description of an institutional form as 'law' could simply mean that it is 'one historical realization of the general practices and institutions from which our own legal culture also developed'. Ronald Dworkin, *Law's Empire* (London: Fontana, 1986) 103.

[55] For example: if 'punishment' must be of one judged 'responsible' for wrongdoing, does this commit us to backward-looking retributive theories rather than forward-looking deterrent theories? Does the latter type of theory need to be married to a backward-looking constraint restricting deterrent punishment to those who actually are responsible for a wrong?

any individual. Such practices inform our values, attachments and forms of sensibility, and the attempt to gain a reflective grasp of their nature may be in itself a deepening of moral understanding.

The fact that practices are forms of human activity may suggest that they embody 'intersubjectivity' but not 'objectivity', and the philosopher might consequently be tempted to seek an intellectual perspective that sets such structures on one side and understands moral and social phenomena from a viewpoint lying outside the range of understandings that an established ethical life makes available to us. The difficulty here lies not only in the thought that no such viewpoint may be available, but also in the thought that this very idea of a detached and value-free inquiry might itself be inseparably bound up with a substantive ethical outlook. Meta-ethical theories concerning morality's status may reflect the substance of commonly accepted ethical values in a way that should lead us to question the basis of their appeal. While claiming to put moral perceptions at a distance for the purposes of inquiry, the 'detached' view derives much of its appeal from its ability to resonate with familiar ideals of the responsible moral agent: the philosophical believer in value-free inquiry seems to embody the person who is undeceived by appearances, who judges for himself and does not uncritically follow the crowd, and so forth.

The thought that moral value is wholly independent of the practices upon which it stands in judgment connects with wider features of our culture, features that are sometimes regarded as peculiarly characteristic of modernity. Many aspects of our moral and political life are portrayed as tools that are to be judged by their serviceability for this or that task, or as empty vehicles for the expression of a meaning that is to be supplied from elsewhere. An essentially technical culture celebrates the knowledge of tools and instrumentalities, rather than the wise understanding of goals and values, and is therefore content to see intrinsic value drained from the practices that we share, to be located instead in an ineffable realm of subjectivity. This celebration can plausibly be seen as a significant erosion of the moral fabric within which we ordinarily conduct our lives. Law is a central part of that fabric, and the question of whether it possesses intrinsic value, or is of purely instrumental significance, therefore raises an issue of great importance.

Ronald Dworkin has suggested that the jurisprudential inquiry into law's nature, when properly conceived, reflects an 'interpretive attitude' that may be adopted in relation to social practices. The interpretive attitude assumes that the practice has some general point or rationale or meaning, and that the requirements of the practice are sensitive to the precise nature of that rationale. The search for univocal meaning within a practice must therefore be conducted from the perspective of one who seeks to follow and continue the practice: for this reason, an acceptable interpretation will try to present the practice in its best light: to make it into the best practice of its kind that it can be (it will be, in other words, a 'constructive' interpretation).[56]

Dworkin is surely right that the search for univocal meaning within a practice must form part of a morally engaged and informed inquiry. But he is wrong to equate this with the outlook of a participant who seeks to follow and continue the particular practice in question. In our comprehension of human practices we must draw upon our moral understanding; but this must be our moral understanding as a whole, not just this or that value underpinning the outlook of some hypothetical supporter of the practice in question. We sometimes wish to say that a practice, while superficially innocuous, actually carries a meaning that is pernicious in one way or another. Some practices of male courtesy towards women, for example, might be said to convey demeaning images of women and in that way to serve as instruments of oppression; or the practices of legal argument, with their emphasis upon principles that apply to everyone equally, might be said to aim at a mystification of social relations, presenting relations of domination and hierarchy as if they were founded upon equality. Negative interpretations of this kind clearly do not present the practice in question in its best light, but they should not be disallowed for that reason. Nor should they have to satisfy the onerous burden of showing that no benign interpretation would be an adequate 'fit' for the practice. Rather, the acceptability of such interpretations is a function of the power and plausibility of the more general understanding of our moral life that they propose. They might succeed in drawing out deep and otherwise unrecognized affinities and resonances between different aspects of our institutions and practices, while deploying some strands of our shared ethical life as a basis for their moral critique (it is hard to see how a critical position could be so radical as to avoid some such dependence).

Practice and Ideal

Perhaps the inquiry into law's nature is not so different from the inquiry into justice after all. We may feel that justice differs fundamentally from law in so far as justice is an abstract standard against which our conventional beliefs and practices are to be measured, while law is composed of those conventional beliefs and practices. But, even if law is in some respects manifest in established social practices, it may also be the embodiment of a certain ideal in the light of which those practices should be understood. Even if justice is an abstract standard against which our institutions are to be measured, it must

---

[56] Dworkin, *Law's Empire*, above n 54, Chapter 2.

also find some expression in our established juridical and ethical life if it is to be more than an arbitrary postulate or empty figment.

Philosophical inquiry into the nature of justice cannot begin by setting on one side all of our conventional beliefs about justice. Even if some sort of escape from the cave of conventional understanding might be an intelligible goal, the basis for the escape must begin in reflection upon the beliefs that shape our lives within the cave. The resulting philosophy might be critical of this or that belief, but the overall enlightenment gained must be a grasp of the conditional nature of the conventional understandings, rather than a denunciation of the totality of such understandings as sheer error.

Suppose, for example, that some profound philosopher were to tell us that all of our ideas about justice were completely wrong: in fact, he had discovered, justice consisted in a consistent practice of painting all medium-sized objects green. We would know straight away that, whatever deep reflections had led the philosopher to this conclusion, they had not led him to an understanding of justice. For the philosopher's theory could not be a theory of *justice* without offering us an explanation and coherent grasp of some at least of the practices that we ourselves regard as practices of justice: practices such as punishing the guilty and protecting the innocent; distributing the benefits and burdens of social life in accordance with criteria of merit, or need, or equality; accepting responsibility for our own freely chosen actions, and being prepared (on appropriate occasions) to compensate those who suffer as a result of those actions.

People sometimes resist the idea that the adequacy of a theory of justice can be assessed in part by the theory's ability to explain and accommodate our ordinary practices and beliefs about justice. For is not justice precisely an abstract standard against which those practices and beliefs are to be measured? Our existing standards are the result of a history that is thoroughly contingent at best, and in places little more than a story of oppression and exploitation. Surely, one might think, a theory of justice must derive its content from a more secure and non-contingent basis: perhaps from basic standards of rationality, or from the very notion of rational agency, or of personal identity. The soundness of the theory should then be a function of the validity of its derivation, and not of the degree to which it accords with our existing ideas and practices.

This line of thought, however, is likely to founder upon the discovery that any notions of rationality, subjectivity, identity and agency that are sufficiently rich to ground a theory of justice will also themselves have a history that is mired in contingency. The philosopher who seeks some Archimedean point outside of history will find that he has nowhere left to stand. What we seek from philosophy, if we are wise, is not a foundation that is secure because it is somehow not part of history, but a reflective understanding of the way in which (and the extent to which) our beliefs can be connected up in a system of mutual supportiveness. Such a philosophy need not lack critical leverage in relation to existing beliefs and practices. Thus, a philosophical theory of justice will be expected to offer a principled basis from which some at least of those beliefs and practices might be seen as unjust. But the principles invoked must be presented as, in some sense, immanent within our existing moral and juridical practices; for, without some such degree of immanence, they could have no claim to be regarded as principles of justice.

Could something analogous be true of law? Perhaps law cannot unproblematically and of itself be treated as an observable social phenomenon. The most relevant social phenomena are characterized by a great many claims, beliefs and expectations about law. The idea of 'law' seems to provide a focal point that gives orderly sense to these claims and expectations. When that focal point is clearly identified and understood, might it not (like the idea of justice) provide an ideal with critical leverage in relation to the practices and understandings within which it is immanent? Could law be an established social institution while also containing within itself a critical ideal? In this book I will explore that possibility.

2

Dualism and Archetype

Law as Instrument and as Aspiration

Most of the time we are inclined to regard law as a set of rather mundane arrangements by which transactions are regulated and the more objectionable forms of conduct are punished. We take for granted the idea that authorities must decide upon the content of the law, and will choose to enact as law those rules that they hope will advance certain goals or implement certain values. If they pursue goals or espouse values that we do not share, we may find that the laws they enact are not to our taste. We may consider the law to be unjust; indeed we may sometimes conclude that laws have been enacted without any genuine belief in their justice on the part of the lawmakers. From this perspective law appears to be a device that can be used for diverse purposes. Law can serve justice but can also be employed as an instrument of exploitation. In itself, therefore, law seems to be morally neutral, deriving any moral properties that it might possess from its variable and contingent content.

There are times, however, when we think of law in a different way: as the embodiment of an elevated aspiration. Consider, for example, the complex and conflicting feelings that surrounded the trials of the Nazi bosses at Nuremberg. Adherence to the forms and processes of law must there have seemed like a proud proclamation of the values for which the Second World War had been fought, rather than a matter of simple efficacy. The trials that resulted were significant as a visible expression of commitment to legality; and, in that way, as an articulation and affirmation of values. They were not seen simply as the best way of establishing the culpability of the accused. In such contexts, law sheds its familiar and workaday garb, and appears on the stage as a lofty ideal. Governance by law is regarded as being in itself a virtue of a just political community: it is not thought of as an instrumentality that derives the entirety of its moral significance from the contingent uses to which it is put.

Law cannot simultaneously be a lofty moral aspiration and a morally neutral instrument that is as serviceable for evil as for good. For that which is intrinsically moral cannot also be morally neutral. When expressed in these terms, our conventional understandings of law seem to embody a fundamental contradiction or antinomy. But is the antinomy genuine or merely apparent?

In this book it will be conceded that there are perfectly straightforward ways in which law may be used as an instrument of evil: laws may be enacted to advance unjust goals, and officials may follow and apply the law for purely self-serving reasons, for example. Yet it will be argued that these various ways in which law may serve evil are all of them fully compatible with law's status as an intrinsically moral idea. In that sense, the argument of the present book might be thought of as aimed at the reconciliation of apparently opposed positions. It is necessary, however, to distinguish between (on the one hand) the pre-theoretical understandings that underpin and motivate the inquiry into law's nature, and (on the other hand) the developed legal theories that try to make systematic sense of those understandings. While seeking to dissolve apparent conflicts within our pre-theoretical understandings, this book opposes outright those positivist legal theories that have denied law's status as an intrinsically moral idea. Such theories have, not infrequently, compared law to a sharp knife or a gun that is available for good purposes or bad: the moral value and significance of law, they argue, is entirely dependent upon the contingency of particular circumstances, contingencies that include the variability of law's possible content.[1] These claims, I shall argue, are false. They derive much of their plausibility from the various ways in which law can indeed be employed in the service of evil; but, as we shall see, these aspects of law are not at all incompatible with law's intrinsically moral status. Positivists portray close assimilations of law to morality as the result of some relatively simple confusions: confusing the law's normative character with its moral bindingness, for example; or confusing the law's concern for rule-application with a concern for justice. This is, however, a shallow diagnosis: opposition to legal positivism is not the result of confusion but of a real appreciation of the place that the idea of law has within our lexicon of moral and political ideas. At the same time, legal positivism is not the modest but soundly-based set of theses that remain once we have shaken off various muddles and ideological distortions: it is itself the distorted representation of features of law that can only properly be understood by their relationship to the ideal.

---

[1] Joseph Raz, *The Authority of Law* (Oxford: Clarendon Press, 1979) Chapter 11; Matthew Kramer, 'On the Moral Status of the Rule of Law' (2004) 63 CLJ 65.

Familiar Debates

Legal positivists have made their own efforts to dissolve the apparent antinomy in our pre-theoretical understanding, but in a manner favourable to
their position. Central to these efforts have been the views of HLA Hart. Hart
sought to show that a non-reductionist version of positivism, preserving and
elucidating the normative character of law while denying any necessary connection with morality, was both possible and attractive. Rather than analysing
propositions of law as purely descriptive, Hart's theory treats them as deriving
their primary sense from a prescriptive attitude, but one that need not be
understood as an attitude of moral approval. He seeks to construct a middle
position between (on the one hand) theories that distinguish law from morality only by a tacit erasure of law's normative character, and (on the other hand)
theories that preserve the law's normativity only by portraying the law as
necessarily grounded in morality.

Hart develops his own position by criticizing the positivist theory of
John Austin. Austin's theory was strongly reductionist in character, treating
propositions of law as predictions of the likelihood of suffering sanctions.[2]
Consequently, Hart's main emphasis is upon a demonstration of the inad-
equacy of such reductionism, and the need to acknowledge the normative
character of propositions of law if the framework of legal thought is properly
to be understood. Opposition to reductionism constitutes only one aspect of
Hart's positivism, however. The other aspect is his claim that law's normativity
can be accommodated without any need to ground law in morality. Here
Hart's suggestion is both simple and very sketchily developed. It consists in the
proposal that legal thought is guided by a basic 'rule of recognition' that can be
treated as normative and action-guiding for either moral or non-moral reasons. From the fact that the basic rule may be followed for diverse reasons, we
are invited to conclude that the normativity of the rule can be separated from
the reasons for following it, and that the normativity of law need not be seen as
necessarily a matter of moral normativity.

Hart's arguments centre upon the suggestion that propositions of law
(propositions about the validity of legal rules, the existence of legal rights and
duties, etc.) can be analysed as expressing action-guiding conclusions about
the applicability of the rules of the system, including the basic 'rule of recognition' by reference to which all the other rules of the system are to be identified.
Since the primary role of such propositions of law is to guide conduct, the

---

[2] John Austin, *The Province of Jurisprudence Determined* (1832) edited and introduced by HLA
Hart (London: Weidenfeld and Nicolson, 1955) 18.

framework of legal thought has to be understood by reference to the viewpoint of those who regard the legal rules as standards that ought to be complied with. This 'internal' viewpoint, Hart argues, need not involve an attitude of moral approval or a belief that the law is morally binding. Just as, in a game, one's reasons for playing the game are separable from the reasons obtaining within the game, so the normativity of propositions of law need not and should not be reduced to the reasons that agents may have for being guided by law in the first place. These latter reasons may be moral reasons, but they may equally be non-moral prudential reasons.

Against those theories that would reject any such separation between law and morality, and would insist that law's normativity can only be a matter of moral bindingness, Hart offers a number of arguments. Each of these arguments seems to do no more than offer an explanation of how the opponents of positivism might, by error, have been led to a contrary view. The error in each case seems to be a relatively simple one.

For example, Hart seems to see much confusion as springing from the shared vocabulary of law and morality. Law employs a vocabulary which echoes that of morality: it confers upon us 'rights', and imposes 'duties', for example. Yet, Hart argues, we should not on this basis conclude that subjection to a legal duty is a matter of the law's moral bindingness, or legal entitlement a matter of moral right. Law is a body of rules, and the language of 'obligation', 'duty' and 'right' may be employed to draw conclusions about the applicability of rules to individual instances, without any assumption that the rules are morally binding. The need to draw such conclusions is characteristic of contexts where we seek to guide our conduct by reference to the rules. But our reasons for taking that attitude towards the rules need not be moral reasons. It is true that, in many cases, our reasons for wishing to comply with the law may be moral reasons, and may be inseparable from our belief that the law is broadly just. But such a basis in morality will not, Hart tells us, be the invariable accompaniment of law. We are advised not to confuse that which happens to be true in some cases with that which must of necessity be true in all cases. While the law may on occasion be an important safeguard of justice or liberty, it should not be concluded that law is of necessity bound up with those values in such a way that law's very nature takes on the character of a moral ideal. Consequently, we should not be too quick to assume that the law's characteristic vocabulary of 'obligation', 'duty' and 'ought' presumes some intrinsic connection between law and morals.

Close associations between the ideas of 'law' and of 'justice' can, Hart argues, become a source of confusion if one lacks a clear grasp of their strictly limited significance. When we follow rules, we act with a certain formal consistency; and we thereby treat people as, in some similarly formal sense, equal. Such consistency and equality play a central role in our notions of 'justice'. Not only is there a strong normative demand that the law *ought* to be just; there is also (in virtue of the conceptual connections between rule-following and formal justice) a sense in which justice prescribes the consistent application of the law. We need only reflect, however, on the frequency with which laws may themselves be unjust to see that merely formal consistency is only (at best) one aspect of justice, and is not to be confused with the whole.

How successful are these arguments in overcoming the tension between an understanding of law as morally neutral and an understanding of law as embodying a moral aspiration? Unduly casual conflations of normativity with morality, or of formal consistency with substantive justice, may indeed be found in many of the theories that oppose legal positivism. Reductive analyses that treat propositions of law as descriptive of the issuing of commands or as predictive of the incidence of sanctions are indeed deficient, but positivists will insist that they are not committed to such reductive analyses: the normativity of law can be preserved, they claim, without acknowledging any necessary conceptual connections between law and morals.

The idea that governance by law is a lofty moral aspiration, however, is a well-established feature of our ordinary pre-theoretical outlook, not just the upshot of legal theoretical oversight or confusion. The positivist's standard repertoire of arguments may serve to identify errors in the work of some who attack legal positivism, but the arguments look implausible when offered as an explanation of a prominent feature of our ordinary understanding. For the tension between mundane and aspirational views of law should be regarded, not simply as a dichotomy within legal theoretical debate, but as an apparent antinomy structuring our established beliefs about law. The positivist reacts to this apparent antinomy by portraying one half of it as grounded in intellectual confusion, but this is unlikely to be an accurate diagnosis. After all, we are familiar with a host of normatively structured social practices which might themselves invite confusion of the kind that the positivist finds in our understanding of law. The rules of games (for example) prescribe our conduct within the game, and confer upon us the right to make certain moves within the game. Yet it seems we do not find an apparent antinomy within our understanding of social practices generally, but merely and specifically in relation to the law. When some feature of our ordinary understanding has given rise to a long-standing philosophical dispute, it is unlikely to spring from confusion of a very superficial sort, which may be dispelled by a few simple reminders.

In this book, it will be argued that the aspirational view of law embodied in our settled beliefs represents truth rather than the fruit of error. Positivism addresses the apparent contradiction between our aspirational and mundane understandings of law by seeking to excise the former from the intellectual landscape, while trying to demonstrate that this act of excision can be achieved at no very high cost, and with a considerable gain in clarity. Here, by contrast, it will be suggested that the aspirational view should be taken seriously, and explored as a source of insight. The more obvious truisms that appear at first to support the mundane over the aspirational view will be shown to do no such thing, but to be fully reconcilable with the aspirational view. Beyond those obvious truisms, when we address stark theoretical claims for the moral neutrality of law, we will find that the aspirational view is entirely sound and its rival straightforwardly false.

Those who oppose legal positivism are apt to embark upon a direct denial of claims that might better be endorsed or assimilated. When legal positivists assert that law may be an instrument of injustice, for example, their opponents might deny that unjust decrees can truly be said to be 'law'. Or those opponents might say that oppressive systems, where law departs from justice or the common good, may meaningfully be spoken of as 'law', but not 'law in a focal sense'.[3] Consequently, positivists and their opponents tend to agree that the debate ultimately involves a choice between alternative theoretical regimentations of our ordinary (somewhat fuzzy and unregimented) concept of 'law'. Positivists favour a wide concept of law that includes grossly unjust rules and systems within its ambit, while the opponents of positivism favour a narrow concept that excludes such systems from the (now honorific) label 'law'.

Once the debate is viewed in this way as a choice between alternative regimentations, it quickly moves up to a 'meta' level where the issue is one concerning the grounds on which we should choose between different concepts of law. Both sides agree that an adequate theory should serve to highlight and elucidate those aspects of the phenomena of law that are most important. But the notion of 'importance' itself requires a judgement of value before it can be given content. The clash between legal positivists and their opponents thus gives rise to a clash between methodological positivists and *their* opponents. Methodological positivists claim that the values invoked as a basis for choosing between rival regimentations of the concept of law can be purely explanatory theoretical values of simplicity and generality, and that the features of legal phenomena chosen for emphasis can be selected without engaging in any form of *moral* evaluation. Opponents of methodological positivism deny these claims. Some such opponents emphasize that we cannot *understand* law's nature without engaging in moral reflection, while others argue that we face a *choice* between different ways of thinking about law, and the choice should be made in the light of moral reflection upon the probable long-term consequences of adopting this or that view.

---

[3] John Finnis, *Natural Law and Natural Rights* (Oxford: Clarendon Press, 1980).

When they accept an invitation to step up to the meta-theoretical level, the opponents of positivism are too quick to endorse the positivist's picture of the debate as one involving a choice between 'wide' and 'narrow' concepts of law. The debate is thereby prematurely transformed into a stark conflict where we must choose between rival sets of assertions, and where we quickly come to feel that such choices are either ungrounded, or grounded by appeal to meta-theoretical considerations that are the real source of disagreement. The conclusion that we have here, not a genuine debate, but an exchange between parties engaged in quite different projects, follows hard on the heels of this discovery.

In this book I try to avoid the rapid collapse of substantive inquiry (concerning the nature of law) into meta-theoretical debate (concerning the nature of legal theory). Instead, I put forward a distinctive account of the general nature of jurisprudential reflection, but I derive this account in large part from provisional substantive conclusions about the nature of law. Thus, a meta-theoretical view is derived from a provisional substantive conclusion, rather than a substantive conclusion being shored up by a meta-theoretical view. I claim to be able to achieve this remarkable feat in so far as the substantive position defended is sufficiently robust to survive attacks that are motivated by quite diverse methodological commitments.

To elucidate the strategy slightly more fully, it is necessary to distinguish between two different phases of the argument. In the first phase, I offer a rather sparse account of law that could easily be viewed as common ground between positivists and some of their opponents. I then show that, even on that sparse account of law's nature, law is in fact an intrinsically moral idea; or, putting the matter slightly differently, law exhibits conceptually necessary connections with morality. In the second phase of the argument, I offer an account of jurisprudential inquiry as a form of moral reflection. This account is not entailed by the earlier claim that 'law' is an intrinsically moral idea, but it is compatible with that claim and helps us to see the potentially rich implications of the claim. I then move towards a gradual enrichment or refinement of the sparse conception of law employed in phase one, such enrichment being warranted by the conception of jurisprudential inquiry developed in phase two, as well as by the intrinsic insights that it yields.

Suppose that we could show that all of the most plausible claims that seem to support positivism are actually fully compatible with a theory that squarely rejects positivism's central thesis.[4] If, for example, we could find a theory that

---

[4] The term 'legal positivism' is now employed in such a diversity of ways that one cannot speak of the theory's 'central thesis' without further explanation. In the text, I am referring to modern analytical positivism, rather than to the classical positivism of Hobbes. I take analytical positivism to centre upon the denial of any necessary connection between law and morality.

presented law as being the embodiment of a moral ideal, and yet also acknowledged that law may be the instrument of injustice in the diverse ways upon which positivists are apt to focus, we would have avoided the need to choose between 'wide' and 'narrow' concepts of law. Suppose further that the theory did not rely on any of the familiar equations between normativity and moral bindingness, legal duty and moral duty, or rule-based consistency and justice. We would then have left the positivist with few shots in his locker, since his standard battery of arguments and examples would have simply missed the target. It is the object of this book to demonstrate that such a theory is readily available, and that it yields a rich source of insight.

No Real Problem?

I have suggested that, on the face of things, we seem to think of law in two mutually incompatible ways. On the one hand, it seems to be a mundane institution that has no intrinsically moral properties but derives its moral status (as good or evil) from the contingencies of particular circumstances. On the other hand, it seems to embody a lofty moral ideal.

There will inevitably be those who suspect that, in setting up this contrast between 'mundane' and 'aspirational' views of law, I have already erred. For it might be suggested that there is no genuine contrast to be made here. When properly identified and understood, the mundane and aspirational aspects of law reveal no tension or conflict, but are mutually compatible in a way that reveals law to be essentially mundane.

It might be suggested, for example, that the profound moral significance attached to the observance of standards of legality does not entail the view that law is itself intrinsically moral. Perhaps law is an instrument available for bad purposes as well as good, while being an essential precondition for the attainment of certain good states of affairs. Suppose, for example, that law is serviceable both for liberal democrats and for fascists, but is an essential precondition of liberal democracy, while being only a useful but dispensable governmental aid for fascism. Our anxious concern, in contexts such as Nuremberg, to ensure that standards of legality are observed might then reflect our appreciation of the important but contingent connection between law and some favoured set of values, rather than reflecting an ascription of intrinsic value to legality itself. A plug spanner is a useful tool for turning various nuts and bolts, but a virtually essential tool for turning spark plugs. The particular utility of plug spanners *vis-à-vis* spark plugs does not alter the fact that plug spanners are tools which are serviceable for many different tasks.

Familiar features of legal thought, however, are hard to reconcile with the idea that law is simply a tool, albeit a tool with particular utility for certain valued political goals. We do not find ourselves reflecting upon the nature of tools, except to consider their serviceability for this or that task. Yet, when law presents itself in the guise of a moral aspiration, its very nature comes to seem a problematic but significant focus for philosophical debate and moral reflection. The Nuremberg trials, for example, might be viewed by some as a triumph of legality over lawless violence, but by others as the reverse. Do courts gain jurisdiction as a result of victory on the battlefield? Does the sheer wickedness of an act render it legally punishable even when it accorded with the statutes in force at the time and place of its performance? Notoriously, these questions force upon us a series of intractable and fundamental puzzles. The puzzles do not primarily concern the serviceability of legality for liberal democracy so much as the nature of legality itself, and the coherence of our various attitudes towards legality. Such questions are hard to envisage in relation to the nature of tools, no matter how indispensable for certain purposes those tools might be.

Furthermore, it is important for us to note that human practices may sometimes be instrumentally valuable for various non-moral goals without it being appropriate to think of those practices as morally neutral tools, or to deny their intrinsically moral status. Take for example, the practice of justice. As Kant points out, a merchant who acts merely from self-interest may eschew opportunities to overcharge the inexperienced, since by maintaining a fixed general price for everyone he makes it possible for all (even children) to deal with him in confidence.[5] We will see in due course that it is possible to argue that even wicked regimes can have self-interested reasons for pursuing justice and the good to a substantial if imperfect extent. But the qualified serviceability of moral practices for self-interested goals does not undermine the claim of those practices to embody moral standards; nor does it suggest that the practices are morally neutral. To think otherwise is simply to confuse the legal positivist separation of law and morals with the quite different distinction between the rectitude of an action and the virtue of the agent. Too easy an equation between practices such as law and tools such as plug spanners invites us to overlook these complexities.[6]

Another way in which we might try to dissolve the apparent conflict between the mundane and aspirational views of law would be by distinguishing the

---

[5] Immanuel Kant, *Groundwork of the Metaphysics of Morals* (1785), translated by Mary J Gregor, *Practical Philosophy: The Cambridge Edition of the Works of Immanuel Kant* (Cambridge: Cambridge University Press, 1996) 4:397. It should be noted that the merchant's aim need not be the maintenance of a reputation for *morality*, but simply a reputation for *consistent pricing*.

[6] See Raz, above n 1, 226 (comparing the rule of law to a knife).

nature of *law* from the nature of one of our guiding ideals, an ideal that we refer to as *the rule of law*. On this approach, the nature of law is to be understood in terms of a set of conditions satisfied by all legal systems; or perhaps as a set of conditions satisfied by central or 'paradigmatic' instances of legal systems, with other possible instances counting as such in virtue of their resemblances to the paradigm cases. The guiding ideal, by contrast, is the ideal of the rule of law, and it is to be understood as a set of conditions to which legal systems *ought* to strive to conform, but from which they are all likely to fall short, albeit in varying degrees.

Such a distinction between 'law' and 'the rule of law' is not an entirely comfortable one, for it aims to separate ideas that, in our ordinary understanding, are not clearly separate but closely linked and perhaps inseparable. Taking words at face value, might we not reasonably assume that 'the rule of law' refers to a state of affairs where law rules? Is it really possible to think of law's existence as one thing and its 'ruling' as another? In so far as the validity of individual legal norms is independent of their efficacy, norms may certainly exist (in the sense of being 'valid') while being disregarded in practice (and so not 'ruling'): in that sense one may have laws that do not 'rule'. Yet this could scarcely be true of the system of norms as a whole: a system of norms that wholly lacks efficacy is not an existing system of law; and a system the valid norms of which are *extensively* disregarded in practice is to that extent a marginal or 'penumbral' instance of a legal system. Consequently, law rules to the extent that it exists as law. Moving beyond the sheer efficacy of norms to those aspects of the rule of law that involve their substantive content, we might wonder whether the very extensive conferment of discretion upon officials (a conferment that, if sufficiently extensive, is understood to detract from the rule of law) might not similarly invite the judgement that the regime in question is but a marginal instance of legal ordering. After all, if the conferment of discretion were to be very extensive, citizens would have to guide their conduct by predictions of official behaviour rather than by legal rules; and a situation where citizens are unable to guide their conduct by reference to rules might well be felt not to be an instance (or not to be a non-marginal instance) of a legal system. This would be so even though the discretion-conferring norms would be perfectly effective in governing the limits of official discretion.

A great many legal theorists seem to concur in separating the idea of 'law' from the idea of 'the rule of law'.[7] The distinction is more often assumed

---

[7] See, for example, Neil MacCormick, *Questioning Sovereignty* (Oxford: Oxford University Press, 1999) 43: 'The concepts of *Rechtsstaat* and of Rule of Law both express certain closely related values that have been advanced in respect of legal order. Some of the proponents of these values in the past and the present may have thought it possible to derive them from pure analyses of the concept of law and have thus been . . . in error.' See also TRS Allan, *Constitutional Justice* (Oxford: Oxford University

without argument than defended, perhaps because philosophers of a certain disposition tend to regard it as obvious that what they take to be the *descriptive* notion of 'law' must be separable from the *value* known as 'the rule of law'. The matter requires more careful attention, however, and it is therefore worth examining an influential defence of the position, offered by Joseph Raz.

Raz on the Rule of Law

In his essay 'The Rule of Law and its Virtue', Raz seeks to identify the virtue that is intrinsic to the rule of law, and to separate this from virtues that the rule of law may contingently possess in particular circumstances. His principal goal is to argue that the intrinsic virtue of the rule of law is a purely 'negative' virtue, in two senses: 'conformity to it does not cause good except through avoiding evil and the evil which is avoided is evil which could only have been caused by the law itself'.[8] For the law 'inevitably creates a great danger of arbitrary power' and the rule of law serves to minimize this danger. When the rule of law exhibits any other moral importance, its importance is purely contingent. Thus, it may be of moral importance to enable the law to perform useful social functions, 'just as it may be of moral importance to produce a sharp knife when it is required for a moral purpose'.[9]

The notion of the rule of law as a 'negative' virtue necessarily requires a distinction to be made between 'law' and 'the rule of law'. For how can the rule of law protect us from evils that only the law can cause, if 'the rule of law' is not a distinct concept from the concept of 'law'?

To Raz's credit, he does not take this separation between ideas as obvious and requiring no argument. In fact, he acknowledges that there are features of our thought that might suggest a rather different picture. He compares law to a knife that is available for good or bad purposes, and the rule of law to the quality of sharpness in a knife. If the law's purposes are to be achieved, the law must be capable of guiding behaviour, 'and the more it conforms to the principles of the rule of law the better it can do so'.[10] Consequently, some minimal degree of compliance with the rule of law is relevant to the status of a form of social organization as law: '[a]s with some other tools, machines, and instruments a thing is not of the kind unless it has at least some ability to perform its function. A knife is not a knife unless it has some ability to cut.'[11] In a later essay, Raz deepens these acknowledgments of interconnectedness between

---

Press, 2001) 62–67. We noted in Chapter 1 that Ronald Dworkin adopts a similar view: see above, p 25.

  [8] Raz, above n 1, 224.   [9] Ibid, 226.   [10] Ibid, 225.   [11] Ibid, 226.

the ideas. He tells us that one of our most 'common images' of the rule of law holds that 'the rule of law is an ideal rooted in the very essence of law', so that '[i]n conforming to it the law does nothing more than be faithful to its own nature'.[12]

Nevertheless, Raz insists upon the importance of separating the two ideas. He takes the 'common image' of their interconnectedness to embody a confusion. He sees nothing but a muddle in the claim that 'the form of law' can be 'an ideal, the ideal of the rule of law, which all law should conform to'. For, 'if it is part of the form of law, then law conforms to it, or it would not be law'.[13] Rather than endorsing this muddled way of thinking, we should acknowledge a certain dualism in our thinking about law, a dualism that can be seen when we try to make sense of the idea that the rule of law can be a constraint upon government.

The dualism in question is one involving a lay sense of 'law' and a technical lawyers' sense: '[f]or the lawyer anything is law if it meets the conditions of validity laid down in the system's rule of recognition or in other rules of the system... To the layman ... the law is essentially a set of open, general, and relatively stable laws.'[14] When we speak of 'the rule of law' we are really speaking of the requirement that the making of particular laws (or legal orders) should be guided by open and relatively stable general rules.[15]

One should not postulate such a dualism in our thinking about law too casually. We should not, without some compelling reason, treat the word 'law' as bearing different senses when it is used generally, and when it is employed in the phrase 'the rule of law'. This follows from general principles of intellectual hygiene, but resistance to such a dualism should be particularly strong in this case. After all, Raz himself concedes that one of our most 'common images' of the rule of law holds that 'the rule of law is an ideal rooted in the very essence of law'.[16] Jurisprudence should be an attempt, so far as possible, to make coherent sense of such settled understandings, which may themselves be constitutive of the social phenomenon of law.

Raz, however, believes that he has such compelling reasons. For, without the dualism of senses, he argues, the idea of government by law would be a tautology rather than a substantive ideal: '[a]ctions not authorised by law cannot be the actions of the government as a government'.[17] Since all governmental

---

[12] Joseph Raz, 'Formalism and the Rule of Law' in Robert P George (ed), *Natural Law Theory* (Oxford: Clarendon Press, 1992) 309, at 309.

[13] Ibid, 320. See also Kelsen, who mutters darkly about erroneous theories wherein 'positive law is justified less by appeal to a higher law . . . than by appeal to the concept of law itself'. Hans Kelsen, *Introduction to the Problems of Legal Theory* (1934), translated by BL Paulson and SL Paulson, (Oxford: Clarendon Press, 1992) 37.   [14] Raz, above n 1, 213.

[15] Ibid.   [16] Raz, 'Formalism and the Rule of Law' above n 12, at 309.

[17] Raz, above n 1, 212.

actions are authorized by law (or they would not be governmental actions) it is impossible, without introducing a second sense of 'law', to account for the idea that the 'rule of law' is a constraint on government.[18] Once we have introduced such a dualism, we can understand how the rule of law can be a constraint on government. In order to count as governmental actions, acts must be authorized by law. But such authorization will not be sufficient to satisfy the requirements of 'the rule of law' if it is authorization by 'law' in the purely technical lawyers' sense: the governmental action must also be guided by relatively stable general rules (by 'law' in the lay sense).

At first glance, Raz's argument seems to rest upon a remarkably legalistic understanding of the notion of government. It is in many contexts perfectly reasonable to speak of legally unauthorized acts of government: as when, for example, the members of the government have acted in a carefully coordinated way to achieve a certain goal, and have presented themselves as acting in their capacity as the government. When we speak of the rule of law as a constraint on government, one might say, it is this sense of government that we generally have in mind. We may speak of it as 'government in the sociological sense'.

Raz anticipates this response, however. He suggests that, if this is what 'the rule of law' means, then it amounts to no more than the requirement that people, including governments, should obey the law. The 'rule of law' in this sense is simply law and order applied to government. But, he tells us '[t]here is more to the rule of law than the law and order interpretation allows.'[19]

There is an important oversight in Raz's argument, however. His argument might be put as follows. The rule of law is taken to be a constraint upon government. Either 'government' is construed legalistically or it is construed sociologically. If it is construed sociologically, the idea of the rule of law is simply the idea that the government, like everyone else, should obey the law; and this 'law and order' view fails to capture much of what we mean by 'the rule of law'. If, on the other hand, the notion of government is construed legalistically, the rule of law (the idea of a government of laws) becomes a tautology rather than a substantive value. It becomes a tautology, that is, if we fail to acknowledge a dualism in the notion of 'law'.

The fallacy in this argument is surely clear. Suppose that we construe the notion of government sociologically, as the coordinated actions of certain individuals or role-occupants who present themselves as acting in their role as members of the government. The idea of the rule of law is not simply the idea that these individuals should obey the law. For it encompasses also the idea that force should not be used against citizens except in response to the breach

---

[18] Ibid.   [19] Raz, ibid.

of some published, prospective rule by that citizen. This is a different idea from the bare notion of obedience to the extant legal provisions. For those provisions might *permit* the use of discretionary violence by governmental officials. In deploying such violence against citizens, the officials would not then be disobeying the law; but the regime of which they are a part would be guilty of a serious departure from the rule of law.

I conclude that it is possible for us to avoid the danger of tautology without adopting Raz's dualism, because it is possible (in our explication of the notion of the rule of law) to define government sociologically without reducing the idea of the rule of law to the bare idea of obedience to law.

Raz's mistake here is closely related to another claim that he makes: one which is not mistaken so much as misleading. It will be recalled that, in proposing a contrast between the lawyerly and lay senses of 'law', Raz tells us that '[f]or the lawyer anything is law if it meets the conditions of validity laid down in the system's rule of recognition or in other rules of the system'.[20] If, for the moment, we accept the positivist account of the rule of recognition, Raz's claim is basically correct. But it is correct only when the system of which we are speaking is a system of law; and it is possible to imagine systems characterized by the existence of a rule of recognition, which nevertheless fail to constitute legal systems. Lon Fuller provides us with some vivid examples: a system where all the rules are kept secret, for example.[21] Or we might imagine a system where the rules spell out sufficient but not necessary conditions for the use of violence against citizens, so that officials feel free to use violence against citizens who have violated no rule. In such systems, citizens would order their conduct by trying to predict the incidence of official sanctions, rather than by reference to publicly available rules: we might with good reason withhold the title of 'law' from such a system. Consequently, the lawyerly and lay senses of 'law' seem to be related after all. The lawyer is (let us assume) applying a rule of recognition. But derivability from such a rule confers legal status only if the rule of recognition is part of a system of law; and it will not be a system of law unless it to some extent approximates to the ideal of the rule of law.

All of this reflects our ordinary understandings. For, do we not think of the rule of law as the situation where law rules? And the situation where law rules is not (as Raz seems to think) simply the situation where the extant rules are obeyed, for it involves a certain content for the law, a content that excludes the conferment of extensive discretionary power upon officers of the state. If the conferment of discretion were to be very extensive, citizens would guide their

[20] Ibid, 213.
[21] Lon Fuller, *The Morality of Law* (revised edition, New Haven, Conn: Yale University Press, 1969).

conduct by prediction of official behaviour rather than by reference to the legal rules: we might well conclude that such a system of governance is not an instance of law at all. Hence, law is realized to the extent that the rule of law obtains.[22]

To some extent Raz seems to acknowledge that the dualistic view he proposes is at odds with our ordinary understanding. As we have already seen, he acknowledges that one of our most 'common images' of the rule of law holds that 'the rule of law is an ideal rooted in the very essence of law'; indeed, '[i]n conforming to it the law does nothing more than be faithful to its own nature'.[23] But he appears to regard this 'common image' as a source of confusion which is to be excised by a clarified theoretical regimentation of our ideas. Perhaps then his overly hasty claims about the relationship between 'government' and 'law', and his erroneous (or at best misleading) assertions to the effect that anything stemming from a rule of recognition will count as 'law', are not the nub of his concerns. Rather, he has a deeper sense that our 'common image' of law embodies a 'muddle', in so far as the criteria by which something qualifies as law cannot also serve as a guiding ideal for law. If this is a muddle, then it must be a mistake to regard law as an intrinsically moral ideal.

But all of this moves much too swiftly. Before acknowledging any need to introduce a dualism into our thinking, and before abandoning one of our most 'common images' of law, we should perhaps explore the alternatives carefully. Is it true that the criteria by which a social ordering counts as law cannot also constitute a guiding ideal for that self-same ordering?

Towards the Archetype

Our ordinary understandings of law seem to embody a contradiction: we think of law as *both* an intrinsically moral idea *and* a morally neutral instrument. One response to this situation is to try and demonstrate that the appearance of contradiction is misleading. Most commonly, this is done by trying to show that our 'aspirational' picture of law is grounded in a misunderstanding of our own settled ideas: we mistake the significance of the law's normative vocabulary; or we confuse the formal justice of rule-application with the substantive justice of the rule's content; or we simply confuse what is *contingently* true of law with what is *necessarily* true.

---

[22] At times, Raz seems unable even to envisage this as a possibility. Thus he contemptuously dismisses Weinrib's suggestion that the form of law is also an ideal to which all law should conform: above n 12, at 320. [23] Ibid, 309.

Another (not incompatible) option imposes a dualism upon our thinking, distinguishing the moral ideal of 'the rule of law' from the concept of 'law' itself. Various arguments are offered in support of such a dualism, but the least obviously flawed of those arguments turns on the impossibility of something being *both* a criterion that must be satisfied by any instance of law, *and* a guiding ideal from which such instances may fall short.

Too quick a regimentation of our thinking may forestall inquiries that need to be carried out, and the fruit of those inquiries might be hard to envisage in advance. The quick regimentation all too often yields a Procrustean theory that is an obstacle rather than a stimulus to further insight. A great deal of analytical jurisprudence is grounded in a disposition to find confusion or emptiness[24] in our ordinary patterns of thought, and to respond to that confusion by the regimentation of our concepts. As we shall see later in this book, what at first appears to be confusion might in fact represent a form of moral reflection that is obscured by the moral voluntarism so deeply rooted in modern jurisprudence. Or apparent confusion might sometimes reflect a sound perception of the complex ways in which our concepts (of justice and legality, for example) can be related. The theorist needs to balance an otherwise admirable desire for clarity against a more submissive respect for the infinite depth of human culture.

In this book I explore the thought that the concept of 'law' might not be best understood in terms of a set of characteristics exhibited by all instances (or all non-marginal instances) of law or legal systems, but in terms of an intellectual archetype to which actual instances of law merely approximate to various degrees. That thought in turn opens up a number of possibilities, including the possibility (rejected as a muddle by Raz) that the idea of law might provide *both* the general criterion whereby instances of law count as such, *and* a guiding ideal by reference to which all such instances ought morally to be judged.

The concept of a 'triangle' is an example of what I shall call an 'archetypal' concept. Triangles are defined by a mathematical definition, but the requirements of the definition will not be fully satisfied by all actual instances of triangles. Indeed, there may be no real-world exemplars of the mathematical archetype. The actual instances of triangles that one comes across in the real world constitute triangles in virtue of the degree to which they approximate to the ideal 'triangle' of mathematical definition. So triangles do not constitute triangles by satisfying a set of criteria, but by approximating to an ideal archetype; and not all triangles are equally triangles: they are triangles to the degree to which they approach the ideal. The triangle I roughly sketch on my pad is

---

[24] See for example Raz's treatment of characteristic features of legal discourse as merely 'rhetorical or ceremonial': Joseph Raz, 'Professor Dworkin's Theory of Rights' (1978) 26 *Political Studies* 123.

only just a triangle, while the diagram of a triangle in the mathematics text-book is much more of a triangle, though still not perfect.

The concept of a 'triangle' may be contrasted with the concept of a 'bach-elor'. Particulars count as bachelors only by fully satisfying a set of criteria (bachelors must be unmarried male human beings) and all particulars that satisfy those criteria will count equally as bachelors. Bachelors do not count as such by degree of approximation to an unattained ideal of bachelorhood; nor do they vary in the extent of their bachelordom. Concepts exhibiting this general type of structure will be referred to here as 'class concepts' in contrast to 'archetypal concepts'. The question then is why should law be identified as the latter and not as a class concept?[25]

If we think of the concept of 'law' as structured by an abstract archetype, we can avoid the need to postulate (with Raz) two meanings for the word 'law': one where it appears in the phrase 'the rule of law', and one where it appears outside that context. For we can see how something can constitute an instance of law (by its approximation to the archetype) while nevertheless falling short of full compliance with the requirements of that concept. We can therefore see how it would be at least *possible* for the concept of law to function as both a descriptive category that serves to identify a distinct form of social ordering, and a guiding ideal of special relevance to social orderings of that type.

To a large extent, the mundane and aspirational views of law simply reflect different aspects of this conceptual structure, and are therefore reconcilable. There is, however, an irreducible core of conflict between them; and, in so far as they do conflict, I will argue that the aspirational view should be preferred. This view, I will suggest, is perfectly compatible with most of the claims that people might have in mind when they casually favour the mundane view, or find it plausible; and this very compatibility constitutes in itself the dissol-ution of any puzzling dualism or contradiction that might be thought to char-acterize our ordinary understanding. Properly understood, the aspirational view makes clear the sense in which the guiding aspiration of 'the rule of law' is

---

[25] I am not, of course, suggesting that these are the only alternatives. Concepts may be structured by family resemblance, to take only one familiar example of a different conceptual form. See Ludwig Wittgenstein, *Philosophical Investigations*, translated by GEM Anscombe (2nd edition, Oxford: Blackwell, 1953) Remarks 65–67.

It is worth noting at this point that defenders of analytical jurisprudence sometimes seem to neglect the possible variety of conceptual forms. Thus Julie Dickson tells us that, given that we recog-nize some forms of social organization as legal systems and some as not being legal systems, it must be the case that law has essential properties, and 'it will be necessarily true that law exhibits those proper-ties'. Julie Dickson, *Evaluation and Legal Theory* (Oxford: Hart Publishing, 2001) 19. By contrast with such claims, my own advocacy of an archetypal concept of law is not based on any thesis about the form that concepts *must* exhibit, but on the ability of the theory as a whole to dissolve apparent antinomies and yield fertile insights.

indeed grounded in 'the essence of law'; and it reveals that the muddle Raz
believes himself to have identified is no muddle at all.

Resistance to an aspirational understanding of law frequently springs from
the thought that, in adopting such an understanding, we will gild and idealize
what, all too often, are sordid realities; realities, indeed, that we need to view in
an undeceiving light. Such concerns, however, to some extent evince a mistake
about the general impetus behind the aspirational view. That impetus is not to
protect established regimes from criticism but to indicate the availability of a
form of immanent critique grounded in the regime's implicit claim to govern
by law. Such a form of critique may, on occasion, be more powerful and pertinent than any criticisms which might be framed in terms of wholly independent values, precisely in so far as it draws upon values to which the regime is
already making a tacit (albeit perhaps cynical) appeal. Moreover, we will see in
due course that the moral idea of law stands in a complex relationship to the
value of justice (a value from which it is otherwise distinct), in such a way that
the intimate connections between law and justice cannot be properly understood if an aspirational understanding of law has been rejected at the outset.

It should not be imagined that, in considering the possibility that the concept of 'law' might exhibit an archetypal structure, I simply beg the question
in favour of the aspirational view. It is certainly true that I thereby create
an intellectual space within which an aspirational understanding of law can
coherently be developed: but the understanding of the concept of 'law' as an
archetypal concept does not in itself commit us to the aspirational view. The
aspirational view is best thought of as composed of two separable theses: first,
the claim that the notion of law is structured by an archetype; and, second, the
claim that the archetype is an intrinsically moral ideal. The essential hallmark
of an archetypal concept is the fact that instantiations of the concept count as
such by resemblance or approximation to the archetype, such resemblance or
approximation being a property that can be exhibited to varying degrees. It
does not follow from this that the archetype must function as a guiding ideal
for the practices that instantiate the archetype; nor does it follow that the
archetype must be intrinsically moral in character.[26]

Our theoretical endeavour is not an articulation of semantic criteria governing our use of the word 'law', but it is nevertheless an error to dismiss, as
some jurists do, a concern for the word's meaning as it ranges over juridical

---

[26] I take Fuller's eight *desiderata* for the rule of law as constituting an adequate (albeit provisional)
account of the archetype of law. These *desiderata* require that law should consist of published prospective rules that are intelligible, free from conflict or contradiction, possible to comply with, stable over
time, and effectively complied with by officials. Fuller's critics have argued that the eight *desiderata*
are morally neutral in character. See Fuller, above n 21, and 'Eight *Desiderata*' later in this chapter. For
criticism of Fuller's view, see Hart, *Essays in Jurisprudence and Philosophy* (Oxford: Clarendon Press,
1983) essay 16.

and non-juridical contexts (e.g. 'the laws of physics'). For the notion of 'law' in that most general (and not specifically juridical) sense involves the ideas of universality, necessity and the governance of particular events. To be laws, human arrangements must consist of general standards rather than particular decisions, the standards must be capable of governing conduct, and they must govern conduct with a degree of 'necessity'. We might profitably view the practices that compose the phenomena of juridical law as an attempt to introduce a domain of universality and necessity into human affairs.

An account of the nature of law must be judged by its ability to yield insight and to make coherent sense of our more settled understandings and beliefs about law. For law is not a phenomenon with a nature wholly independent of our beliefs about it, but one that is constituted by our understandings and expectations. Real or apparent conflicts within that body of understandings generate both intellectual puzzlement and practical juridical problems. The case for thinking of 'law' as an archetypal concept depends in the end upon the insight that is yielded by a theory developing such an approach; and the extent, depth and importance of such insight can be judged only at the conclusion of the theoretical argument, not at its outset. At the outset, however, it is necessary for us to motivate the exploration of this intellectual possibility; and this we can do, even if the reasons offered for favouring an archetypal notion of law must at this stage seem no more than mildly persuasive.

By thinking of law as an archetypal concept we can eliminate the dualism between different senses of 'law'. We do not need to follow Raz's view that the idea of the rule of law involves a lay understanding of law's nature that departs from the lawyer's understanding; nor do we need to regard the word 'law' as bearing a quite different sense when it is employed to describe extant systems and when it is employed in the context of discussions of 'the rule of law'. We also create room for what Raz himself concedes to be one of our most 'common images' of the rule of law as 'an ideal rooted in the very essence of law' so that '[i]n conforming to it the law does nothing more than be faithful to its own nature'.[27] If the idea of an archetype does not exhibit clear intellectual deficiencies that render it obviously unsound, then it merits our consideration on these grounds (of eliminating a dualism, and admitting room for the intelligibility of a common understanding) without more.

I will suggest that such an approach can to a considerable extent dissolve the dualism of mundane and aspirational understandings of law by revealing how all of the more plausible theses that might incline us towards the mundane view are in fact fully compatible with the aspirational view (something that we cannot discern so long as we are thinking in terms of concepts defined by flat

---

[27] Above n 12, 309.

criteria). Later in the book I argue that the approach offers us a more plausible analysis of the nature of judicial judgment than can be offered by Hart's positivism, and reveals otherwise overlooked distinctions between possible forms of legal thought (that I dub 'reflexive' and 'non-reflexive' realizations of the archetype). The approach can also provide us with a plausible basis for solving the intractable problem of the nature of doctrinal legal analysis. In the background to all of this, I wish to place the suggestion that an understanding of 'law' as an archetype moves us away from the sterility of much modern jurisprudential debate towards a stronger and more coherent engagement with the classical tradition of philosophy of law.

A Lost Tradition

Why does the notion of law as an archetypal concept create puzzlement (of the type articulated by Raz) within contemporary jurisprudence? Lon Fuller and Ernest Weinrib[28] have both taken up the idea, but this very reliance has tended to mystify rather than enlighten some of their critics.[29]

Although tracing its ancestry to the nineteenth century, analytical jurisprudence assumed its present dominance in the work of HLA Hart, whose principal book was published in 1961.[30] When Hart's work first appeared, it was not unknown for some of his readers to complain that his enterprise was an inquiry into words rather than an inquiry into the nature of law, as

---

[28] Fuller, above n 21; Ernest Weinrib, 'Law as a Kantian Idea of Reason' (1987) 87 *Columbia Law Review* 472. There are also certain resemblances between this approach and the views of Ronald Dworkin, as presented in *Law's Empire* (London: Fontana, 1986), and the idea of 'focal meaning' as invoked by Finnis, above n 3. Full consideration of the relationship between these approaches would be a complex matter taking us too far from the main line of inquiry explored in this book. It is worth noting, however, that Finnis adopts the strategy criticized earlier, of seeking to underpin his substantive conclusion by reference to a highly contestable methodological argument. Thus, the first chapter of his book argues that legal theory must be grounded in the practical understanding of the *phronimos*; the subsequent chapters then argue that, as a consequence of this, 'law' must be understood by reference to the 'focal instances' where law serves the common good. This makes it easy for those who reject Finnis's methodological claims to choose a different account of the relevant 'focal instances'. See e.g. Matthew Kramer, *In Defense of Legal Positivism* (Oxford: Oxford University Press, 1999) 237–239.

Dworkin also builds substantive conclusions upon methodological claims that positivists are likely to reject. But his theory differs still more fundamentally from the present theory, in so far as he does not claim that instances of law 'in a pre-interpretive sense' count as such in virtue of their participation in the guiding idea of integrity. It is this that explains the common accusation that Dworkin offers a theory of adjudication, not a theory of the nature of law. See *Law's Empire*, 103.

I criticize Weinrib's theory in 'Justice, Causation and Private Law' in Maurizio Passerin d'Entreves and Ursula Vogel (eds), *Public and Private: Legal, Political and Philosophical Perspectives* (London: Routledge, 2000). [29] Above n 12.

[30] HLA Hart, *The Concept of Law* (1961), (2nd edition, Oxford: Clarendon Press, 1994).

jurisprudence had traditionally been conceived. The complainants, however, were uneasily aware that inquiry into the nature of law might well be considered an empirical, rather than a philosophical, matter. Earlier philosophers were not infrequently accused of a vice labelled 'essentialism', which was taken to consist in the belief that general words such as 'law' derive their meaning from an abstract essence with a metaphysical status independent of linguistic usage, and available for investigation by philosophical argument rather than empirical inquiry.[31] Once essentialism of this kind was avoided as an option, it became hard to see how an investigation of law's nature could be anything other than an empirical matter. Hart appeared to answer this question by relying upon the traditional philosophical distinction between the necessary and the contingent, while rejecting as unduly mysterious any idea of a metaphysical essence or 'nature' of law in which such necessities might be grounded. The relevant form of necessity was taken to be grounded in the structure of our concepts and language.

The middle decades of the twentieth century did not provide an intellectual environment within which the sympathetic reconstruction and recovery of an older tradition of philosophical reflection upon law seemed possible or desirable. The dismissal of great swathes of political philosophy as embodying the errors of 'essentialism' was conducive to a high-handed attitude which made it well-nigh impossible for the present to learn from the past.[32] Thus we find one theorist suggesting (admittedly *en passant*) that the older tradition rested upon a convention requiring 'political and moral ideals' to be put forward 'as versions of the meaning, definition, or function of law'.[33] The invocation of such a mysterious and seemingly pointless convention as a way of making sense of the history of philosophy of law is an eloquent admission of inability to make better sense of that tradition of inquiry, and evinces a quite remarkable lack of interest in historical continuity with the tradition. The emergence of analytical jurisprudence is quite widely perceived as amounting to a major advance over earlier reflections upon the nature of law, precisely in so far as it clearly separates inquiry into law's nature from substantive moral reflection upon law's justice and binding force. Analytical jurists tend to construe older writings on the philosophy of law as the embodiment of confusions that have now been dispelled, and exhibit in consequence a striking lack of interest in the history of that subject. In this way they severely impoverish the intellectual resources that they have at their disposal.

---

[31] For an influential discussion, dating from the same period as Hart's theory, see Karl Popper, *The Poverty of Historicism* (London: Routledge, 1957) 26–34.

[32] See, for example, TD Weldon, *The Vocabulary of Politics* (Harmondsworth: Penguin Books, 1953).

[33] Tony Honoré, *Making Law Bind* (Oxford: Clarendon Press, 1987) 32.

Perhaps resistance to the idea of an archetype is based upon the assumption that such archetypes would have to inhabit a strange metaphysical realm accessible only to the Platonic philosopher who has escaped from the cave. But such an assumption would surely be a mistake. The notion of 'law' is not one that simply *describes* certain independent practices, but a concept that plays a role *within* the relevant practices. In the last chapter I compared the idea of law to a notional point in space that gives coherence to a drawing. In trying to locate and depict this orienting idea, we are faced by the problem that our ordinary understandings ascribe to law a multiplicity of features that are not easily reconcilable: law is an established institution, but also an ideal for such institutions; an apparatus of force, but also the negation of force; a product of authority, but also the source of any such authority; a huge assemblage of enactments and pronouncements but also a system of ideas that is not reducible to the totality of enactments and pronouncements, serving to control their meaning and juridical effect. The question we are asking is 'what must law be for these various beliefs and understandings to be true of law's nature?' If the most coherent solution to this problem is provided by an abstract archetype, no problematic metaphysical commitments are involved: our practices themselves *create* the archetype in so far as they are structured by ideas that are best understood as pointing to the archetype.[34]

The thought that our concept of law may be structured by an archetype requires no commitment to a strange or luxuriant ontology. Yet it would nevertheless be a mistake to underestimate the substantial connections that obtain between this thought and the Platonic or Hegelian tradition of idealism. For our enterprise lies solidly within the tradition of philosophical reflection upon the *logos*: reflection, that is, upon the world as it becomes clear to us in our speaking of it.[35] In distinguishing his transcendental idealism from the older tradition of idealism, Kant tells us that the central proposition of the older tradition was that 'all knowledge through the senses and through experience is nothing but illusion, and only in the ideas of pure understanding and reason is truth'.[36]

---

[34] It will be argued in due course that the archetype of law is recognizable as a moral idea, representing the conditions within which one can live in a political community while enjoying a degree of independence from the power of others. These conditions reflect permanent features of the human condition. Their range and content is not exhausted by the provisional understanding of them that we might possess at any one time. There is, of course, a question to be raised about the metaphysics involved in any such idea of moral knowledge: but it is not a question specific to the idea of the archetype, and it cannot properly be addressed in this context.

[35] Hans-Georg Gadamer, *The Idea of the Good in Platonic–Aristotelian Philosophy* (1976), translated by P Christopher Smith (New Haven, Conn: Yale University Press, 1986); Hans-Georg Gadamer, *Hegel's Dialectic* (1971), translated by P Christopher Smith (New Haven, Conn: Yale University Press, 1976).

[36] Immanuel Kant, *Prolegomena to Any Future Metaphysics*, Appendix, translated by Peter G Lucas, (Manchester: Manchester University Press, 1953) 145.

If this is our idea of the tradition of idealism, then it would clearly be an error to assimilate the present theory to that tradition. There are, however, other aspects to idealism, aspects that link Plato to Kant, and that achieve great prominence in the aftermath of Kant's work. Far from being an embarrassment, these connections with the idealist tradition mark out the extent to which the present theory restores the substantial concerns of the philosophy of law, and overcomes the sterility of more recent legal theoretical debates.

Support for the Mundane View?

The term 'legal positivism' is now used to refer to a great diversity of different theories and theses. Not all of these entail what I have labelled the 'mundane' view of law as an instrument that is equally serviceable for good purposes and bad. It may well be the case, however, that acceptance of the mundane view entails several of the theses associated with legal positivism. If law is as serviceable for evil as for good, it would seem (for example) that there can be no necessary connection between law and morality, or at least no necessary connection grounded in the concept of law itself. Similarly, if law is as serviceable for evil as for good, it would seem that law is capable of being identified without reliance upon moral judgement. In this way, acceptance of the mundane view of law tends to support legal positivism in at least some of its various versions. The mundane view of law itself gains much credibility from certain fairly obvious features of law. In this way, legal positivism can come to seem the clear and obvious truth, and its opponents may appear to be the victims of confusion or intellectual perversity.

It is important at the outset, therefore, to identify certain obvious ways in which law can indeed be the instrument of evil, and to explain why these ways are in reality not at all germane to the fundamental issue. This procedure will help us to focus the question that must be addressed in choosing between the mundane and aspirational views of law, in so far as such a choice must be made. Having achieved a clear formulation of the question at issue, however, I will suggest that it is not at all hard to answer that question: the mundane view is simply wrong.

The most obvious respect in which law may be thought to be as serviceable for evil as for good is visible when we focus our attention upon the possible content of laws within an established legal system. Some theorists hold that law is essentially a product of authority, in the sense that individual rules become law by being deliberately posited or enacted by those who occupy positions of law-making authority. Whether or not enactment by authority truly represents law's essence, enactment of laws by authority is certainly a familiar and pervasive feature of modern legal systems. Such authorities may well have good reasons, of justice or the common good, for choosing to enact the laws that they do in fact enact. Nevertheless (we might hold) it is the fact of enactment that makes a rule a law, and not the fact of its being just or good. Consequently, it is entirely conceivable that the authorities might enact as law rules that are in fact unjust or even downright wicked.[37] What follows from that is that the justice and reasonableness of the law's content is at best a contingency, dependent upon the rules that the authorities have chosen to enact: had the authorities chosen to enact unjust and exploitative rules, those rules would have become valid laws in virtue of the fact of enactment.

What we have been referring to as the 'mundane' view of law holds that law is not, in itself, a moral ideal but rather a tool that is equally serviceable for good and bad purposes. Does the mundane view follow from the thought that law is enacted by authority? It might seem that it *does* so follow, for we have just seen that the view of law as enacted by authority yields the conclusion that authorities may enact unjust rules as law. If unjust rules may be enacted as law, does that not show that law may be used as an instrument for the advancement of unjust goals? And does that not show the mundane view to be correct?

The short answer is 'no'. For, to count as a law, the decree issued by some powerful person must form part of a *system* of governance by law. Hence, when we ask whether law is equally serviceable for good and for evil, we are asking whether a regime devoted to wicked goals would find that the general maintenance of a system of governance by law was an appropriate way of advancing its evil objectives. Given the existence of a system of governance by law, persons possessed of law-making authority within that system might find that their goals can be best advanced by suitable legislation; but it may nevertheless be the case that certain moral commitments are inherent in the maintenance of the general scheme of governance into which the legislation fits. Perhaps one would govern by law only if one was motivated by certain moral considerations, or if one wanted to pretend to be so motivated. The issue dividing the mundane and aspirational views of law concerns the serviceability of *law* for evil goals, not the serviceability of individual *laws* within the context of a system that we simply take for granted.

---

[37] I set on one side here the possibility of defending Radbruch's thesis that the gross injustice of an enactment should deprive the enactment of legal validity. Alexy has shown that this thesis is far more defensible than positivists tend to assume. See Robert Alexy, *The Argument from Injustice* (1992), translated by SL Paulson and BL Paulson (Oxford: Oxford University Press, 2002). See also the essays by Alexy and Julian Rivers in David Dyzenhaus (ed), *Recrafting the Rule of Law* (Oxford: Hart Publishing, 1999).

Contrary to appearances, therefore, the prominence of authority and enactment within the law does not provide a basis from which we might declare an easy victory for the mundane view.

Similarly, one should not imagine that the mundane view of law is supported by the possibility that officials such as judges might fulfil the requirements of their role while being motivated by entirely wicked goals; for the motives of individual officials may be parasitic upon the practice of others in rather the same way that the possibility of wicked individual laws is parasitic upon the existence of the legal system as a whole. That is to say, given the existence of a legal system that is sustained by the shared and orderly practices of officials, individual officials might see the performance of their role within that structure as serving their selfish interests or wicked goals. This may be simply a matter of earning a large judicial salary, or sustaining a state of affairs that is in general beneficial to the official and his class. The possibility of such self-interested motivation, however, does not cast any real light upon the nature of law as such: for it does not serve to explain why the regime as a whole should choose to pursue its goals through the institutions of law.

We might even envisage possible situations where the rule of law is maintained within a regime where *all* of the officials are motivated by purely self-interested goals. The possibility of such regimes is nevertheless compatible with the aspirational view. For maintenance of the rule of law might best be explained here, not by reference to the regime choosing the rule of law as a serviceable instrument for wicked goals, but by the regime's inability co-operatively to secure the gains that might flow from (total or partial) abandonment of the rule of law. Consider, for example, a well-established legal system that comes to be taken over by officials who are entirely self-seeking, but who do not openly acknowledge this fact, even in their dealings with each other. Any deviation from the rule of law by a particular official might, in these circumstances, leave that official open to damaging criticism. The criticism would be motivated by a desire to defeat the deviant official in the competition to secure a greater proportion of the regime's monetary or other benefits; and it would be effective in so far as other officials did not wish to expose themselves to similar criticism by a failure to sanction the deviant. Even if this scenario describes a possible situation, it nevertheless fails to demonstrate the soundness of the mundane view: for it fails to present law as a serviceable instrument for the regime's wicked goals. Quite to the contrary, in fact, the law operates in the example as a constraint upon the governing officials' ability to advance their collective interests: the law is sustained by the inability of the officials to secure those gains, in consequence of their own strategic behaviour.

Suppose that someone offered the following claim: 'a wicked regime might pursue its objectives through law precisely in order to conceal its wicked character. By operating with a careful respect for legality, it might succeed in appearing (at least to superficial examination) as a benign regime that is motivated by considerations of justice.' Such a claim would be misguided as a defence of the mundane view. For, as an integral part of its account of the reasons a wicked regime might have for establishing and respecting the institutions of law, it invokes an assumed connection between those institutions and moral motivation of precisely the kind that the mundane view seeks to question. There is no denying that a wicked regime may find it *possible* to pursue its goals through law (I will in due course argue that the choice of law as the favoured instrument of government would come at a substantial cost in terms of the regime's wicked goals); but will it have good reasons of a non-parasitic sort for choosing law in preference to other governmental instrumentalities? Or will the only good reasons for choosing law as the medium by which government is conducted be reasons that assume a belief in some intrinsic connection between law and morality?

Before moving on it should be noted that defenders of the mundane view need to establish (at a minimum) that the practices of law are *equally* serviceable for good and for evil: it would clearly be insufficient to establish (even if this were possible) that law is serviceable for evil to a substantial extent, but not equally serviceable for good and for evil. For a demonstration of substantial, as opposed to equal, serviceability would not serve to negate law's status as an intrinsically moral idea rather than a morally neutral instrument. Consider once again Kant's merchant (mentioned above) who charges everyone the same price, but who does so from a concern for his own self-interest. The merchant observes the practice of justice, but his conduct is not motivated by a concern for justice. His practice will be just to the extent that just practice serves his self-interested goals, but the possibility of divergence between those goals and the requirements of justice will always be present. Consequently, just practice may be highly serviceable for the merchant's self-interested goals while nevertheless being less serviceable for those goals than for the goal of justice as such. The fact that the practice of justice may at times, and purely contingently, be serviceable for some non-moral goal does nothing to demonstrate that the practice of justice is not the embodiment of a moral ideal. Similarly, a demonstration that observance of the rule of law may at times, and to some extent, be serviceable for evil goals does nothing to negate law's status as an intrinsically moral idea. We will see in due course that this raises some serious problems for legal positivism.

Asking the Right Question

The preceding section suggests that there are certain respects in which it is obvious[38] that laws may be employed in the service of evil; yet, it is argued, none of this actually does much to support the mundane view of law as a morally neutral instrument that is as serviceable for evil as for good. Within a legal system, individual laws may be enacted and enforced for wicked, unjust or self-serving reasons; and judges or officials may follow and apply the law for similar motives: but all of this is quite compatible with the claim that the institution of law as such can be rendered intelligible only when we discern its relationship to certain moral values.[39]

Theories that assert the existence of a necessary conceptual relationship between law and morality commonly encounter an objection centring upon real or imaginary examples of wicked legal systems. Where real examples are cited, they may sometimes be disposed of by the arguments set out in the preceding section. Perhaps, for example, the system includes a great many wicked laws; but the regime's faithful adherence to law as its chosen instrument of governance may nevertheless be explicable only by certain moral commitments, or by the hypocritical desire to hide behind such apparent moral commitments.

A rather different problem is posed by the invocation of purely imaginary examples. Someone might, for example, concede that actual wicked regimes tend to make extensive use of extra-legal violence as their favoured instrument; and where those regimes do observe the rule of law, this observance cannot be disconnected from the regime's cynical claim to govern justly. Yet it might nevertheless be pointed out that, if we *were* to encounter a wicked regime that did in fact follow the rule of law closely, while making no pretence of governing justly, we would have good reason to think of it and speak of it as a legal system. Such imaginary examples may well seem to be relevant, in so far

---

[38] Subject to the qualification in n 37.

[39] We discern a relationship between the rule of law and moral values when we see how the pursuit or observance of the rule of law is rendered intelligible by values that we recognize as forming part of our inherited vocabulary of moral ideas. This does not necessarily involve endorsement of the value in question. Thus one might hold that the rule of law embodies a commitment to a certain abstract idea of equality that is a recognizable constituent of our moral tradition, while nevertheless rejecting the value of equality as essentially empty or mystificatory. When one rejects such a value, however, one does so by invoking other elements in our shared moral understanding. The endorsement of a value is therefore a matter of judgement, not an ungrounded exercise of will. For this reason amongst others, an adequate jurisprudence should be constructed in such a way as to provide space for dialogue with theories that view law in a negative light. See Simmonds, 'Bringing the Outside In' (1993) 13 OJLS 147.

as we are concerned with the alleged existence of conceptually necessary connections between law and morality. If our semantic intuitions indicate that we would apply the label 'law' to a system that exhibited certain formal features while being unremittingly wicked, it might seem that our ordinary concept of 'law' exhibits no necessary connection with morality.[40]

It must be remembered, however, that such semantic intuitions can be explained in different ways. Suppose that the legal theorist reflects upon an imagined example of an openly wicked but formally meticulous regime, and concludes that his settled semantic intuitions incline him to judge the regime to be an instance of 'law'. Contrary to some very common assumptions, such a conclusion would not serve to support the mundane against the aspirational view of law, but would be completely neutral between the two views. For a theorist inclined to the aspirational view would simply say that the judgement about the imaginary wicked regime was shaped by the fact that the regime possessed formal features that made it closely resemble the archetype of 'law', an archetype that the aspirational theorist would regard as intrinsically moral.

Claims about the applicability of the concept of 'law' to real or imaginary examples, therefore, are not very germane to the ultimate issue. Our question is whether law should be understood as the embodiment of a moral aspiration, or as a neutral instrument that is as serviceable for evil as for good. A situation where wicked rulers oppress a subject population, but also adhere to the rule of law, is of course logically conceivable. The question, however, is not whether it is logically conceivable, but whether the said wicked rulers would have any good reason for acting in that way. To decide between the mundane and aspirational views, therefore, we need to address the following question: would a regime devoted to wicked or self-serving ends have good reason to establish and maintain the institutions of law?

Eight *Desiderata*

As we have already seen, the archetypal view opens up the *possibility* of a coherent aspirational understanding of law (thereby giving it the potential to capture some familiar assumptions, such as those involved at Nuremberg) while not begging the question *in favour of* an aspirational view. However, much depends here upon how we construct our account of the archetype. The aspirational view of law might not be entailed by the general idea that instances of law may count as such in virtue of their approximation to an abstract archetype; but it

---

[40] If we feel that we have no stable semantic intuitions on such an issue, we might nevertheless feel (for reasons of descriptive or explanatory clarity) that 'law' is a label most appropriately applied on the basis of the said formal features, and reach the same conclusion by this slightly longer route.

might be entailed by the particular account of the archetype that we choose to construct. Thus, for example, if the 'archetype' of law were to be a matter of the law's compliance with justice or equality, or its serving the common good,[41] we could scarcely expect legal positivists to agree that law is best understood by reference to that archetype. We need to construct an account of the archetype of law that serves to order our more settled understandings of law, while not simply begging the question against positivism.

Fortunately, our work is already done for us. For we can proceed by adopting Fuller's account of the eight 'precepts' or '*desiderata*' of what he called the 'inner morality of law'. According to Fuller, for a legal system to exist, there must be (i) rules, and the rules must be (ii) published, (iii) prospective, (iv) intelligible, (v) free from conflict and contradiction, (vi) possible to comply with, (vii) not constantly changing, and there should be (viii) congruence between the declared rule and official action.[42] Fuller's argument, which is frequently misunderstood, is best understood as consisting of two steps. In the first step, he claims that no social ordering will count as a legal system if it fails entirely in respect of any one of the eight *desiderata*: that is to say, if it has no rules; or if all the rules are kept secret; or if all the rules are retrospective; and so forth. Legal systems count as such by how closely they approximate to the situation of total compliance with all eight. This state of total compliance, however, is never attained by any actual legal system. The second step of his argument then claims that the eight *desiderata*, when taken collectively, are recognizable as a moral aspiration. Putting the two steps together, we have the thesis that, since instances of law count as such by their degree of approximation to a moral aspiration, law is an intrinsically moral phenomenon.

Fuller's critics have tended to dispute the second step in this argument, rather than the first. That is to say, they have claimed that his eight precepts or *desiderata* have no claim to represent a moral ideal of any sort: the connections between those precepts and morality are entirely contingent. Fuller made it easy for his critics to draw this conclusion, for he tended to argue that compliance with the eight precepts would make it harder to pursue wicked goals than to pursue virtuous goals. Thus he claimed that wicked regimes will not want to make their aims open and obvious by working through published rules, and even that wicked aims cannot in principle be formulated clearly.[43] Such arguments seek to explain the moral significance of the rule of law by reference to moral goals that are analytically distinguishable from actual compliance with the rule of law: they commit one to search for connections that are necessary yet fundamentally instrumental in character, and they thereby invite the conclusion that only contingent connections have been established.

---

[41] See Dworkin, above n 28; Finnis, above n 3.   [42] Above n 21.
[43] Ibid, Chapter 4.

In this book no such vulnerable claims as those made by Fuller will be relied upon. The argument will not be that wicked goals cannot be pursued through the rule of law, nor that the pursuit of such goals through the rule of law will be more difficult than the pursuit of virtuous goals. Instead it will be argued that compliance with the rule of law is not a matter of instrumental efficacy at all, whether the goals in question are good or bad. Governments pursue various objectives and employ the law as an instrument in that pursuit. But a government's compliance with the requirements of the rule of law is not best explained by considerations of instrumental efficacy. Rather, it must be explained by reference to a concern to maintain an intrinsically valuable form of moral association that is embodied in the rule of law, or by a desire hypocritically to assume the appearance of such a concern.[44] Wicked goals *can* be pursued through the rule of law, but non-hypocritical compliance with the rule of law can be motivated only by a concern for a particular form of moral association and not by a concern for instrumental efficacy.[45]

The first step in Fuller's argument has attracted less criticism than the second. This may to some extent be the result of a failure to see that there are indeed *two* separable steps in his argument, but it also reflects the fact that Fuller's account of the archetype of law is calculated to capture a conception of law's nature that positivists are unlikely to dispute. To this end, Fuller employs a story about a ruler called Rex, whose efforts at lawmaking go astray in a variety of ways. The story is intended to trigger some of our most settled intuitions about the limits of applicability of the concepts of 'law' or 'legal system'. We are invited to conclude that a system where (for example) all rules are kept secret, or where officials never act in accordance with rules, or where rules are published but turn out to be impossible to comply with, would not constitute a legal system.

Fuller's story of Rex seeks to activate and explore our intuitive grasp of the concept of law.[46] Fuller relies upon our willingness to say that a form of governance that is wholly devoid of rules, or in which none of the rules are possible to comply with (and so forth, for the rest of the eight *desiderata*), is not a system of law. This seems to be a direct appeal to semantic intuition, and some will view it with suspicion for that reason. Do we really share Fuller's intuitions? And, if we do, how much importance can properly be attached to that fact? A theory of law must apply to the phenomena we ordinarily think of as law, or

---

[44] There is a third possibility. As explained above, if a government composed entirely of self-serving individuals were to gain control of a state within which the rule of law already obtained, the government might continue to comply with the rule of law in consequence of an inability to capture the gains that would flow from departures from the rule of law. Such an inability could be the consequence of the strategic behaviour of the individual officials. See above, p 61.

[45] This is subject to the qualification in the preceding footnote.   [46] Above n 21, Chapter 2.

forfeit its claim to *be* a theory of law. To that extent, legal theory is constrained by semantic intuition. But the constraint need not be very substantial, for individual semantic intuitions may be challenged and revised in the light of general theoretical analyses, provided that the analysis exhibits some correspondence with our ordinary understanding as a whole, and affords a degree of insight or clarity not otherwise attainable.

We saw in Chapter 1 that Ronald Dworkin has suggested that there cannot be a meaningful philosophical debate about the nature of law as a type of institutional social structure. In his view, we lack sufficiently rich and determinate semantic intuitions to dictate any more than a very rough answer to such a question (our intuitions will not be 'outraged' by any of the rival answers on offer) and law is not a 'natural kind' with empirical or moral boundaries that await exploration. Only in the context of specific research projects, and in relation to the needs of such projects, does it make sense to look for a more precise account of the nature of law in the sociological sense.

But we saw also in Chapter 1 that this argument is misguided, for it neglects or underestimates the extent to which our concepts are interconnected, so that conclusions about the applicability of the sociological concept of law may dictate or suggest or require a particular analysis of rights and duties (for example). It is because the analysis of each concept has consequences for the analysis of its neighbours that philosophical reflection need not be rendered empty and indeterminate by the allegedly sparse and inconclusive nature of those semantic intuitions that bear directly upon the applicability of any particular concept that is under discussion. A conceptual analysis might be unacceptable, even though it does not 'outrage' discrete semantic intuitions,[47] if the totality of its implications and consequences is contrived, artificial and capable of casting little light. Moreover, when settled and determinate intuitions are directly in point, they need not be viewed as an incontestable bedrock but are always in principle open to revision: everything depends upon the clarificatory power and persuasiveness of the analysis as a whole.

In this book, I will assume the correctness of Fuller's judgements concerning the inapplicability of the concept of law to systems that wholly lack rules, or contain only impossible rules, or rules that are secret, and so forth. That is to say, I will assume that these judgements do indeed reflect our own intuitive grasp of the concept of law as embodied in the natural reactions we would exhibit when invited to apply the label 'law' to such imaginary systems. But I should also say that, in my belief, each of these judgements could be defended by reference to the intellectually troubling consequences that would flow from an alternative decision. To insist that a system of wholly retrospective

---

47 Ronald Dworkin, *Justice in Robes* (Cambridge, Mass: Harvard University Press, 2006) 3.

enactments (for example) might constitute a legal order would inevitably commit us to a series of increasingly artificial and unenlightening positions on other issues, such as the nature of rights and duties, the sense in which law is an ordering of human conduct, and so forth.

By adopting Fuller's account of the eight *desiderata* as a (provisional) understanding of the archetype of law, we can work from ground that positivists are likely to endorse, and that some positivists have in fact explicitly endorsed. This reduces the need to offer, at the outset, a fully worked-out defence of the intuitions from which Fuller's argument proceeds. But I will show that this starting point ultimately leads to a conclusion that is fatal to positivism. From that conclusion, I will derive a radically revised understanding of the nature of jurisprudential inquiry: an understanding which reveals the settled intuitions from which Fuller proceeds to be inchoate moral insights rather than (as they might at first seem) semantic intuitions. From that revised understanding, I will move towards a revision of Fuller's account of the archetype.

3

Evil Regimes and the Rule of Law

We are currently exploring the resources of a legal theory constructed in terms of an abstract archetype of law. We are also assuming that we have arrived at an initial understanding of that archetype by consulting our settled intuitions as to what would and would not count as an instance of 'law'. I have in mind here the semantic intuitions that are activated by Fuller's famous story of Rex's efforts at law-making: thus, we would not apply the label 'law' to a system that contained no rules at all, or in which all the rules were retrospective, or unintelligible, or contradictory, or impossible to comply with, or constantly changing, or where the officials never acted in accordance with the rules. Later we will have good reason to conclude that these settled understandings reflect inchoate moral insights, but for the present they can be taken as reflecting our pre-theoretical grasp of the concept of 'law'.

Not only does Fuller's account of the eight *desiderata* seem very plausible as an (at least preliminary) analysis of the archetype informing our concept of law, but it could also be seen as more or less common ground between the mundane and aspirational views. The notion of law as consisting of published, prospective, intelligible and followable rules, to which official conduct generally conforms, is a conception of law which should create no particular conflict with the outlook of the legal positivist. One might, of course, object to Fuller's account on a variety of grounds; and, later in this book, I will myself acknowledge the desirability of revising Fuller's account in a number of respects. But there is no obvious reason why positivists as opposed to other legal theorists should take special exception to the account.

When legal positivists have criticized Fuller they have typically concentrated their fire, not on the content of the eight *desiderata*, but on Fuller's characterization of those precepts as an 'inner morality of law'. The classic source for this line of criticism is, of course, the work of HLA Hart. When we examine Hart's observations closely, however, we find that their import is not entirely clear. Consequently, this chapter must begin with an exegetical discussion before we can get to the real meat of the debate.

In *The Concept of Law*, Hart tells us that the formal features of governance by rule are 'closely related to the requirements of justice which lawyers term principles of legality.' He then tells us that 'one critic of positivism' (presumably Fuller) has seen here 'something amounting to a necessary connection between law and morality'. Hart's conclusion is that 'if this is what the necessary connection of law and morality means, we may accept it. It is unfortunately compatible with very great iniquity.'[1]

Hart seems to be saying that 'we may accept' Fuller's thesis that there is a necessary connection between law and morals. But is this willingness to 'accept' Fuller's view ironic or genuine? Is Hart suggesting that, in the light of their compatibility with great iniquity, the formal features of governance by rule cannot really constitute a necessary connection with morality, at least in any substantial or significant sense? Or is he suggesting that there *is indeed* here a significant and necessary connection between law and morality, but not the type that his theory seeks to deny?

Let us call the first reading the 'ironic' reading, and the second reading the 'concession' reading. If we construe Hart's observation on the concession reading, we thereby call into question the conventional understanding that Hart disagrees with Fuller's main thesis: for we would have to take Hart as agreeing with that thesis. If we construe his observation on the ironic reading, we preserve the conventional view that Hart disagrees with Fuller's main thesis.

The Concession Reading

At first, some people might be very puzzled by the concession reading, for it seems to ascribe to Hart a view that is at odds with his legal positivism. Legal positivism is frequently taken to involve the denial of *any* necessary connection between law and morals. Yet the concession reading takes Hart to be acknowledging precisely such a necessary connection. In fact, the position is a little more complicated than this, partly in consequence of the vagueness and ambiguity of the term 'legal positivism'. Hart does speak of legal positivism as denying the existence of necessary connections between law and morals. But he tends to equate this with a denial of any connection between law as it is and as it ought to be.[2] Consequently, one might perhaps read Hart, not as denying all necessary connections between law and morals, but simply as denying any necessary connection between the validity of a law and its substantive justice or injustice. On this reading, Hart might concede that there is a necessary connection between law and morals, but not a connection that would guarantee the substantive justice of the law. Since Fuller's eight *desiderata* appear to

---

[1] HLA Hart, *The Concept of Law* (2nd edition, Oxford: Clarendon Press, 1994) 207.
[2] See HLA Hart, *Essays in Jurisprudence and Philosophy* (Oxford: Clarendon Press, 1983) 57ff.

concern the formal features of law (such as its publicity and prospectivity) rather than its substantive content, Hart might coherently acknowledge the intrinsically moral significance of those formal features while sustaining a clear separation between legal validity and substantive justice.

However, if we construe Hart's positivism in this way, it becomes hard to understand why Hart seemed to think that his positivism necessitated a defence of the thesis that the acceptance of the rule of recognition by officials can be based upon purely non-moral considerations. For, according to Hart, such acceptance need not be based upon moral reasons, nor do we need to view the officials as *purporting* to be motivated by moral considerations.[3] This thesis gives rise to some serious deficiencies in Hart's theory, for (as we shall see in the next chapter) it is hard to see how officials could intelligibly invoke, as a justification for the ordering of sanctions, a rule that they accept for purely self-interested reasons. If Hart's aim was simply to defend a clear separation between legal validity and substantive justice, he might have restricted himself to the more limited thesis that officials need not accept the rule of recognition for reasons grounded in the substantive justice of the laws stemming from that rule: their acceptance could stem from (for example) a moral concern for the maintenance of a shared fabric of publicly ascertainable rules as a basis for social order. The stronger thesis that Hart chose to defend forms an essential part of any version of legal positivism that denies *any* necessary connection between law and morals; but it would be superfluous to a theory that only denies necessary connections between legal validity and substantive justice. Perhaps Hart's attachment to the thesis in question could be portrayed as simply a discrete error: perhaps he saw that self-interested guidance by the rule of recognition was a possibility, but failed to see how it was always parasitic upon the acceptance of the rule by others for moral reasons (in the various ways that I explained in the last chapter). But his position is given greater coherence if we treat it as an integral part of a broad denial of necessary connections between law and morals.

In any case, if the concession reading were correct, we would expect Hart to endorse Fuller's idea of an 'inner morality of law' rather than to reject it. Fuller distinguished the 'inner' morality of law from its 'external' morality, and he took the latter to be represented by (amongst other things) the law's substantive justice or injustice. Admittedly, he was inclined to argue that a concern for the inner morality of law tends to flow over into a concern for substantive justice (external morality). On the 'concession' reading, Hart would have to be read as departing from Fuller at this latter point, but as accepting the core idea of an inner morality forming an integral part of the concept of law itself. If this

---

[3] HLA Hart, *Essays on Bentham* (Oxford: Clarendon Press, 1982) 159.

was indeed the central point of Hart's disagreement with Fuller, we would have expected him to make this clear in his review of Fuller's book.[4] Instead, we find Hart insisting that Fuller has no warrant for treating his eight *desiderata* as in any sense 'moral'. He appears wholly to reject Fuller's central thesis. If the 'concession' reading were correct, we would have expected Hart to endorse the idea of an inner morality of law, but to insist upon a firm separation between the inner morality and the 'external' morality of substantive justice.

There are other difficulties with the 'concession' reading. For example, at one point in his review of Fuller, Hart tells us that Fuller has offered no 'cogent argument in support of his claim that these principles are not neutral as between good and evil substantive aims'.[5] The insertion of the word 'substantive' might at first seem to be an important qualification here, for it will be argued in the present book that the intrinsic moral importance of the rule of law (Hart's 'principles of legality') is to be found in its embodiment of a form of moral association wherein one may enjoy a degree of independence from the power of others. Someone might say that this, although a moral value, is not a 'substantive aim' of the law. In that sense, one might argue, the law may be intrinsically moral while nevertheless being neutral between good and evil 'substantive aims'.[6] If Hart had intended the qualification 'substantive' to bear this meaning, one would have expected him to acknowledge that the qualification leaves ample space for a claim that law is intrinsically moral in character; but he provides no such acknowledgment.

A few pages later in the same review, Hart compares Fuller's attitude towards the 'principles of legality' with the attitude of those legal positivist writers who are criticized by Fuller. Hart's sympathies are clearly with the positivists. The passage is as follows:

The difference between the author and those he criticizes in this matter is that the activity of controlling men by rules and the principles designed to maximize its efficiency are not valued by the latter for their own sake, and are not dignified by them with the title of a 'morality'. They are valued so far only as they contribute to human happiness or other moral substantive aims of the law.[7]

To understand the significance of this passage for the present exegetical issue, we must compare it with the passage from page 351, where Hart appears to be saying that the principles of legality are neutral as between good and evil 'substantive aims'. We saw above that the passage from page 351 might be

[4] See Hart, above n 2, essay 16.   [5] Ibid, 351.
[6] Readers will recall from the last chapter that I do not deny that the use of law in pursuit of wicked goals is perfectly possible. The present chapter will claim that regimes motivated solely by non-moral goals will have no good interest-based reason to observe the rule of law, but it does not deny that it would be *possible* for them to observe the rule of law.   [7] Hart, above n 2, 357.

rendered compatible with the idea that the principles of legality embody 'a necessary connection between law and morality' if we were to contrast 'substantive' aims of the law with the valuable form of moral association implicit in the law's status as a structure of binding rules. On the face of things, that seems a good way to read the passage, for it treats the word 'substantive' as contributing to the meaning of the passage when, on other readings, it might seem to be redundant. However, if we construe the word 'substantive' in this non-redundant way, we find that Hart's later claim (on page 357) must then be construed as denying the possibility that the principles of legality could derive their moral value from anything *other than* a 'substantive' aim (at least if we take Hart to be endorsing the positivist view that he describes). The two passages combined therefore seem to be incompatible with the 'concession' reading of Hart whichever way we construe them. For Hart seems to be saying that the principles of legality are, in themselves, neutral between the only things that could give them value. This is, of course, not to say that the principles of legality are *without* value, but that their value is not *intrinsic* to them, being always *contingent* upon the circumstances. That is clearly inconsistent with treating the principles of legality as embodying a *necessary* connection between law and morals. We therefore have good reason to reject the concession reading and to adopt the ironic reading.

John Gardner has asserted that no significant legal positivist has ever denied the existence of necessary connections between law and morality.[8] The concession reading of Hart's remarks on Fuller might seem to sit well with Gardner's claim. But Hart later acknowledged that, in his earlier works, he had 'failed to discuss adequately different forms of the claim that there is a conceptual connection between law and morality which are compatible with the distinction between law as it is and as it ought to be'.[9] If Gardner was correct, Hart had here a good opportunity to make it clear that his positivism asserts the distinction between law as it is and as it ought to be, but does not offer a general denial of the existence of other forms of necessary connection between law and morality. Hart does not take this opportunity, just as he does not take the opportunity when he reviews the work of Fuller. Indeed, it seems clear from the context that Hart is regretting, not only his earlier neglect of an important distinction, but also his lack of a suitable opportunity to make clear his opposition to theories of the indicated type; he goes on to 'briefly indicate' his objections to such theories.[10] This seems to reinforce our other reasons for rejecting the 'concession' reading of Hart.

---

[8] John Gardner, 'Legal Positivism: 5½ Myths' (2001) 46 *American Journal of Jurisprudence* 199.
[9] Above n 2, 8.   [10] Ibid, 9.

Foxes, Hedgehogs, and the Ironic Reading

On the 'ironic' reading Hart's observation must be taken to say that formal features of law cannot be the embodiment of a moral ideal if they are in fact compatible with great iniquity. This seems open to an obvious counter-argument, however. For it is possible that we should think of legal systems, like people, as capable of possessing distinct moral virtues. Perhaps legality is one moral virtue for legal systems and justice is another. Now it may well be that a high degree of compliance with the requirements of legality is compatible with considerable injustice in the law. But it is not at all clear that this possibility does anything to suggest that legality is not a moral virtue. By way of comparison, consider the virtues (for individuals) of kindness and honesty. Since these are distinct virtues, it may well be that scrupulous honesty is compatible with a most serious lack of kindness. Perhaps scrupulous honesty is compatible with extreme cruelty. Even if this is so, however, it would not show that honesty is not a moral virtue.

It might be said that we would hesitate to ascribe the virtue of courage to one who exhibits fearlessness in combat but who fights for an evil cause. Our hesitation might be thought to reflect a core of truth in one ancient line of philosophical thought according to which all the virtues form a unity, so that genuine manifestations of a virtue cannot be combined with great wickedness. We should be careful to note, however, that our doubts concerning such wicked manifestations of fearlessness can be interpreted in different ways. On the one hand it might be said that the virtue of courage is constituted by some set of characteristics that are fully exhibited by the soldier who fights for evil, but we withhold from him the title of 'good' or 'virtuous' because the virtuous aspect of his conduct is massively outweighed by the evil aspects. On the other hand, it might be said that the virtue of 'courage' cannot be identified with any set of characteristics that are fully exhibited by the soldier in question: a proper understanding of any virtue requires a grasp of its inseparable connections with all the other virtues.

On the first approach, the fact that a set of characteristics is compatible with great iniquity would not show that those characteristics are not constitutive of a genuine moral virtue. On the second approach, however, compatibility with great iniquity would indeed demonstrate that the characteristics in question do not constitute a moral virtue. If the second approach represents Hart's own view, it would explain his apparent suggestion that the compatibility of Fuller's eight *desiderata* with wickedness shows that those *desiderata* are not constitutive of any moral virtue in law. If this is his basic assumption, however, it reveals the dependence of his legal positivism upon an excessively demanding account of morality which he nowhere articulates or seeks to defend.[11]

In fact, not only does Hart fail to defend such a view, he sometimes appears to take for granted a view of morality that is very much at odds with any strong assumption of unity in the moral virtues. When he criticizes Gustav Radbruch, for example, Hart adopts both the outlook and the language of Isaiah Berlin's pluralism. Hart is considering the denial of legal validity to a duly enacted statute, on the ground that the statute was grossly unjust. He asserts that such a denial of validity serves 'to cloak the true nature of the problems with which we are faced and will encourage the romantic optimism that all the values we cherish ultimately will fit into a single system, that no one of them has to be sacrificed or compromised to accommodate another'.[12]

Thus, in his criticism of Radbruch, Hart seems to adopt a pluralistic understanding of moral value and to emphasize the extent to which the values that we endorse might compete and conflict. Following Berlin's famous quotation from the poet Archilochus, we will call this the position of the fox.[13] Yet, in his debate with Fuller, the possibility of such a pluralistic outlook seems not even to be considered: the compatibility of legality with iniquity is taken as indicating that legality is not an intrinsically moral idea. Here Hart seems to assume the position of the hedgehog.

Is this a simple inconsistency in Hart? Perhaps not, you may say. Perhaps Hart adopts the outlook of the fox in some contexts, and the hedgehog in others, because he perceives the balance of danger to vary with the particular situation. In the context of his debate with Radbruch, the principal risk is that we will allow a desire for the punishment of the morally culpable to obscure the moral loss that would be integral to such punishment. In the context of the debate with Fuller, however, the principal danger is that we will allow an idea of the intrinsic moral value of legality to lend undeserved ethical weight to iniquitous laws.

Certainly it is not uncommon to be reminded that there are dangers on both sides. The dangers of hedgehog-like monism (on which Berlin concentrates) are balanced by dangers intrinsic to the fox's pluralism. For the idea that values compete, and necessitate a choice between them, contains its own moral hazards. As Ronald Dworkin has pointed out, it may invite too easy a preparedness, in critical situations, to abandon or qualify important principles, offering us the plea that in a world of plural values no such principle can

---

[11] Later in this book it will be argued that a full understanding of the requirements of legality reveals an intimate bond between legality and justice, even though the two remain distinct values. This line of thought serves to subvert Hart's positivism rather than to sustain it, however.

[12] Above n 2, 77.   [13] 'The fox knows many things, but the hedgehog knows one big thing.'

be treated as absolute.[14] Still more perniciously, it can ground a single-minded commitment to a limited range of political values by the argument that every community must make a radical choice between the various competing goods that it might conceivably pursue, such choice entailing the total neglect of other ideals, acknowledged to be genuine and important. More generally and pervasively, the pluralist outlook can encourage an anti-rationalist and voluntarist approach to politics that emphasizes the need for sovereign decision and discourages reasoned reflection on politics. It is possible for some self-proclaimed foxes to resemble hedgehogs, whose one big idea is the need for radically ungrounded choice.

Yet we should be suspicious of the suggestion that the choice between monism and pluralism might be made in terms of this balance of danger. For it is pluralism that tells us that ethical and political decisions will sometimes involve choices where there is a moral cost to whatever we choose; and, in taking this view, pluralism embodies a particular understanding of our shared ethical life. The 'balance of danger' approach seems to treat the adoption of pluralism in preference to monism as itself such a choice, to be determined by our decision as to which set of costs we are most willing to bear. It therefore presupposes the ethical outlook of pluralism. Clearly, pluralism cannot provide the framework for its own justification in this way.

Purposes and Moral Reasons

Hart's principal arguments against Fuller are put forward in his critical review of Fuller's book *The Morality of Law*.[15] Here Hart tells us that it is a mistake to assume (as he thinks Fuller does) that just because law is a purposive activity, it must therefore be somehow 'moral'. He observes that poisoning is a purposive activity, and has its own principles of efficacy, yet it would clearly be a mistake to insist that the 'principles of the poisoner's art' constitute an inner 'morality of poisoning'.[16] It is unclear whether Hart intends his 'morality of poisoning' example simply to illustrate his (surely uncontentious) thesis that we cannot

---

[14] 'Just as tyrants have tried to justify great crimes by appealing to the idea that all moral and political values come together in some harmonious vision so transcendently important that murder is justified in its service, so other moral crimes have been justified by appeal to the opposite idea, that important political values necessarily conflict, that no choice among these can be defended as the only right choice, and that sacrifices in some of the things we care about are therefore inevitable.'

Ronald Dworkin, 'Do Liberal Values Conflict?' in Ronald Dworkin, Mark Lilla, and Robert B Silvers (eds), *The Legacy of Isaiah Berlin* (New York: New York Review of Books, 2001) 75.

[15] Above n 2, essay 16; Lon Fuller *The Morality of Law* (revised edition, New Haven, Conn: Yale University Press, 1969).   [16] Hart, above n 2, 350.

infer the morality of an activity from its purposive nature, or whether he is suggesting that Fuller's eight *desiderata* of legality are in fact simple principles of efficacy that are devoid of any moral status. This ambiguity mirrors the ambiguity of his observations in *The Concept of Law*, mentioned above.

In Chapter 2, I emphasized the fact that many aspects of the serviceability of law for evil aims are fully compatible with the thesis that the archetype of law is an intrinsically moral idea. The aspirational view of law need not claim that law *cannot* be used for wicked goals. Compliance with the rule of law is logically compatible with laws that serve wicked goals, in the following sense: if we were to encounter a regime that openly and consistently pursued wicked goals, but was nevertheless meticulously observant of the rule of law, an aspirational view of law is not committed to denying the label 'law' to such a system. We can acknowledge that the system closely approximates to the archetype of legality (Fuller's eight precepts), and nevertheless claim that that archetype is itself intrinsically moral, without our claim being in any way undercut by the wickedness of the law's substantive content. Similarly, we saw in the same chapter various other ways in which the moral status of law's archetype may be compatible with evil: individual laws within a system might be enacted in the service of wicked goals; individual judges might have wicked or self-interested reasons for complying with the rule of law; and *all* of the judges might comply with the rule of law from self-interested reasons, if strategic behaviour makes it impossible for them (as members or supporters of the governing regime) to capture the gains consequent upon departure from the rule of law.

I can now add a further gloss to the fact that an evil regime's compliance with the rule of law may be compatible with the intrinsic moral status of law. For, if legality is but one virtue amongst others (such as justice), it is conceivable that a regime might wholly fail to exhibit some such virtues while nevertheless exhibiting others. The possibility that a very unjust regime might nevertheless comply meticulously with the requirements of the rule of law does nothing, therefore, to refute the thesis that law is an intrinsically moral idea.

Hart's critical observations on Fuller are considerably more circumspect and ambiguous than they might at first seem: so circumspect, in fact, that it is not entirely clear that Hart disagrees with Fuller on the key point that separates aspirational and mundane views of the nature of law. For, on one possible reading, Hart acknowledges that Fuller has succeeded in identifying a necessary connection between law and morality, and seeks to resist only those misguided parts of Fuller's argument where he claims that observance of the principles of legality will confine the law to relatively just purposes and prevent the pursuit of wicked goals. In this book, I am not trying to defend or develop these latter aspects of Fuller's argument. In any case, Hart's dismissive yet evasive discussion of Fuller makes him too ambiguous an opponent. We must therefore turn to one who is somewhat less wary in his defence of legal positivism, and who therefore succeeds in clearly articulating the thesis that many readers would unhesitatingly ascribe to Hart.

Matthew Kramer takes the rule of law to be 'admirably encapsulated in Lon Fuller's eight principles of legality', but he nevertheless argues that 'the rule of law is not an inherently moral ideal'. Wicked rulers who are solely concerned to advance their own interests, and who make no pretence of serving justice or the common good, will nevertheless (Kramer argues) have good reason to maintain the rule of law to a substantial extent.[17] Kramer's thesis enables us to raise in a stark form the clash between mundane and aspirational views of law. For, in defending the aspirational view, it is my intention to argue that, while wicked rulers will have good reason to publish rules and enforce them, they will have no reasons of self-interest[18] for respecting a most fundamental requirement of the rule of law: the requirement that official violence should be used only in response to the violation of the law by others. Wicked rulers, I argue, will have powerful reasons for departing from this requirement, while the only good reasons for respecting the requirement are grounded in moral considerations of a kind that I will explore later in the chapter.

Stated in this way, the engagement between Kramer and myself promises to be refreshingly direct. A similar engagement with Hart would, as we have seen, of necessity be much less direct. I focus on Kramer, therefore, not because he is a relatively soft target, but because he definitely opposes the thesis for which I wish to argue, while it is not entirely clear whether Hart is an enemy or a friend on this issue. One senses that Hart saw the dangers ahead and hesitated.

As always in jurisprudence, things are not quite as straightforward as we might wish, and some initial ambiguities and uncertainties must be addressed before we can proceed to the main engagement.

Between Threshold and Archetype

Fuller acknowledges throughout *The Morality of Law* that even the most benevolent and just regimes will fall short of perfect compliance with his eight *desiderata*. Much of that book is taken up with an exploration of the way in

---

[17] Kramer, 'On the Moral Status of the Rule of Law' (2004) 63 CLJ 65.
[18] For the purposes of this argument I assume a clear contrast between prudential reasons grounded in self-interest and moral reasons grounded in some sort of impartial concern for the interests of everyone. However, I do not at all seek to oppose those philosophical positions that would refuse to recognize any such distinction at a fundamental level, arguing that a well-grounded concern for one's own well-being is always bound up with the well-being of others. I simply set such positions on one side for present purposes.

which, when applied to the circumstances of a real political community, the eight precepts place upon the judge or lawmaker cross-cutting demands. This recognition of inevitable shortfall is closely allied to Fuller's acknowledgment that the eight precepts themselves may in the end be inadequate as an expression of the 'impulse towards legality',[19] an acknowledgment the full significance of which will be explored later in this book. At this point, the fact of inevitable shortfall raises a rather different problem.

Kramer hopes to show that the rule of law 'is not an inherently moral ideal'. Let us call that his 'moral neutrality' thesis. The thesis follows, Kramer believes, from what he takes to be the following fact: wicked regimes motivated solely by the self-interest of the rulers will nevertheless have good reason for complying with the requirements of the rule of law to a substantial extent. Now suppose that Kramer could justify his claim about wicked regimes (we will see in due course that he cannot). Would that be sufficient to demonstrate the truth of his moral neutrality thesis?

Since just and benevolent regimes will fall short of complete compliance with Fuller's eight *desiderata*, it might be thought unreasonable to expect Kramer to demonstrate that wicked regimes will have good reasons for aiming at *perfect* compliance. This is in fact not so unreasonable as one might at first think. After all, the shortfall contemplated by Fuller does not appear to arise, for the most part, from a willingness on the part of benevolent regimes to balance rule-of-law values against other considerations; rather, it springs from the cross-cutting demands inherent in those rule-of-law values when they are applied to the circumstances of the real world. Even if rule-of-law values must be traded off against other competing values, this does not demonstrate that we do not have good reason for pursuing the ideal of perfect compliance with those rule-of-law values: it merely shows that those good reasons must be balanced against other competing reasons. Consequently, even though shortfall may be inevitable, it may nevertheless be true to say that benevolent regimes will have good reason for pursuing the goal of perfect compliance. It might actually be possible to end our debate with Kramer at this point. For perhaps he is simply confused in thinking that the moral neutrality of the rule of law can be demonstrated by showing that evil regimes could have self-interested reasons for a substantial but not perfect degree of compliance with the rule of law. But I will place no reliance on these possibilities, for there are a number of other respects in which Kramer's argument can be seen to fail.

Let us therefore accept for the purposes of argument that, in proposing that the rule of law (as represented by the eight precepts) is not an intrinsically moral idea, Kramer should not have to demonstrate that wicked rulers will have

---

[19] Fuller, above n 15, 41, 45.

good reasons for aiming at perfect compliance. The question then becomes one concerning the standard of compliance, falling short of perfect compliance, which should form the focus for debate.

In his book *In Defense of Legal Positivism*, Kramer seems to claim that wicked regimes will have good reason for adhering to the rule of law to the same extent as benevolent regimes.[20] Writing of officials in wicked regimes, he makes the following claim:

> [T]here will be strong reasons for those officials to endow their regime with the essential characteristics of law ... to just as great an extent as would be undertaken by the officials in a benevolent legal system.[21]

On other occasions, however, Kramer appears to retreat to a much weaker thesis. In an essay written some years after his principal book, for example, he tells us that '[a] repressive and exploitative regime will frequently fall even further short than a liberal-democratic regime in the degree of its conformity with most of the precepts of legality'.[22] A little further on in the same essay we find him saying that 'heinous incarnations of the rule of law are very likely marked by aberrations that would not occur—or would not occur on the same scale—under a liberal-democratic scheme of governance.'[23] Such assertions might at first lead us to suspect Kramer of watering down his thesis. Indeed, 'watering down' is hardly an adequate description, for these claims appear to amount to a concession that the rule of law is more serviceable for good than for evil (a proposition with which I am, of course, happy to agree). When we return to the key passage (quoted above) from Kramer's book, however, we find a certain latent ambiguity that could be important in this context.

The passage could be construed in two different ways. On one interpretation, Kramer is saying that a wicked regime will have good reason to comply with the rule of law to the same extent as a benevolent regime. On another interpretation (let us call it the 'threshold' view) Kramer is saying that a wicked regime will have good reason to comply with the requirements of the rule of law up to the point where the regime qualifies as a clear (non-marginal) instance of a legal system: the regime will, in other words, reach some notional threshold for constituting a clear instance of a legal system, and will cross that threshold as decisively as would a benevolent regime. Even though the benevolent regime might approximate more closely to the ideal of full compliance with the rule of law, the benevolent and wicked regimes will be equal in regard to their threshold-crossing. Just as all bachelors are equally bachelors, all threshold-crossing regimes are equally threshold-crossing regimes: the fact

---

[20] Matthew Kramer, *In Defense of Legal Positivism* (Oxford: Oxford University Press, 1999) 238.
[21] Ibid.   [22] Above n 17, 74.   [23] Ibid, 75.

that, beyond the threshold, the regimes differ in their degree of compliance with the rule of law is (on this interpretation) treated as irrelevant.

The ambiguity seems to infect Kramer's main thesis. In claiming that 'the rule of law is not an inherently moral ideal', is Kramer disputing the moral status of the idea represented by the basic precepts of legality, from which all systems will fall short to a greater or lesser extent? Or is he simply arguing that wicked officials would have good reason to comply with those precepts to an extent sufficient to qualify their regimes as 'legal systems'? In asserting that 'the rule of law is not an inherently moral ideal', Kramer gives the impression that he is addressing the guiding ideal that goes by that traditional name, an ideal from which all legal systems fall short to varying degrees. On the other hand, he tells us that, by the phrase 'the rule of law' he means 'nothing more and nothing less than the state of affairs that obtains when a legal system exists and functions'.[24]

Fuller's view was that particular legal systems count as such in virtue of their approximation to the idea of full compliance with the eight *desiderata*. This ideal, he argued, is an intrinsically moral ideal. We must remember that Fuller's theory consists essentially of two steps: in the first step he argues that the concept of law is to be understood by reference to an intellectual archetype; in the second step he argues that the archetype is itself recognizable as a moral ideal. Fuller's eight precepts, when taken collectively, represent the archetype for the concept of law. That is to say, particular instances of law count as such in virtue of their approximation to the ideal of full compliance with the eight principles. The necessary connection between law and morals that Fuller sought to delineate is grounded in the fact that instances of law count as such by their approximation to an archetype that constitutes a moral ideal.

There are two ways in which one might attack Fuller's theory. One might argue that the concept of law is not best understood by reference to the structuring archetype of the eight precepts: perhaps law is a class concept; perhaps it exhibits some other type of structure; or perhaps it is best understood by reference to an archetype quite different from the one we find in Fuller's eight precepts. On the other hand, one might attack Fuller's second step, by claiming that the archetype in question is not in fact a moral ideal. But one cannot attack Fuller simply by pointing out that wicked regimes may sometimes properly be regarded as instances of law, for Fuller need not deny this. Fuller would simply say that when such regimes count as law, they do so in virtue of their approximation to the (intrinsically moral) archetype.

[24] Ibid, 65.

Fuller tells us little or nothing about the standard of compliance that must be satisfied by a regime if it is to count as a legal system. It is possible that he regards this as in itself a trivial and uninteresting question that merits consideration only in so far as our conceptual intuitions about what does or does not count as a legal system can point us to the archetype that in his view informs and underlies those intuitions. Once we have grasped the archetype, we see that qualifying as a legal system is a matter of degree and not a matter of a boundary that can fruitfully become a subject of intellectual contestation in the abstract. Or it is possible that he regards the question as one that can meaningfully be addressed only within specific contexts of moral deliberation, and not as a general theoretical issue.

Suppose that a critic of Fuller had no wish to challenge his claim that the concept of law is to be understood by reference to an archetype; but they did wish to challenge his claim that the archetype is a moral ideal. They wished to argue, let us suppose, that (even when understood by reference to the archetype of compliance with the eight precepts) law is equally serviceable for good and for evil. What would such a critic need to establish?

Let us accept for the purposes of the present argument that it would be unreasonable to expect Fuller's critic to show that wicked regimes will have good reason *fully* to comply with the eight precepts. If the argument is that law is equally serviceable for evil and for good, the natural standard to apply would seem to be the standard of compliance that would ordinarily be attained by a just and benevolent regime. One would need to show that wicked regimes have good reason to comply with the rule of law to the same extent as just regimes. Let us call this the 'mundane archetype thesis'.

At times, Kramer seems to adopt the mundane archetype thesis. At other times his argument is suggestive of the somewhat different threshold thesis: that wicked regimes have good reason to comply with the eight principles to a degree that would qualify them as legal systems. As outlined above, this thesis focuses upon the regime's passing of a certain threshold which may fall short of the level of compliance typically attained by benevolent regimes. I will call it the 'threshold thesis.'

The difficulty with ascribing the mundane archetype thesis to Kramer is that it appears to conflict with his acknowledgment that wicked regimes will not comply with the rule of law to the same extent as benevolent regimes. On the 'threshold' reading, however, Kramer's views seem equally problematic. For Kramer tells us that a social formation will count as an instance of law when it exhibits a substantial degree of compliance with Fuller's eight precepts. He therefore accepts that particulars count as instances of the concept by resemblance or approximation, which is inherently a matter of degree. Once we have agreed that instances of law count as such instances by approximating to the ideal of Fuller's eight *desiderata*, nothing is lost if we dispense with the notion of a domain of equal threshold-crossers. Since the criterion for legal status is a matter of approximation to the Fullerian ideal, the 'threshold' is really but a shadow cast by our application of that criterion: it plays, as it were, no working part in our thinking. The notion of a conceptual domain within which all instances are equally threshold-crossing can therefore be seen to be a superfluity, which seeks to preserve the structure of a class concept within a context where it is inappropriate.[25] The very features in virtue of which regimes cross the threshold are features that those regimes exhibit to varying degrees.

Kramer accepts that social formations count as instances of law when they substantially approximate to the model of compliance with Fuller's eight precepts. He appears now to be saying that wicked regimes will approximate to that ideal less closely than will benevolent regimes. This concedes that wicked regimes are likely to differ from benevolent regimes in, amongst other things, the extent to which they exhibit the characteristic features of law. Kramer's positivism appears therefore to consist in an uninteresting postscript to this concession. For it amounts to saying that, although wicked and benevolent regimes differ in the extent to which they exhibit the features constitutive of legality, they nevertheless attain the relevant threshold, and are therefore co-equal in their threshold-crossing. This is exactly like saying that Jack and Jill got an equal result in their exams when, although Jack got a Third and Jill got a First, they both passed and therefore equally exhibit the quality of 'having passed'. In both the case of law and the case of the exam, the criteria in terms of which one passes or fails were satisfied to varying degrees.

This is not to say that the threshold is devoid of significance. Perhaps the judgement that a particular system counts as 'law' can, at least in some contexts, embody conclusions about the extent to which the system derives moral legitimacy from its approximation to the archetype. If one concedes that the concept of 'law' is structured by an archetype, and one also concedes that wicked regimes will have reason to comply with the archetype to a lesser extent than regimes that are guided by moral considerations, one has already conceded that the concept is not morally neutral. The significance of the threshold consists in the fact that compliance to a substantial extent with the requirements of the archetype constitutes a moral virtue for systems of governance,[26] and our judgements on the threshold may be expressive of intuitions about the

---

[25] In relation to certain concepts and in certain contexts, of course, a focus on the threshold may be entirely appropriate. My point is specific to the context of the present debate.

[26] A moral virtue for the systems, but not necessarily a moral virtue in those who establish and maintain such systems, who may be motivated by wholly non-moral aims (such as a desire hypocritically to assume the mantle of moral legitimacy).

point at which the degree of compliance has become sufficiently substantial to register in the moral scale.

In suggesting that Kramer's thesis (on the threshold reading) is trivial, I am of course not conceding that (on that reading) it is *true*. I feel that it would be hard to argue that a regime that very extensively employs violence against law-abiding citizens is a clear and non-marginal instance of what Kramer calls 'the rule of law'. As we will see in a moment, Kramer himself appears to share this view, for he argues strenuously that even wicked regimes will have good reason to avoid the extensive use of official violence.

The rule of law, Kramer tells us, is not an inherently moral ideal.[27] Wicked regimes aiming solely at their own profit, and devoid even of a pretence to serve justice and the common good, will nevertheless have good reason[28] to abide by the requirements of the rule of law. Opposing his thesis, I say that wicked regimes will have good reason to publish rules and enforce them, but will have no good reason for respecting one of the most fundamental requirements of the rule of law: confining the use of official violence against citizens to circumstances where a legal rule has been violated. Kramer replies by arguing that, if people are frequently punished even when they have obeyed the law, their incentives to comply with the law will be 'markedly sapped'.[29]

We should begin by noticing that, if he is to support his claim that the rule of law is not an inherently moral ideal, Kramer has to overcome at least four distinct problems. In the first place, he needs to establish that the governmental use of extra-legal violence (by contrast with the enactment of coercively-enforced legal prohibitions) will sap incentives for compliance with the law. Second, he needs to show that the cost represented by such incentive-impairing effects outweighs the benefits to the regime of the use of extra-legal violence. Third, he needs to establish that appropriate incentives for compliance might not be maintained at lower cost simply by increasing penalties.

If Kramer could establish all three of these claims (which, in my view, he cannot) a further obstacle would remain. For he would still have to demonstrate that the serviceability for evil of a certain practice demonstrates the moral neutrality of that practice. This may not be as easy as Kramer sometimes seems to imagine, for he has recently clarified his argument[30] in a way that

---

[27] Above n 17, 65.

[28] Throughout this chapter I follow Kramer in his focus upon interest-dependent prudential reasons; I also assume for present purposes the soundness of the conventional contrast between moral and prudential reasons.   [29] Above n 20, 69.

[30] Matthew Kramer, 'The Big Bad Wolf: Legal Positivism and its Detractors' (2004) 49 *American Journal of Jurisprudence* 1. See also Hamish Stewart, 'Incentives and the Rule of Law' (2006) 51 *American Journal of Jurisprudence* (forthcoming, with accompanying comments from Kramer and Simmonds).

commits him to a potentially embarrassing set of claims. In his latest clarification he fails to establish that departures from the rule of law would have incentive-impairing effects, but his argument does inadvertently suggest certain respects in which serious departures from *justice* could be said to have incentive-impairing effects. What follows from this is that substantial compliance with the requirements of justice or the public good might be highly serviceable for wicked regimes. If substantial serviceability for evil entails moral neutrality, the serviceability for evil of substantial compliance with justice and the public good entails the moral neutrality of justice and the public good. Thus, the thesis that serviceability for evil entails moral neutrality would be refuted by *reductio ad absurdum*.

Reasons for Violence

My argument involves two main claims. First I need to show that wicked regimes would typically have reasons for deploying violence against acts that have not been prohibited in any published and prospective rule. Then I need to show that these reasons are not typically outweighed by any countervailing reasons: in particular that a use of violence outside the published rules will not weaken incentives for compliance with the published rules.

Why might a wicked regime wish to punish acts that have not in fact been prohibited by the published rules? After all, we might well share Kramer's view that such publication of rules is generally the best way 'directly and perspicuously' to convey to the populace an understanding of what the regime requires in the way of conduct.[31]

I have elsewhere offered various examples by way of response to this question.[32] The examples can be divided into three or four broad categories, as follows.

(1) *The chilling effect.* No regime, be it good or bad, can anticipate all of the multifarious ways in which the conduct of citizens may subvert or obstruct the regime's attainment of its objectives. Activities that are consciously directed towards such obstructive effects, or that will foreseeably have those effects, might however be deterred even when the activities have not been specifically anticipated and prohibited. Appropriate deterrence may be achieved by ensuring that activities contrary to the governing regime's interests are punished regardless of whether they violate any existing prospective prohibition. Citizens contemplating some proposed course

---

[31] Above n 17, 83.
[32] Simmonds, 'Straightforwardly False: The Collapse of Kramer's Positivism' (2004) 63 CLJ 98.

of conduct will thereby be encouraged to consider the likely impact of that conduct upon the governing regime's interests and concerns, or (more accurately) the regime's probable perception of that impact. The prospect of being punished, should the regime believe its interests and objectives to have been threatened by the conduct in question, will deter citizens from engaging in conduct that might prejudice the regime's interests; it will also have a chilling effect upon attempts to devise new and therefore non-prohibited ways of subverting the regime's agenda.

(2) *Blocking visibility.* One of the most important weapons in the armoury of any repressive regime is its ability to structure social interaction in such a way that it becomes very difficult for opponents of the regime to identify one another, such mutual identification being an essential precondition for the coordination of oppositional activity. Thus, a repressive regime might be concerned to discourage the wearing of certain clothes or cultural symbols or even the adoption of certain postures that could be construed as expressive of values opposed to those of the regime.[33] A fundamentalist religious regime that is hostile to American-style liberalism, for example, might view in this light the carrying of Coca-Cola bottles or the wearing of baseball caps. A prohibition on the display of such cultural symbols is, of course, possible; but, in so far as such a prohibition meets the requirements of the rule of law, it must have ascertainable limits, and those limits create the possibility of new vehicles for the symbolic expression of allegiance being developed beyond the bounds of existing prohibitions. Subtle semiotic connections and cultural bonds might enable new forms of expression to develop and mutate with surprising ease. Beyond the domain of cultural symbols, all sorts of subtle messages can be conveyed by forms of body language that, for all their eloquence, would be hard to define and proscribe. A puritanical regime might dislike fluid and rhythmical modes of walking that are suggestive of the dance; a militaristic regime might feel threatened by those who adopt conspicuously slouching postures; wholly non-ideological but exploitative regimes might have similar feelings about those who look officials in the eye and do not adopt a posture of cowed subservience. A wicked regime that sought to address such issues through the rule of law would find itself enacting a long series of prohibitions to meet the constantly evolving forms of cultural expression. This would not only make the regime appear to be excessively concerned about dissent, but would also makes its repressive measures look ineffective.

---

[33] Ibid.

(3) *Blocking visibility by requiring enthusiasm.* One of the most effective ways in which a repressive regime can render its opponents invisible (and thereby block their attempts to identify one another) is by ensuring, through a background threat of violence, that everyone has a strong prudential interest in the expression of support for the regime. Spies and informers will assist in maintaining the pervasive nature of the threat, and in robbing potential dissenters of any sense of secure domains within which opposition might safely be voiced. Furthermore, the extensive use of *agents provocateur* might encourage even those who are opponents of the regime to serve as informers on other opponents: for when you voice your (genuine) loathing for the government, how am I to know that you are not an agent of the government, testing my willingness to inform on such dissidents? One option for the regime would be the enactment of a law requiring the giving of Nazi-style salutes in certain (frequent) circumstances. Another way would be to make it clear, by action rather than words, that people who do not seem genuinely enthusiastic about the Party (and therefore fail to evince their support by the giving of heart-felt salutes) are likely to suffer violence at the hands of government thugs. Which course would be adopted by a well-advised and thoroughly wicked regime? The legislative course would almost certainly be counter-productive. For, if the legal prohibition is to be clear and followable, it must define what is to count as a salute, what are the appropriate circumstances for giving a salute, and so forth. Such definitions will almost certainly create the possibility of performing ironic or mocking forms of salute that would nevertheless count as complying with the legal requirement. A salute with the arm raised rather limply, or a quiet smile accompanying the stiffly raised arm, might actually serve to proclaim one's opposition, and so assist dissenting individuals to identify their like-minded potential allies. Where Party thugs hold sway, by contrast, all but the most heroic people will be concerned to do everything they can to convince the regime of their loyalty: your slightly unenthusiastic salute might be combined with other items of information about you to convince the regime that you are due for a beating.

(4) *Dealing with strategic behaviour amongst supporters.* The reasons for departure from the rule of law examined up to this point have concerned the relationship between the governing regime and the governed population. Once we consider the relationship between various individual members of the governing regime (and between individual members and the regime as a collectivity) a whole new crop of reasons for violence comes to light. Individual members of the regime might all stand to profit from the

maintenance of the regime (and so have shared interests) while being locked in conflict over the division of the spoils; or individuals might be united in their support for the government's objectives, but construe those objectives in slightly different ways, or wish to emphasize slightly different aspects of the regime's overall agenda. In relation to such conflicting interests, observance of the rule of law will help to determine the forms of strategic behaviour that are available to various individual members of the governing regime. A regime's choice between observance and non-observance of the rule of law will therefore serve to structure the strategic opportunities enjoyed by individual members of the regime. Suppose, for example, that our regime observes the rule of law, and that this observance takes the form of rules being enacted by a legislature and then being interpreted and enforced by the courts. There is an obvious risk here that judges might use their role within the institutions of law to extract large personal gains; or to shape the Party's agenda in ways that would not be favoured by the non-judicial members of the regime. In deciding whether to enact general rules for judicial enforcement, or to rely upon the violence of the regime's thugs, therefore, a wicked regime will have to rely upon an assessment of which groups of officials or supporters occupy the strategically most powerful bargaining position for the extraction of personal or policy gains. There will consequently be occasions when reliance upon Party thugs might seem preferable to reliance upon the judges.

As a result of these diverse considerations, wicked regimes will have good reasons to deploy violence against those who have violated no published prospective law. Such reasons for the use of extra-legal violence are not the result of any inability or unwillingness to formulate wicked goals with clarity or to pursue them openly: in this respect the present argument differs fundamentally from that of Lon Fuller. Indeed, the *wickedness* of the regime's goals is in a sense irrelevant to the reasons favouring extra-legal violence. Those reasons spring from the fact that extra-legal violence provides an array of effective techniques by which a regime can retain power and render its opponents impotent: such techniques are in principle serviceable for virtuous governmental objectives as well as wicked ones. But it is only wicked regimes that will regard the instrumental efficacy of such techniques as providing a general and weighty reason for adopting them. Morally upright regimes will see the use of extra-legal violence as violating the form of moral association that finds expression in the idea of the rule of law, and it is for this reason that the rule of law is generally perceived as a moral constraint upon governmental power, rather than as a matter of instrumental efficacy.

Incentives

The question we must now ask is whether these reasons for violence are out-weighed by any competing reasons (of a non-moral sort) that support govern-mental compliance with the rule of law.

Kramer insists that 'if people often undergo punishment even when they have conformed closely to the prevailing legal norms ... the inducements for them to abide by those norms will be markedly sapped.'[34] He argues that a threat of unlawful punishment to which the law-abiding and the disobedient stand equally exposed will reduce incentives for compliance with the law not by reducing the quantitative disparity between the expected level of punish-ments for law-abiding and for disobedient persons, but by reducing the ratio between those expectations. In a regime practising extra-legal violence, com-pliance with the law will achieve a proportionally smaller reduction in the overall level of risk than it would in a regime that observes the rule of law.

Although at first seeming to be both sound and obvious in its claims, this argument is in fact quite irrelevant to the issue of the disincentive effects of extra-legal violence. At the same time, it entangles Kramer in some intractable problems that he does not seem to anticipate and address.

Let us begin slowly, by considering the situation of Joe. Suppose that Joe faces a 50 per cent chance of an extra-legal beating in the next year; he is now also faced by a 90 per cent chance of a short term in prison if he violates a law that requires him to display a Party flag.[35] Clearly, the risk of the beating has not reduced in any way the risk of prison consequent upon violation of the flag-display law. Kramer's point, however, is that the potential beating has reduced the value to Joe of compliance with the flag-display law in the following sense. If we ask, not about the risk of *prison* but about the risk of *punishment* (under-stood in a sense that would cover both the lawful imprisonment and the unlawful beating) we get a different and, to Kramer's mind, more revealing result. In the absence of any risk of an unlawful beating (and ignoring all other factors, such as other legal prohibitions), compliance with the flag-display law would greatly reduce Joe's risk of suffering a punishment. But, given the risk of a beating, compliance with the flag-display law will reduce Joe's exposure to the risk of punishment by much less. Kramer concludes that Joe's incentives for compliance with the flag-display law have been greatly reduced.

---

[34] *In Defense of Legal Positivism*, above n 20, 69. The argument is clarified in 'The Big Bad Wolf', above n 30.

[35] In my original discussion of this example (see above n 32) the punishment for violation of the flag-display law was a beating. As will become obvious in a moment, I have altered the nature of the punishment to improve clarity. No issue of substance turns on the change.

The problem with this argument is that it seems unrelated to the very feature upon which Kramer should be focusing: namely, the *extra-legal* nature of the beating to which Joe stands exposed. For it would make no difference to the argument if this beating were in fact prescribed by law in consequence of some prohibition other than the flag-display requirement. Kramer needs to establish that departures from the rule of law will sap incentives, not that additional threats of punishment will sap incentives.

In analysing the alleged incentive-sapping effects of departures from the rule of law, we must tread carefully if we are not to err. Kramer's most recent clarification of his argument is less terse than his earlier pronouncements: but it is nevertheless over-simplistic. It therefore fails to overcome the errors that I have already pointed out in earlier criticisms of Kramer.[36] It does, however, enable us to identify more precisely the particular mis-steps that generate Kramer's mistakes.

In examining Joe's incentive to obey the flag-display law, we must compare his situation under a regime that observes the rule of law with his situation under a regime that exposes him to the risk of extra-legal punishments; but we must be very careful to compare like with like. We should not, for example, assume that (in the regime that observes the rule of law) Joe will have done what he can to reduce his risk of punishment under laws other than the flag-display law, but then assume that (in the situation of departure from the rule of law) Joe will not have done what he can to reduce his risk of exposure to extra-legal violence.

In a regime that departs from the rule of law, the governmental use of violence will not be constrained by law: but it does not follow from this that the incidence of extra-legal violence will be wholly unpredictable. Governmental actions may be reasonably predictable without being governed by binding rules: to think otherwise is to assume that extra-legal violence must of necessity be wild and chaotic, rather than a carefully measured tool of policy.[37] The virtue of the rule of law consists in its embodiment of our independence of the power of others, not in its realization of mere predictability in governmental action: even when we are fully under the power of the unconstrained will of our governors, the exercise of that power may be highly predictable.[38] Perhaps government officials and Party bosses will follow general 'rules of thumb' in

---

[36] Above n 32.

[37] A tendency to overlook this point pervades Kramer's discussion, as I have elsewhere pointed out: ibid.

[38] Kramer confuses predictability with the rule of law when, in his earlier essay, he suggests that the existence of 'clear and established patterns' in the government's punitive measures would be sufficient to constitute governance through the rule of law. See above n 17, 91.

pursuing their objectives: but this is a very different matter from viewing rules as a binding constraint.

Consequently, governmental departures from the rule of law need not entail an absence of available strategies that will very effectively reduce Joe's exposure to the risk of an extra-legal beating. Just as there are things Joe could do to reduce his exposure to a legal punishment, so there are things he could do to reduce his exposure to extra-legal beatings: in the former case, he might try to comply with whatever law prescribes the punishment; in the latter case, he might try to look like a loyal Party member, and generally keep his head below the parapet. In the case of both the legal prohibition and the extra-legal beating, there will be various courses of action that Joe might adopt that will alter the risks to which he is exposed: adoption of a toadying and supportive attitude towards the Party will greatly reduce but not eliminate his risks of a beating, while meticulous compliance with the law will greatly reduce but not eliminate his risk of prison (he is still exposed to a risk of wrongful conviction).[39] In the case of either the law or the extra-legal beating, reduction of the risk of punishment might or might not be difficult; but the difficulty or ease with which the risk may be reduced depends upon a host of considerations, of which the form that the punitive threat takes (legal prohibition, or known disposition to use extra-legal violence) is only one. Published and prospective laws may embody severe demands that some or all individuals might find hard to meet; while substantial reduction in the risk of an extra-legal beating might require little beyond a preparedness to abstain from oppositional activity. Published and prospective laws may collectively make a host of discrete demands upon the individual, for each law will specify various actions the performance of which will trigger a large increase in the risk of punishment for the actor. By contrast, given the reasons that a regime will have for the use of extra-legal violence, the risks of an extra-legal beating can be anticipated to exhibit a certain underlying coherence, so that the adoption of a subservient or supportive (or simply apathetic and quiescent) attitude should in many circumstances be enough virtually to ensure one's security from all manifestations of extra-legal violence. In short, the differences between legal prohibitions and practices of extra-legal beating, from the viewpoint of risk reduction, are entirely contingent and dependent upon all of the circumstances. Kramer has therefore failed to identify any general reasons for expecting departures

---

[39] One might ask whether punishment as a result of an erroneous conviction should be regarded as a lawful punishment for the purposes of this debate. The answer is that it should. Even within a regime that is meticulously observant of the rule of law, one is still exposed to a certain risk of conviction in error; and that risk must be taken account of in our deliberations upon the punishment-based incentives faced by the citizen.

from the rule of law to weaken incentives any more than would the enactment of additional legal prohibitions.

What follows from this is that, in so far as Kramer's argument is correct, it shows that each additional threat of punishment (and, therefore, each additional sanction-backed law) will affect the extent to which any individual act of compliance with the law reduces one's overall exposure to the risk of punishment. But it does not necessarily make any difference, from this point of view, whether the additional threats of punishment are contained in legal prohibitions, or are constituted by practices of extra-legal beating. Kramer's argument therefore fails to establish anything at all about the allegedly necessary incentive-impairing effects of departures from the rule of law.

The only circumstance in which extra-legal violence would necessarily weaken incentives would be a situation where the extra-legal violence was made conditional on one's compliance with the law. That is to say, if one is to be lawfully punished if one breaks the law, but beaten up if one obeys it, the risk of the beating will clearly weaken one's incentives for compliance.[40] The importance of this point will be seen later in this chapter, where it is pointed out that the state's monopoly of force serves to sustain incentives for compliance by seeking to prevent forms of extra-legal violence that *would* be conditional upon one's compliance with the law. But extra-legal *governmental* violence of the kind that my argument contemplates will not be conditional upon one's compliance with the law in this way.

Of course, the employment of extra-legal governmental violence will (as Kramer points out) reduce the ratio between the expectations of punishment of the law-abiding and of the law-breakers. That ratio will be higher in a regime that observes the rule of law than in a regime that does not. This is surely obvious. But we must remember that, given shared goals for the two regimes (so that they differ only in their degree of compliance with the rule of law) the set of legal prohibitions in the former regime will be more extensive in its scope than the set of legal prohibitions in the latter regime, precisely because a regime that violates the rule of law will sometimes employ extra-legal violence when a regime observing principles of legality would enact legal prohibitions. Each of those additional legal prohibitions will itself have had an incentive-reducing effect, and the totality of such effects may be more or may be less substantial than the incentive-reducing effect of a practice of extra-legal

[40] According to Kramer, I erroneously attribute to him the assumption that extra-legal penalties will be conditional upon a person's law-abidingness. He points out that the examples he discusses clearly show that he makes no such assumption: above n 30. As any moderately careful reader of my original essay will discern, however, I do not ascribe the relevant assumption to Kramer (to him I ascribe only confusion) but to his *argument*, in the sense that the argument cannot sustain its conclusion without that assumption. The soundness of this claim is unaffected by the content of Kramer's examples, and is also unaffected by the substantive argument of his essay.

beating adopted in the regime that does not observe the rule of law. When we compare the situations of the law-abiding in the two regimes, therefore, we do not really compare like with like: for some of those who count as law-abiding in the regime that departs from the rule of law would (on the basis of the same conduct) count as law-violators in the regime that observes principles of legality. General comparison of the law-abiding and the law-violating in the two regimes is therefore inherently misleading and problematic. To eliminate its misleading features, we would need to formulate the comparison in much more complex terms that discriminate between different laws, some of which are substituting for extra-legal violence. If we do not do this we will confuse the incentive-reducing effects attaching to *all* additional threats of punishment, be they lawful or unlawful, with the incentive-reducing effects of extra-legal violence as such. Kramer's analysis ignores this fact, and the oversight is fatal to his argument.

While doing nothing to sustain legal positivism, Kramer's argument does, however, do something to *undermine* positivism. He argues (unsuccessfully) that wicked regimes have good reasons substantially, though not perfectly, to comply with the rule of law; and he concludes from this that the rule of law is not inherently moral. What his arguments *do* indicate, however, is the extent to which wicked regimes might have good reasons to enact substantially just and good laws aimed at the well-being of the governed. If the (qualified) serviceability of the rule of law for evil demonstrates the moral neutrality of law, then the (qualified) serviceability of justice and the good for evil demonstrates the moral neutrality of justice and the good. Since this is an absurd conclusion, Kramer's argument can be refuted in two ways: his thesis that the rule of law is highly serviceable for evil can be rejected as straightforwardly false; and his assumption that this thesis yields a conclusion about moral neutrality can be refuted by *reductio ad absurdum*.

Evil Contingencies

Kramer's argument on probabilities is, as we have seen, irrelevant to the issue he purports to be addressing: that is, the question of whether departures from the rule of law weaken incentives for compliance with the law. His argument does, however, raise some serious difficulties for positivism, which he does not seem to perceive or address. For, precisely in being of such a high degree of generality, Kramer's argument not only fails to distinguish extra-legal violence from lawful violence, but also fails to distinguish the risk of extra-legal violence from all other evil contingencies. To the difficulties raised by this I now turn.

Recall once again the situation of Joe. Joe faces a 90 per cent chance of prison if he breaks a law requiring him to display the Party flag. This chance of prison is unaffected by the fact that he also faces a 50 per cent chance of a beating. Kramer's argument requires us to ask about the effect of Joe's compliance with the flag-display law in reducing, not his risk of prison, but his risk of *punishment*, where 'punishment' is understood to cover both prison and beating. Once we move from a focus on the risk of prison to a focus on the risk of punishment, we can see that the risk of a beating has weakened Joe's incentives for compliance with the flag-display law by reducing the extent to which an act of compliance with the flag-display law will lower the risk of punishment that Joe faces.

The problem with this argument is that it is, in principle, applicable to *all* evil contingencies, and not simply to those constituted by the threat of unlawful punishment. In considering the possible incentive-impairing effects of unlawful punishment, we are really abstracting one limited slice from a much more complex calculation. Once we remind ourselves of this fact, we will see that exposure to *any* evil contingency (the incidence of which is independent of one's compliance or non-compliance with the law) could be factored into the calculation to produce exactly the same result as the risk of unlawful punishment: and the effect upon incentives for compliance would be exactly the same. Consequently, Kramer's argument commits him to the claim that evil regimes have sound reasons to remove such evil contingencies from the lives of their citizens.

What evil contingencies do I have in mind here? The list is in fact endless, but some examples would include disease, premature death, injury, poverty and unemployment. If a government could greatly reduce or even eliminate our exposure to such contingencies, it would (on Kramer's argument) greatly stiffen our incentives for compliance with the law. But a government that adopts laws and policies greatly reducing our exposure to such risks complies to a high degree with the moral requirement, incumbent upon governments, to advance justice or the good.

Some readers may at first be confused by the rapid moves made in the last couple of paragraphs: so let me explain. In applying Kramer's analysis to Joe's case, we needed to move from talking about the risk of 'prison' to talking about the risk of 'punishment', the latter term being understood to cover both prison and extra-legal beatings. But nothing, from the viewpoint of incentives, turns upon the availability or otherwise of a conventional word. Let us invent a couple of new words: 'flutishment' and 'unempunishment'. 'Flutishment' is a type of event that can be instantiated either by one's catching the flu, or by one's being punished; while 'unempunishment' is a type of event that can be instantiated either by one's being made unemployed, or by one's being punished. Now we can see (following Kramer's argument) that incentives for compliance with the law will be reduced by our exposure to evil contingencies such as flu and unemployment. For while compliance with the law may reduce our exposure to the risk of punishment to some very considerable extent, it will reduce our exposure to the risk of flutishment or unempunishment much less. As I have already said, the fact that there are no such words as 'flutishment' and 'unempunishment' can have no bearing upon incentives: the words describe evil contingencies, which could be analysed into various more refined categories of evil contingency, but the same is true of the risk of 'punishment' faced by Joe (this could be analysed into discrete risks of a beating and a prison sentence).

It must at this point be remembered that the key point in dispute between Kramer and myself concerns the moral status of the rule of law. Is the rule of law (as represented by Fuller's eight precepts) an intrinsically moral ideal? Kramer claims that it is not, and supports this claim by arguing that a substantial (though less than perfect) degree of compliance with the eight precepts is highly serviceable for the aims of wicked regimes as well as good regimes. His argument,[41] however, seems to undermine rather than reinforce his general thesis, for it has the implication that a substantial (though less than perfect) degree of governmental compliance with the requirements of justice and the good will also be highly serviceable for the aims of wicked regimes. The problem here is not that the substance of this implication is false: it may well be true that wicked regimes have sound interest-based reasons for the (qualified) pursuit of justice and the good. The problem is rather that it would be odd to argue on this ground that justice and the good do not represent moral ideals. So in what way would the (qualified) serviceability of the rule of law for evil (if Kramer could demonstrate such serviceability: which, of course, I say he cannot) demonstrate the moral neutrality of law?

Outside the realms of the Prince of Darkness, wicked regimes do not usually take wickedness *as such* to be their goal. Setting that possibility on one side, therefore, we will see that the goals of a wicked regime will typically allow some room for laws and policies aimed at improving the overall expectations of the populace, so as to stiffen incentives for compliance with the law. How extensively such laws and policies are adopted by a wicked regime will depend upon the extent to which the stiffening of incentives by their adoption competes with the regime's goals (particularly relevant in this context is the question of whether the same stiffening of incentives could be

[41] Above n 30.

achieved at lower cost in other ways: by, for example, increasing the brutality of the punishments prescribed by law).

If Kramer could establish that departures from the rule of law by the use of extra-legal violence necessarily weaken incentives for compliance with the law (more than sanction-backed legal prohibitions would), he would still need to establish, as a quite separate step in his argument, that a substantial degree of compliance with the rule of law would be serviceable for the interests of wicked regimes. This is because he would need to establish that any incentive-impairing effects of departure from the rule of law would outweigh the benefits to be secured by departing from the rule of law,[42] and that incentives could not be sustained at lower cost simply by increasing the severity of the threatened punishments for lawbreaking.

If departures from the rule of law did have any incentive-impairing effects, the status of the rule of law (as represented by Fuller's eight precepts) would be very much on a par with the status of justice or the good. The extent to which a wicked regime has good reason to conform to the requirements of those ideals would depend upon the strength of the reasons for departure from those requirements, and the possibility of securing in other ways (such as heavier punishments) the incentive-strengthening effects of conformity to their requirements. Kramer has failed to establish that departures from the rule of law have incentive-impairing effects; but even if he overcame this problem, some difficult obstacles would continue to lie in his path.

I have argued at length, both here and elsewhere, that wicked regimes will have powerful reasons for extensive departures from the rule of law. The cost of observing the rule of law will include the loss of the benefits that flow from such departures. Meanwhile, the benefits of observing the rule of law (in so far as they are connected to the issue of the sapping of incentives) will be represented primarily by the avoidance of additional costs attaching to an increase in penalties designed to rectify any impairment of incentives. Kramer's confidence that these sums will come out favouring his main thesis (that wicked regimes will have good reasons for substantial compliance with the rule of law) is implausible and wholly ungrounded in argument. My confidence that they will not is grounded primarily, though by no means entirely, in Kramer's failure even to get past the starting post by showing that departures from the rule of law will tend to sap incentives.

Finally, after he has overcome these various problems, Kramer would need to explain why his theory supports the claim that the rule of law is morally neutral while not committing him to the ridiculous thesis that justice and the good are also morally neutral.

---

[42] Benefits that I summarize above, pp 85–88.

Managing Violence

Might serious departures from the rule of law undermine the preparedness of citizens to comply with the regime's diktats in other ways? For example, might the population begin to feel insecure in consequence of the regime's departures from the rule of law? After all, a regime's commitment to comply with published rules gives us one basis for feeling that we are secure from the regime's coercive interference. A widespread sense of insecurity in the bulk of the population, it might be argued, creates at least one of the preconditions for revolution. Perhaps, then, the best way to prevent revolution is for the regime to comply with the rule of law.

This argument, it seems to me, is ineffective. For it assumes that those who feel insecure will also have available to them ways of organizing oppositional activity. In fact a wicked regime may have little reason to foster and protect a sense of security in the population at large. Insecurity may make people feel unhappy, and disposed to hope for a change of regime; but it will also make people far less likely to put their heads above the parapet by expressing their opposition. If people are cowed into a desire to avoid expressing their opposition, opponents of the regime will be unable to identify each other, and to coordinate their conduct. In this way, general insecurity may serve the purposes of the regime well. Regimes can survive very succesfully with little in the way of active support from their subject populations, provided that the regime is able to structure interaction in ways that make it very difficult for opponents of the regime to identify each other and so organize oppositional activity. As we saw above, the deployment of extra-legal violence is an important technique in this structuring of interaction. Individuals will have little to gain and much to lose (their lives, for example) by voicing opposition in such a context; and where very few reveal their opposition, opponents of the regime cannot cooperate and organize.

Even if a widespread sense of insecurity would pose a danger to the regime, however, there is no reason for thinking that compliance with the rule of law is the most appropriate way to avoid generating such a sense. Compliance with the rule of law, it must be remembered, would come at a heavy cost: namely, the loss of all of those advantages that may be gained by departure from the rule of law. The benefits that might flow from compliance with the rule of law (in terms of security) can quite feasibly be obtained in other ways, and at lower cost. To imagine that this is not so is to imagine that a regime that departs from the rule of law will *ipso facto* be a regime of wild and chaotic violence. In reality, however, the organization of the regime's workings can be very sophisticated. It is of course true that, within regimes committed to the rule of law, this very commitment provides the basis for the coordination of official conduct; but it does not follow from this that commitment to the rule of law is the only, or even the best, way in which official conduct might be coordinated. A wicked regime that finds good reasons to depart from the rule of law could (in relation to those departures) coordinate its internal workings in other ways: it may have suitable procedures, management structures and information gathering systems, without observance of the rule of law in relation to the populace. The regime's use of violence could be closely monitored and controlled. Decisions on the use of violence in individual cases could be the result of carefully considered management decisions, responsive to the particular features of each situation and to the overall political context. In this way the regime could avoid giving any grounds for alarm amongst its loyal supporters, or within the ruling class that generally receives the benefits flowing from the regime's governance. Such management decisions on the use of extra-legal violence could be based on carefully collected and cross-checked evidence. Indeed, any such regime, if well-advised, would inevitably be alert to the need for this monitoring and scrutiny.

We must be careful to avoid confusing the *predictability* of governmental action with the rule of law. The rule of law obtains when the agents of government are *constrained* to act in certain ways by a general framework of rules and principles, not when they follow general rules of thumb serving as provisional guides to policy. Governmental action may be highly *predictable* without any such constraint by rules, but simply in virtue of the constancy and simplicity of governmental objectives. It is simply an error to claim that, where governmental action is predictable, the rule of law obtains.[43]

If a wicked and oppressive regime is to observe the rule of law, problems that might otherwise be addressed by the intervention of the regime's thugs will be addressed instead by the publication and enforcement of legal prohibitions. To the extent that the rule of law is observed, rules must be enforced with some reliability. If statutes are enforced only occasionally, there will be extensive reliance upon official discretion; the rule-of-law requirement of 'congruence between the declared rule and the official action'[44] will not be properly observed. But where legal prohibitions are enforced in a fairly reliable way, those who violate the relevant prohibitions will thereby trigger a sharp increase in the risk of punishment to which they are exposed. If extra-legal violence is never to be used, but oppositional activity is to be effectively suppressed, there might be many such prohibited forms of conduct, each one of which will trigger a substantial risk of punishment. Since a thorough knowledge of all the relevant prohibitions may not be easy to maintain, even those citizens who do

---

[43] A claim made by Kramer, above n 17, 91.   [44] Fuller, above n 15.

not actively oppose the regime may run the risk of unknowingly violating some such prohibition. Where carefully monitored extra-legal violence is used, by contrast, evidence of a consistent pattern of oppositional activity (rather than an isolated violation of a single prohibition) might be required before one would be exposed to a substantially increased risk of punishment. It is therefore by no means clear that a sense of insecurity will be more widespread in regimes that violate the rule of law than in wicked and oppressive regimes that do not violate the rule of law.

Could it be argued that violent departures from the rule of law might so accustom citizens to the occurrence of violence, that their fear of being the victim of violence is greatly reduced? (This seems an implausible claim to me, but I mention it because I have heard it seriously pressed as an argument.) The thought that this might give a wicked regime good reason for compliance with the rule of law simply confuses different issues. One is the overall level of violence in the society in question, while the other is the degree of compliance with the rule of law. A regime might comply with the rule of law and yet have a very high level of violence: regular executions, public beatings, and so forth. On the other hand, a regime might deploy violence outside the published rules, and yet use that violence in a carefully measured and monitored way.

Liberty and the Rule of Law

We noted earlier the confident assertion by positivists such as Kelsen, Raz and MacCormick of a clear distinction between the concept of 'law' and the ideal of 'the rule of law'. Raz in particular dismisses with scorn the idea that 'the form of law' can be 'an ideal, the ideal of the rule of law, that all law should conform to'. For, 'if it is part of the form of law, then law conforms to it, or it would not be law'.[45]

Once we have seen how a concept may be structured by an archetype, however, Raz's problem disappears. To count as an instance of law, a regime must approximate to the archetype to some degree: it must, so to speak, participate in the form of law. Yet the very fact that such participation can be instantiated to varying degrees means that the archetype can nevertheless constitute a guiding ideal to which legal systems ought to strive to conform more closely.

A theoretical approach that views the concept of law as structured by an archetype has a number of virtues. In the first place, an understanding of the

---

[45] Joseph Raz, 'Formalism and the Rule of Law' in Robert P George, *Natural Law Theory* (Oxford: Clarendon Press, 1992) 320.

concept of law as structured by an archetype captures our intuitive sense (acknowledged by Raz) that the ideal of the rule of law 'is an ideal rooted in the very essence of law' such that '[i]n conforming to it the law does nothing more than be faithful to its own nature'.[46] Second, it enables us to see how the basic truth of the aspirational view of law is nevertheless compatible with many of the features of law that might at first seem to support the mundane view. Thus, individual laws might be enacted in the service of wickedly self-interested goals, and entire legal systems might be permeated by gross injustice; yet it remains the case that the establishment and maintenance of the institutions of law is explicable only by reference to impartial moral motives, or by the pretence so to be motivated.

These virtues come at a certain cost, however. For my argument is that instances of law count as such in virtue of their approximation to an archetype which is an intrinsically moral ideal. It is therefore incumbent upon me, not only to explain the nature of this moral ideal, but also to explain how all instances of law participate in the ideal to some extent.[47] I suggested earlier that the main impetus behind the aspirational theory of law is not to gild and sanctify ugly realities but to ground a form of immanent critique. However, the aspirational view acknowledges that, where those ugly realities are found conjoined with a substantial degree of respect for the rule of law, they incorporate genuine moral virtues along with their all too evident vices.

The argument thus far aims to demonstrate that observance of the rule of law is not a neutral instrumentality that is serviceable for diverse goals, be they good or evil. Wicked rulers motivated by pure self-interest are unlikely to find that observance of the rule of law is in their interests, for a willingness to deploy violence outside the bounds of the published rules is a highly effective device for the securing and entrenching of a regime's grip on power, and one that comes at no cost in terms of the 'sapping' of incentives for compliance. However, we have as yet said nothing positive about what the value of the rule of law might be. If the establishment and maintenance of institutions that respect and are guided by those requirements is to be viewed as rational, it must be understood in terms of impersonal moral or political values, rather than in terms of instrumental considerations that are as serviceable for evil as for good. What I now wish to argue is that the value served by the rule of law is the value of liberty.

---

[46] Ibid, 309.

[47] It seems to me that this is a problem that Dworkin's theory of law is able to avoid, since Dworkin does not claim that instances of law 'in a pre-interpretive sense' count as such in virtue of their participation in the ideal of integrity. At the same time, this feature of Dworkin's theory suggests that he never directly engages with his positivist opponents, but simply abandons their debates for a different inquiry. See Ronald Dworkin, *Law's Empire* (London: Fontana, 1986) 103.

For present purposes I take the rule of law to be adequately represented by Fuller's eight *desiderata*.[48] I therefore accept that regimes may observe the rule of law and yet narrowly restrict the repertoire of actions lawfully available to the citizen. However, the concept of liberty is not a simple idea that can helpfully be equated with the availability of a range of choices. It is conceivable that a free man might have fewer options available to him than a slave; and this is so whether we judge the availability of options by reference to the number of normative prohibitions bearing upon the agent, or the number of factual restrictions. The connection between slavery and a restricted set of options is therefore purely contingent, yet we do not think that slavery is only contingently connected with freedom: we think of slavery as the very embodiment of unfreedom. Even when the slave has an extensive range of options available to him, we think of him as unfree. This is presumably because of the conditions under which he enjoys that extensive range of options, for they are fully dependent upon the will of the master.

There are, as it were, two different dimensions to freedom: one concerning the range of options available to us without interference, and the other concerning the degree to which that range of options is itself dependent upon the will of another. In claiming that the rule of law is intrinsically linked to liberty, we rely upon the same concept of liberty that is invoked in treating slavery as intrinsically violative of liberty.

When a citizen lives under the rule of law, it is conceivable that the duties imposed upon him or her will be very extensive and onerous, and the interstices between these duties might leave very few options available. Yet, if the rule of law is a reality, the duties will have limits and the limits will not be dependent upon the will of any other person. Might they be dependent upon the will of a sovereign lawmaker? One needs to remember here that laws must be prospective, and must not be subject to constant change. At any one time, therefore, the law may conflict with the present will of the sovereign lawmaker.

The law might, of course, serve to establish slavery: but slaves are objects of proprietary right, not the bearers of legal rights and duties; to that extent they stand outside the system of jural relationships.[49] If, however, the slaves enjoy certain legal protections (against the violence of their masters, for example[50]), those protections are independent of the will of others, and dependent upon the law. To be governed by law is to enjoy a degree of independence from the will of others.

---

[48] Elsewhere I suggest that those precepts stand in need of revision. Furthermore, I suggest that the need (acknowledged by Fuller) for benevolent regimes on occasion to depart from the requirements of the individual precepts reflects some significant features of moral thought. See below, Chapter 5.

[49] See Simmonds, 'Rights at the Cutting Edge' in Matthew Kramer, NE Simmonds and Hillel Steiner, *A Debate Over Rights* (Oxford: Clarendon Press, 1998) 113 and 165–167.

[50] See Gaius 1.53.

Independence of the will of others could scarcely constitute any form of liberty, of course, if it encompassed no domain of optional conduct protected from the coercive interference of others. Simply in consisting of followable rules, however, the law must allow me to retain certain optional areas of conduct. What we now need to perceive is that any government seeking to advance a range of objectives (be they good or bad) will have good reason to protect those domains of optional conduct from the coercive interference of citizens.

We saw earlier that extra-legal violence would have necessary incentive-impairing effects only if it were to be conditional upon the victim's compliance with the law, so that the citizen considering a legal prohibition faced two alternatives: disobey and be lawfully punished, or obey and be beaten up. Governmental violence will, of course, not take this form of conditionality upon compliance with the law, and the need to maintain strong incentives for compliance will therefore not give a wicked regime good reason for avoiding the use of extra-legal violence. On the other hand, any regime will have good reason to prevent the coercive interference of one citizen with another. This will typically take the form of the enactment of general prohibitions upon trespass and assault, such laws providing a protective perimeter for domains of optional conduct.[51]

The existence of such laws might be said to be a contingent, rather than a necessary, feature of legal systems; but the notion of 'necessity' here simply refers to the fact that a system without such laws may coherently be imagined as an abstract possibility.[52] Suppose, however, that we acknowledge that any governing regime will have certain reasons for what it does, including the laws that it chooses to enact and enforce. There is then a strong case for saying that, regardless of the regime's particular set of policy objectives (or exploitative goals) it will have good reason to enact and enforce such general prohibitions on trespass and assault, thereby providing a protective perimeter for liberty. This is because leaving people exposed to the threat of lawless violence against person or property would undermine incentives for compliance with the governing regime's diktats, and thereby impede the regime's pursuit of its objectives, regardless of their content.

You may well think that I have now contradicted myself. For did I not claim, only a moment ago, that lawless violence would *not* undermine such incentives for compliance? Not so. For earlier I was discussing the governmental

[51] Hart, above n 3, Chapter 7.

[52] A regime that did not seek to regulate the use of force by one citizen against another might be said not to claim or possess a monopoly over the use of force. On a standard Weberian analysis of the state, therefore, the regime would not constitute a state. The relationship between the concepts of 'state' and 'law' is too complex a matter to discuss here, however.

deployment of violence against those who have violated no published rule; and my argument was that such violence would undermine incentives for compliance only if the violence was made conditional upon compliance with the rules. Only if there is one penalty conditional upon non-compliance, and another penalty conditional upon compliance, will the citizen face a comparative judgement between the two penalties, such that the penalty for compliance will weaken or negate the force of the incentive to comply. In the case of lawless violence by citizen against citizen, however, the situation is quite different. There is a far stronger case for thinking that the latter (private) interferences will be capable of 'sapping' incentives for compliance with the law than there is for anticipating such an effect from the former (public) interferences. This is because the performance of the citizens' legal duties might expose them to the risk of violence from other citizens who object to the performance of the duty: citizens annoyed by the performance of the duty of early morning bell-ringing, for example; or opponents of the regime who seek to obstruct the regime's pursuit of its objectives by penalizing any compliance with the regime's diktats.

Now it might be suggested that this argument yields only a very limited and therefore ineffective point: that a governing regime will have good reason to prohibit assault and trespass upon citizens *while they are engaged in the performance of their legal duty*. The suggestion is misguided, however. For violence that is conditional upon the citizen's performance of his legal duty need not be inflicted *in the course of that performance*: it may take the form of reprisals in another context. Nor would a law framed by reference to the *motive* for the assault or trespass be likely to be very effective; or, at least it would be less effective than a simple prohibition on trespass and assault, because it would require proof of motive.

Governments stand to benefit from the citizen's exercise of liberties, as well as from the performance of his duties. Such liberties enable markets to operate, producing wealth (to be extracted in the form of taxes) and generating prices (to be employed in the government's cost/benefit monitoring of its own policies). Specific and carefully controlled governmental violence could be conducted without any substantial market distortions, but a wholesale failure to protect citizens from the coercive interference of other citizens is a very different matter. For these reasons, even a wicked regime will have good reason to grant citizens a perimeter of legal protections against interference. A state's claim to monopolize the use of force is but one facet of the state's deployment of force in the service of its goals. The sanctions that back the state's decrees may be reduced in efficacy if the deployment of coercive threats by citizens (and the performance of acts that might amount to the execution of such threats) is left unregulated.

Simply in consisting of followable rules, the law must recognize certain areas of optional (non-obligatory) conduct, however narrowly circumscribed those areas may be: for the law's demands cannot be *limitless* while also being possible to comply with. Even if my daily round is entirely absorbed by the performance of legal duties, I must enjoy certain options about how I perform those duties (e.g. should I wear a hat whilst doing so?) if the duties are to be performable at all. Such domains of optional conduct[53] are likely to enjoy a protective perimeter either in the form of claim-rights against certain forms of interference, or in the form of criminal prohibitions on such forms of interference (or both).

To make its governance effective, and to retain a substantive[54] monopoly over the use of force, a regime must prohibit potentially coercive interferences, and will thereby create a protective perimeter for the said domains of optional conduct. *To the extent that* the law leaves me with such options, it renders the existence of those options secure and independent of the will of others. Similarly, *to the extent that* the law grants me certain protections against interference (a 'protective perimeter' of claim-rights, for example) the existence of those protections is secure and independent of the will of others.

These options and protections are not simply juridical abstractions. For we will see in due course that the archetype of law is fully realized only to the extent that the rules are effectively enforced. Consequently, to the extent that law exists, citizens will not only enjoy juridical liberties and juridical protections (in the form of claim-rights against interference) but these liberties and protections will (through effective enforcement) give rise to domains of conduct that are genuinely free from the most common and effective forms of coercive interference.

Freedom and Rights

To the extent that law governs, citizens will enjoy certain zones of optional conduct where the state will not interfere; and they will benefit from certain general prohibitions on the most general forms of interference that might be

---

[53] Hohfeldian liberties to perform an action consist simply in the absence of a duty not to perform the action. Bilateral Hohfeldian liberties consist of a liberty to perform a certain action combined with a liberty not to perform it. Domains of optional conduct are constituted by bilateral Hohfeldian liberties. When such domains are effectively protected against violent or coercive interference, we may speak of them as domains of liberty. This analysis is considered further in the next section of this chapter.

[54] That is to say, the regime must actually prohibit potentially coercive interferences by citizens against each other: it is not enough to claim a *formal* monopoly by permitting such conduct, while pointing out that the conduct derives its legitimacy from the regime's will. We may set on one side the

attempted by their fellow citizens. These two features of the rule of law, taken in conjunction, are presupposed by many of the concepts that make up the characteristic framework of legal thought. This is best seen by examining a well-worn and influential, but nevertheless misguided, criticism that has been made of Hohfeld's analysis of rights.[55] By seeing how the criticism misfires we can come to perceive a deeper point that partially motivates it but which has been inadequately grasped (and which, when properly understood, is not at all damaging to Hohfeld's analysis, but rather the reverse).

The principal significance of Hohfeld's analysis is to be found in his demonstration that legal rights lack the internal complexity that has often been ascribed to them.[56] 'Internal complexity' is ascribed to rights when possession of a right is taken to entail a number of distinct juridical consequences. Thus, for example, it might be assumed that the right to free speech entails both the permissibility of certain actions of the right-holder, and also the impermissibility of certain actions that might be performed by other parties, particularly actions interfering with the right-holder's exercise of his right. Hohfeld's analysis reveals that such diverse juridical consequences should not be treated as entailed by a single concept of right. Rather than being internally complex, the notion of a right is ambiguous between several analytically distinguishable ideas. One such idea is the idea of a 'liberty', which is simply the absence of a duty: thus I have a liberty to wear a hat in so far as I am under no duty not to wear a hat.[57] Another, distinct, idea is that of a 'claim-right'. This is correlative to a duty in some other person. Thus, if I have a claim-right against you that you should pay me £500, you have a duty to pay me £500.

Once we have made the distinction between liberties and claim-rights, we can see that the existence of a right of free speech does not in itself entail the conclusion that other persons are under a duty not to interfere with the right-holder's speaking freely. Whether a liberty is or should be protected by a claim-right, and what the content of any such claim-right is or should be, is a separate issue from the existence of the liberty itself. A liberty to speak freely,

question of whether such a purely formal monopoly would satisfy the Weberian analysis: the real point is that the Weberian analysis derives its plausibility from the way in which the monopoly of force is one facet of the state's instrumentalization of force in the service of its goals, and that instrumentalization requires a substantive monopoly, not a formal one.

[55] WN Hohfeld, *Fundamental Legal Conceptions as Applied in Judicial Reasoning* (New Haven, Conn: Yale University Press, 1923). In what follows I ignore, for simplicity, the fact that Hohfeldian rights obtain only as against specific individuals.

[56] See Simmonds, *Central Issues in Jurisprudence* (2nd edition, London: Sweet and Maxwell, 2002) Chapter 8.

[57] Hohfeld employed the term 'privilege' rather than 'liberty'. I am following the majority of modern theorists in substituting the term 'liberty'. In fact, Hohfeld has good reason to avoid the term 'liberty' even if his own choice of 'privilege' is less than ideal.

for example, in itself consists simply in the absence of any duty not to speak freely. This liberty may or may not be protected by the imposition of a duty on others not to interfere with the right-holder's free speech, or not to interfere with that freedom of speech in certain ways. To the extent that no such duty exists, it may be the case that X has a liberty to speak freely while Y has a liberty to prevent X from speaking freely.

Critics of Hohfeld's analysis have very often resisted the idea that the bare absence of a duty can constitute a right. But in doing so they have tended to confuse different issues, and so obscure a real insight that proves on reflection to be perfectly compatible with Hohfeld's analysis.

Consider, for example, the following claim made by Joseph Raz:

> The absence of a duty does not amount to a right. A person who says to another 'I have a right to do it' is not saying that he has no duty not to or that it is not wrong to do it. He is claiming that the other has a duty not to interfere.[58]

The claim seems obviously unsound. For it is easy to offer examples where the claim to possess a right would naturally be construed as pointing out the absence of any duty on the right-holder, rather than the presence of a duty of non-interference on others. Suppose, for example, that in the context of a ball game someone erroneously suggests that it is a foul deliberately to kick the ball into touch. A player might well reply by saying that there is a right to kick the ball into touch. The context makes it clear that this is intended to deny the existence of a duty not to kick the ball into touch. It is not intended to assert the existence of a duty of non-interference on others, for they are in all probability under no such duty: the opposition players are permitted to prevent me kicking into touch if they are able to.

Raz continues the quoted passage, however, with some observations that he no doubt believes will provide an effective response to this type of example. Having told us that anyone who claims a right to act in a certain way is really asserting the existence of a duty of non-interference on others, he adds the following qualification:

> It is not necessarily a duty not to interfere in any way whatsoever. It is, however, a claim that there are some ways of interference which would be wrong because they are against an interest of the right holder. 'I have a right to do it and you have a right to stop me if you can' is paradoxical only if it means 'if you can with no holds barred'.[59]

Now, clearly a ball game is not a state of nature where there are no legal protections whatever. Ball games take place within the context of a legal system which includes certain general prohibitions upon forms of interference such as

[58] Joseph Raz, *Ethics in the Public Domain* (Oxford: Clarendon Press, 1994) 259.   [59] Ibid.

assault. The prohibition on assault continues to apply to the players of the game, only slightly modified by the fact that certain acts which might constitute an assault outside the context of the game will be held to have been consented to (and so will not constitute an assault) if they occur within the game. Acts which go quite beyond anything permitted by the rules of the game are certainly capable of amounting to an illegal assault. If, for example, you try to prevent me from kicking the ball into touch by striking me on the head with an axe, or by shooting me, you will certainly have broken the legal prohibition on assault.

But it is clearly preposterous to suggest that, when I assert the existence of a right to kick the ball into touch, I am really asserting the existence of a duty on others not to carry out a criminal assault upon me: such a possibility has in all probability never entered my head. My object in asserting the right is to negate the suggestion that I am under a duty not to kick the ball into touch deliberately, while I may fully acknowledge that opposition players are free to try and prevent me from doing so (provided that they do not criminally assault me by using violence that goes well beyond anything contemplated in the rules of the game).

Someone might say 'but Raz does have a point to this extent: if people were free to interfere with my conduct in any way at all (if there was not even a prohibition on violent assault) there would be little point in describing the absence of a duty as a right.' The answer is that there is indeed a sound point here, but not the point articulated by Raz. Rather, it is a point that is best understood by considering an example drawn from Hart.

Hart pointed out that the general prohibitions on trespass and assault provide a 'perimeter of protection' for liberties by prohibiting the most obvious ways in which an exercise of a liberty can be interfered with. He pointed out that the existence of such a perimeter of protection formed an essential element in our willingness to describe a Hohfeldian liberty (the absence of a duty) as a right. After all, Hart observed, it would be odd to say 'that a class of helots whom free citizens were allowed to treat as they wished or interfere with at will, yet had rights to do those acts which they were not forbidden by law to do'.[60]

It would indeed be odd to speak of the helots as possessing rights in such a context. But is this because (as Raz tells us) 'the absence of a duty is not a right' and whenever someone speaks of their right to act in a particular way they are really asserting the existence of a duty on others not to interfere? Or is it because the helots would not really stand within juridical relationships at all, and so could not be said to possess rights of any sort, nor be subject to duties?

[60] Above n 3, 173.

The applicability of legal concepts seems to presuppose an interest in determining the exact requirements of the law as applied in particular circumstances. Such an interest could spring from a belief in a moral duty to obey the law, or from a concern to avoid sanctions. But neither of these bases for the interest would seem to be applicable to the helots. By complying with the law, a helot might considerably reduce (though not eliminate) the risk of being subjected to interference by officials. But such compliance might also considerably increase the risk of being penalized by other citizens (citizens annoyed by the helots' compliance with their duty of early morning bell-ringing, for example). Given the absence of any general protection even for their lawful conduct, the helots would be likely to find a policy of being guided by legal rules inferior to a strategy of ad hoc prediction of the likelihood of interference.

We can of course imagine a situation where officials are charged with a duty of applying rules to the conduct of the helots and punishing violations of those rules. Here, the violation of a rule by a helot would provide the occasion for the performance of the official's duty of punishment. But if the rules or the officials describe the conduct of the helots in terms of 'duty' and 'breach of duty', such language will strike us as odd and inappropriate in precisely the same way that it would seem odd to speak of the helots as possessing 'rights'. Hart suggests that the language of legal rights and duties does not presuppose a belief that the duty-bearers morally ought to perform their duty, but simply expresses a conclusion about the fact that certain actions are 'due' or 'demandable' under the rules.[61] But even if this is so, such language nevertheless assumes that the scope of the demands is limited: it is odd to speak of certain actions as 'demandable' when anything at all can be demanded, and the demand backed by sanctions.

A Hohfeldian liberty is not the liberty possessed by people in a Hobbesian state of nature where there are no duties at all. It is not a residual island of freedom left by the incoming tide of legal regulation. For the introduction of law fundamentally changes the status even of those areas of conduct that are not subjected to legal duties, by providing them with a general perimeter of protection against the most common forms of interference such as assault. This perimeter of protection is a basic underpinning for the applicability of legal concepts. Helots who received no such protection would simply be outside the governance of law, being governed by force alone.

Raz offers a further argument against the idea that a Hohfeldian liberty (the mere absence of a duty) can constitute a right. He points out that we sometimes regard people as having a right to do things that we consider to be

----

[61] Ibid, 266.

wrong. He thinks that this feature of our discourse supports his thesis that, in saying that someone has a right to perform an act, we are really saying that others are under a duty not to interfere in certain ways. His point seems to be that we cannot, in such contexts, be interpreted as asserting the absence of a duty because this would conflict with our view that the right-holder does wrong in exercising his right.[62]

We can now see, however, the sense in which it is intrinsic to law to create certain domains of permissible protected conduct that are independent of the will of others and dependent solely upon the law. This inevitably means that people may sometimes have legal rights (Hohfeldian liberties) to act in certain ways that other people (or even the right-holder himself) may consider to be wrong. An understanding of this situation should not lead us to conclude that all assertions of such a right are really assertions that others have a duty of non-interference, for they may equally be assertions of the legal permissibility of the action. Recognition of the legal permissibility of an action is compatible with a recognition of its immorality.[63]

Final Remark

The rule-based independence of the will of others that is intrinsic to the rule of law will confer areas of permissibility (Hohfeldian liberties) upon us. But it will of course also serve to entrench the totality of legal *restrictions* upon our conduct: these too will be rendered invulnerable to the choices and preferences of our fellows. Are my assertions about liberty and the rule of law not then ultimately arbitrary? For I claim that the rule of law is an intrinsically moral idea in that the rule of law serves to protect liberty; but might I not with equal justification claim that the rule of law serves to entrench the restriction of liberty? Even after all that has been said, does it not remain the case that the rule of law is a morally neutral instrument which can be used for good purposes (the protection of liberty) or bad (the entrenchment of oppressive restrictions on conduct)?

It must be remembered at this point that, to reveal the status of the rule of law as an inherently moral idea, what we need to show is (in the first place)

---

[62] Above n 58, 259.

[63] In any case, morality should not be viewed as, in its entirety, a matter of rights and duties: some types of ethical consideration are not a matter of right or of duty. Consequently, I may have a moral right to perform an action in the sense that I have no moral duty not to perform it, while there are powerful moral considerations not amounting to a duty that count against performance of the act (e.g. it would be ungenerous).

that practices observing and pursuing the rule of law cannot be rendered intelligible by the idea that they are instrumentally effective techniques for the pursuit of non-moral goals. Second, we need to show how the features of the rule of law may be rendered intelligible by the way in which they serve certain recognizably moral goals. Securing independence from the will of others for the liberties that we enjoy is in itself an intelligible goal that serves to explain the characteristic features of the rule of law. The project of securing such independence for our liberties is intimately linked with the imposition and entrenchment of duty. If our liberties are to be independent of the will of others, it must be impossible for others to extend the scope of our duties, or to reduce the scope of the duties on others not to interfere coercively with us.

Let us imagine, however, a regime that does not regard the securing of duty as a means to, or a condition of, the securing of liberty: rather it takes *as its object* the securing and stabilizing of restrictions on conduct, perhaps in consequence of a puritanical love for severe discipline, or a life-denying fervour for the suppression of what the regime considers to be vice. Such a regime, motivated not at all by considerations of liberty, would have good reason to punish rule-violators, but no good reason to refrain from punishing (vicious or ill-disciplined) rule-compliers. The maintenance of that key component of the rule of law that consists in the restriction of official violence to circumstances where a rule has been breached seems intelligible only in the light of a concern for the value of liberty, in the full sense that we have explored.

In Chapter 2 we examined an apparent antinomy that haunts our perceptions of law and motivates much theoretical reflection: the antinomy between an understanding of law as a substantive moral aspiration and as a morally neutral instrument, serviceable for wicked purposes as well as good. We considered and dismissed some relatively superficial ways of trying to dissolve the antinomy, by treating aspirational views of law as grounded in simple confusion, or by postulating a dualism between different senses of 'law'. It was then proposed that we should think of the concept of law as structured by an abstract archetype to which all actual instances of law approximate in varying degrees. This proposal does not itself beg the question in favour of the aspirational understanding of law, for it leaves open the possibility of understanding the abstract archetype to be itself morally neutral in character. At the same time, the proposal does rob the mundane view of law (as a morally neutral instrument) of much of its initial plausibility, by demonstrating that most of the more obvious ways in which legality is compatible with evil are perfectly consistent with 'law' being an intrinsically moral idea.

In the present chapter, we turned to consider the question of whether the archetype of law (provisionally equated with Fuller's eight *desiderata*) should be thought of as a moral idea, or as devoid of intrinsic moral significance. My strategy was to consider the arguments recently offered by Kramer in defence of the latter claim. Having rejected those arguments, I then sought briefly to indicate certain respects in which the notion of legality (even when understood in a quite thin and formalistic way) is logically tied to one of the most important aspects of liberty: independence from the power of others. In the chapters to come, I explore some of the further consequences of this approach.

4

Normativity, Legality and Judgment

There are things that we ought to do, and these may differ from the things we are currently doing or are likely to do or have any intention or desire to do. The world contains many facts about what we are doing, have done and (perhaps) will do. But it also contains, it would seem, facts about what we *ought* to do. These '*oughts*' need not be a matter of moral requirement. They may be the requirements of logic, of grammar, of good manners, of good cooking and (of course) of law. We write books about them, and set examinations (in logic, grammar, cooking, law) to test knowledge of them. In that sense, they are a familiar part of our everyday world.

Yet, at the same time, such normative requirements can seem deeply problematic. For they make a certain *claim* upon our conduct, requiring or at least inviting our compliance; and they envisage a state of affairs which may differ from the state that currently obtains. How can such claims be themselves amongst the existing features of the world? How can the existing state of affairs point beyond itself and demand that something other than itself should be brought into existence?

Different 'oughts' may be explained in different ways, of course. The norms of good cooking, for example, may simply reflect facts about the physical and chemical processes of cooking, together with certain common though not invariable uniformities in human culinary preferences. The norms of logic are considerably more problematic, but they might perhaps be seen as stemming from the character of assertions about the world. After all, to contradict oneself is both to assert something and to deny the assertion: in contradicting oneself, one has not so much violated a norm as failed to achieve the object of saying something about the world. Someone who wishes to express a mood or to arouse certain feelings in his audience, rather than to describe an independent state of the world, may find self-contradiction helpful and may therefore have no reason to avoid it. Similarly, someone who enjoys eating smoked mackerel with custard has no reason to follow the norms of good cooking. These norms are sometimes described as 'hypothetical', for their force is contingent upon our goals or desires: if you want to say something about the world, you had better observe the norms of logic; if you share the food preferences of most people, you had better observe the norms of cooking.

Other norms, however, are not dependent in this way upon the goals of the persons to whom they are addressed. The norms of morality, for example, do not tell me to keep my promises and avoid gratuitous injury to others *if* I am aiming at certain objectives (such as remaining popular with my neighbours): they tell me that I *must* keep my promises and avoid gratuitous injury *regardless* of my personal wishes and goals. Moral norms are therefore said to be 'categorical'. This is one reason why the basis of morality has provided such a central and enduring problem for philosophers: for how can the world contain such things as categorical norms?

Ancient philosophers such as Plato and Aristotle took normativity to be grounded in the nature of reality. To understand the nature of something was to comprehend its *telos*: the goal or ideal toward which the thing (if healthily constituted) had a tendency to strive. The norms applicable to conduct reflected the requirements of a fully flourishing existence wherein one realized the specific excellences of a human being. What one *ought* to do was in this way related to what one fundamentally *is*.

Early modern philosophers came to think of nature as the domain of causal laws rather than guiding ideal goals. Consequently, it was less easy for them to see how the '*ought*' could be fitted into an acceptable picture of the world. One tempting option for them was to think of norms as imposed upon the world by an act of will. The attractiveness of explaining *norms* by reference to the *will* springs from the fact that, in exercising the will, we envisage the possibility of a state of affairs that is different from the current situation, and different also from any state of affairs that is likely to obtain in the absence of our intervention. The will, as it were, contains within itself an implicit contrast between the facts as they are at present and the facts that we, in making our choice, have decided *ought to be*. The will therefore seems to be one feature of the world that sits upon the cusp between what is and what ought to be. Something similar is true of the notion of 'desire', which also contains an implicit contrast between the state of the world as currently constituted and the situation that is desired.

Thus, natural law theorists such as Pufendorf sought to reconcile the normative character of morality (or natural law) with a Cartesian or Baconian view of nature by deriving morality's binding force from the divine will.[1] Later theories, such as those of Hume and Smith, transferred the source of normativity from God's will to the human breast with its desires: morality on these

---

[1] Such voluntarist theories had their medieval forebears, especially in the work of Ockham and his followers. For an interesting discussion, see David Cooper, *The Measure of Things* (Oxford: Clarendon Press, 2002) Chapter 2.

accounts derived its normative character from the tendency to approve or disapprove of different actions in ways that reflect the serviceability of those actions for human wants and passions.

Neither approach is ultimately very satisfactory, at least for anyone who believes that there genuinely are categorical requirements upon conduct. For the first (theocentric) approach leaves us asking why we should be bound by God's will. The standard answers (such as 'because God is good', or 'because God created us') assume a deeper norm which cannot itself be derived from God's will ('you ought to obey supreme beings that are good', 'you ought to obey your creator'). Attempts to overcome this problem sometimes endanger the status of morality as categorically binding on everyone. Thus it can be argued that to know God is to love him, and if one loves him one will wish to do his will. But what if I do not want to do his will? This may demonstrate that I do not love God, and perhaps do not 'know' him. But it also takes me outside the scope of the relevant norms, leaving me with no reason for following God's will.

The second (desire-based) approach gives me no reason to comply with moral norms if I do not share the relevant desires: if, for example, I do not *care* about the disapproval of others, and have no fear of the sanctions that they might impose upon me. Consequently, the approach seems to reduce the norms of morality to hypothetical status.

The philosophical problem of normativity is often framed as a question concerning the relationship between normativity and the outlook of modern science: how can norms and the 'ought' find a place in the world as described by science? It is not entirely clear that this is the most appropriate question to ask. We stand to the world both as spectators, who seek to know and understand, and as agents, who try to choose the best and most appropriate course of action. It is possible to think of these postures as equally fundamental but irreducibly distinct, so that the categories in terms of which we deliberate and choose cannot be accommodated into the same logical space as the categories in terms of which we causally explain events: on the one hand, freedom, meaning, responsibility, value and the 'ought'; on the other, necessity and causality. Other philosophers reject this idea of a fundamental bifurcation in human thought, and defend a 'naturalistic' view that gives priority to the scientific understanding of nature in terms of causality yet seeks to accommodate the 'ought' within the space so constructed (the 'desire-based' approach is one expression of this outlook).

Of course, if we adopt the approach of asking how 'oughts' can be fitted into the world as described by science, one possibility that immediately presents itself is an outright denial of the existence of normativity. Denials of this sort seem familiar when they concern the norms of morality: all of us have at some time or other encountered the view that moral standards are a myth foisted on us by those who seek to manipulate our conduct, or a device whereby people try to browbeat each other. Such views are represented by the character Thrasymachos in Plato's *Republic*, and they have always played a role in both sophisticated philosophical discussions and in popular culture. Any approach that seeks wholly to eschew reliance upon the normative, however, faces some severe problems: for the language in which we describe human conduct seems to be intimately entangled with values and norms, and our ascription to others of attitudes and beliefs seems to involve a similar dependency. It is significant that views resembling those of Thrasymachos are almost invariably bound up with (explicit or tacit) ethical recommendations about how the wise and rational man who is not to be duped ought to live. Scepticism about morality therefore seems most commonly to be grounded in a prioritization of the norms of rational self-interest rather than in a rejection of normativity generally.

Could we go further and reject the norms of rational self-interest along with those of morality? Although the precise prescriptions of rational self-interest might be *relative* to what I desire, they are not themselves *reducible* to my present desires: they require me, for example, to consider the effects of my present actions upon my long-term interests, even if at present I care only about the next few minutes. Beliefs about what I 'ought' to do can be experienced as constraints just as surely here as in the context of moral deliberation. If at present I truly care only for the present moment, the belief that I *ought* to be concerned for my future is perhaps a conventional fetter rather than a requirement of reason. Thrasymachos and his philosophical heirs have extolled the clear-sighted person who pursues self-interest without being deluded by ideas of morality; but this critique of normative constraints may be less thoroughgoing than it seems. For why should a clear-sighted concern for my long-term self-interest be taken as a model? Why not choose instead the spontaneity of acting on present desires without regard to the future?

If we always acted on present desires without regard to the future, would each of us not become a mere chaos of transient desires, lacking the identity and continuity that constitutes us as persons? Perhaps then it is a mistake to think of prudential reason as a fetter: perhaps it is the concern for prudential reason that sustains our identity. If this is a plausible thought in relation to long-term prudence, might it not also be a plausible thought in relation to the requirements of moral reason? For could we really be *persons* apart from our participation in community with others (including the communally sustained structures of language and culture)? Might this participation not itself rest upon a certain acceptance of the status of others as sources of normative claims equivalent to our own?

The wholesale rejection of normativity is, in any case, not an option that is open to us. The posture that we adopt towards the world can never be a wholly disengaged and contemplative one. We have lives to lead, and must therefore decide what is to be done. One may avoid making plans and projects, but will still need to decide what one ought to do next. Sometimes people speak of 'letting fate decide', but this is still a practical strategy, chosen because it is believed to have some features that recommend it. If a detached attitude is attainable at all, it is so only intermittently, and then only on the basis of a resolution as to its desirability. The question of what *ought* to be done (and of the stance that we *ought* to adopt) seems, for us humans, to be both inescapable and pervasive.

Understanding and action are always entangled one with another, for our knowledge of the world is always mediated by concepts and categories that are themselves the product of human history (*res gestae*) and sustained by social practice.[2] We cannot inscribe chosen categories upon a clean slate, selecting them for their capacity accurately to represent the contents of an independently available reality. Rather, we must always work from within the categories that we inherit, revising them as we go along. The most general and seemingly detached set of categories may embody a practical ethical orientation: even the outlook of modern science was, in its early-modern origins, bound up with a desire for the practical mastery of nature and perhaps with a new individualism that sought to overturn the authority of established traditions and hierarchies. The philosopher who insists that values are products of the human will rarely succeeds in presenting this thought as a neutral insight into the state of the world as he finds it: more commonly, the voluntarist account of value is *celebrated* as liberating (we are not to be governed by values not of our own making) and as expressing a mature acceptance of our own responsibilities (it is up to us to *create* values). Here it is tacitly accepted that the liberation in question is *good*, or at least that such responsibilities *ought* to be faced up to.

Our conduct is subject to various requirements, drawn from considerations of prudent self-interest, morality, law, logic and perhaps many other sources. But not all of these requirements need be equally fundamental: perhaps the normativity of some standards is derivative rather than original. As we have already seen, some moral sceptics might claim that a completely rational individual would reject the claims of morality and be guided only by self-interest. But, by contrast with such scepticism, some philosophical traditions have sought to demonstrate that considerations of long-term rational self-interest

---

[2] This is of some importance for the later argument of this book, for it helps us to see how the adoption of certain political practices can enable us to deepen our understanding of the values that those practices serve. See below, pp 145–150.

underpin and justify moral requirements rather than conflicting with them. The argument can be developed in quite different ways. One version (associated with Hobbes) offers us an account of well-being which is intelligible quite independently of any moral understanding (well-being as the satisfaction of desire), and then argues that well-being on that conception will best be attained by each individual if that individual complies with certain moral standards, given a reasonable expectation of similar compliance by others. Another version (associated with Plato) claims that moral understanding gives us an insight into the true nature of well-being, revealing such a flourishing existence to be attainable only in community and only by compliance with moral standards.

Many philosophers treat moral reasons as quite distinct from prudential considerations of self-interest. On this view, someone who asks 'why should I be moral?', and seeks thereby a reason of self-interest, has really misunderstood the whole nature of morality. Morality requires us to act on the basis of reasons that are in some sense[3] impartial, weighing our own interests equally along with those of all other persons.

We can therefore distinguish between two problems of normativity which, although by no means wholly distinct, nevertheless represent different focal points for discussion. On the one hand is a metaphysical problem concerning the way in which normativity can or should be thought of as part of the existing world. Are norms and values, for example, integral to the categories in terms of which we describe and understand human conduct, and which therefore render humans mutually intelligible? Or can the value-neutral *facts* of human conduct be disentangled from the values that we choose to attach to them?

On the other hand is an enterprise that, so far as possible, sets the metaphysical question on one side and tries to reflect upon the *structure* of our ideas about normativity: can the normativity of morality be reduced to the normativity of rational self-interest, for example?

The philosophy of law tends to concern itself with this second, structural, type of question. For we ascribe to law a normative character. Even though the law's content may be a function of statutes that have been enacted, or of rules articulated in judicial decisions, propositions of law are not simple reports of the facts of enactment or decision. When lawyers, judges and citizens speak of the law as imposing duties and conferring rights, the language employed cannot plausibly be construed as describing historical events such as the issuing of orders, nor as predicting the likelihood of suffering sanctions in certain

---

[3] It is often argued that morality nevertheless leaves room for some degree of self-preference, as well as special concern for loved ones and other members of one's own community.

circumstances. The judge might (for example) outline the legal obligations that were incumbent upon the defendant, and point to the defendant's breach of those obligations as justifying the judge's order, requiring the defendant to compensate the plaintiff to whom the obligations were owed. The relevant law might be set out in a statute, but the judge does not simply report the fact that such a statute was enacted: he treats the statute as a *reason* for ascribing certain *obligations* to the defendant, and he invokes those obligations as a *reason* why the defendant *ought* to have behaved in a certain way, and as a *justification* for the judge's ordering a sanction against the defendant.

Legal discourse of this kind is intelligible only if we grasp the way in which it is bound up with the guidance of conduct by norms: laws are intended to *prescribe* our conduct, and statements about legal rights and duties draw conclusions about what *ought* to be done, or what is *justified*, in the light of such prescriptions. Even if our object is simply to identify the distinctive characteristics of the practices composing a legal order, there is nevertheless a need to understand the ascription of normativity to law, for that ascription of normativity is central to the entire framework of thought that makes up the relevant practices.

The questions which arise at this point concern the nature and basis of the law's normativity. When lawyers speak of the law as conferring rights and imposing duties, are they assuming that the law binds us morally? Is legal validity a matter of moral bindingness? Is a legal obligation a specific type of *moral* obligation, such as a moral obligation that we bear in consequence of the enactment of certain laws? Or might the law's normativity be somehow distinctive and independent of morality: is being *legally* bound nothing to do with being *morally* bound? Does law perhaps altogether lack genuine normativity, so that the characteristic forms of legal discourse are misleading? Is the law no more than an apparatus of threats grounded in power and organized force? Is its normativity simply a deceptive myth that should clearly be acknowledged as such by a reformation of our legal language?

Hart's Middle Way

HLA Hart is often regarded as having cast a great deal of light upon the problem of law's normative character. Hart saw himself as confronting a jurisprudential debate structured by two main positions. On the one hand were legal positivists such as John Austin who asserted a clear separation between law and morality, but who defended this separation by offering a reductive analysis of propositions of law as descriptive or predictive statements. That is to say, they treated propositions about the legal validity of rules, or about the existence of legal rights, duties and powers, as descriptive or predictive statements concerning the likelihood of suffering sanctions, the issuing of commands, and the willingness of subject populations to comply.

On the other hand were theorists who pointed out the inadequacies of all such reductive analyses. Austin had equated the existence of legal duties with the likelihood of the duty-bearer suffering a sanction. But his critics noted that one might have a legal duty even though one is in fact unlikely to suffer any sanction: some legal duties might be too unimportant for anyone to enforce, given the costs of litigation; or one might be out of the jurisdiction, and not planning on returning. The impossibility of analysing the principal legal concepts in the reductive terms proposed by Austin was perceived to spring from the fact that concepts such as 'obligation', 'right' and 'validity' have their primary role within *normative* discourse: they are concerned with what *ought to happen*, rather than with what probably will happen, or has in fact happened.

Austin's critics, however, took the failure of such reductive analyses to indicate a more general failure of legal positivism. Positivists, they believed, were forced to deny or obscure the normative character of law because the most plausible way to account for that normative character was by grounding law in morality. On this basis, many theorists who grasped the irreducibly normative character of law were led to reject legal positivism, insisting that any adequate analysis of the concept of law would reveal its necessary connections with justice and morality. Others, such as Kelsen, wished to defend legal positivism, but concluded that positivism could sustain the normative character of law only by treating legal discourse as grounded in a basic assumption of law's bindingness, an assumption that Kelsen called the *Grundnorm*. Much earlier, and in a different context, Kant had pointed out that, although it is possible to conceive of a system containing only positive laws, 'a natural law would still have to precede it, which would establish the authority of the lawgiver'.[4] Kelsen did not deny that his *Grundnorm*, although entirely formal in character, might well be considered a residual element of natural law, and to that extent inconsistent with legal positivism's strict separation of law from morality. But he believed that the *Grundnorm* represented a founding presupposition that could be adopted for the strictly limited purposes of legal science, thereby making possible a knowledge of law's content as a body of norms: it was (as he put it) simply the minimum of natural law without which a cognition of law would be impossible.[5]

---

[4] Immanuel Kant, *Metaphysics of Morals* (1797), translated by Mary J Gregor, *Practical Philosophy: The Cambridge Edition of the Works of Immanuel Kant* (Cambridge: Cambridge University Press, 1996) 6:224.

[5] Hans Kelsen, *General Theory of Law and State* (Cambridge, Mass: Harvard University Press, 1945) 437.

Hart endeavoured to show that, while reductivism was certainly to be rejected for its failure to capture the normative character of law, the rejection of reductivism should not lead to a rejection of legal positivism, nor to a version of legal positivism dependent upon the presupposition of Kelsen's *Grundnorm*. Hart tried to demonstrate that the prescriptive action-guiding character of propositions of law can be preserved without grounding law in morality. The central core of his theory consists in a demonstration that it is possible to have a distinct body of normative reasons that is not reducible to some more familiar domain of normative reasoning such as morality or prudence.

This solution depends upon the idea of a basic rule of recognition accepted by officials. Such a rule provides criteria whereby other rules of the system in question may be identified. When a rule of recognition exists, it creates a field of normative reasoning characterized by a distinctive set of concepts and bounded by the basic criteria of recognition. Propositions of law have to be understood within that field of reasoning. Propositions concerning the legal validity of rules, for example, cannot be analysed as claims about the morally binding character of the rules, but nor do they describe the acceptance or effective enforcement of the rules. Rather, they are a distinctive type of proposition, the meaning of which can only be understood by reference to the function of validity claims within the context of a rule of recognition: to say that a rule is legally valid is to express a conclusion about the applicability of the basic rule of recognition. Similarly, propositions concerning legal rights and duties express action-guiding conclusions about the applicability of the rules stemming from the basic rule of recognition. Thus, propositions of law do not assume the moral bindingness of law, but nor are they descriptive statements about the issuing of orders, the likelihood of suffering sanctions, or any other configuration of non-normative facts of that sort.

In Hart's theory, the domain of legal reasons might be said to enjoy a degree of autonomy: we can report legal requirements, and speak of legal rights and duties, while setting on one side all questions concerning our moral or prudential reasons for complying with the law. But this autonomy is only *partial*, for it is limited by two important considerations. In the first place, Hart acknowledges that there will always be cases that fall within what he calls the *penumbra* of the existing legal rules. Penumbral cases of this sort, Hart argues, cannot be resolved by simply applying legal rules, but require reliance upon considerations that go beyond the existing body of law.[6] But secondly (and more importantly for present purposes) legal reasons can only possess practical force when they are supported by moral or prudential reasons for guiding one's conduct by the law.

---

[6] HLA Hart, *The Concept of Law* (2nd edition, Oxford: Clarendon Press, 1994) Chapter 7.

Laws can provide reasons for action only if people have moral or prudential reasons for guiding their conduct by reference to the law. In this sense,
the distinctness of legal reasons can only ever be partial. Moreover, a practice
of normative reasoning, bounded by a rule of recognition, could not be sustained if people had no reason to engage in it. In this sense, the social existence of such a practice of reasoning depends upon the agents' reasons for
participation. Hart, however, thinks that reasons for engaging in the practice need not be moral reasons. Officials must regard the rule of recognition
as a common public standard for judicial decision, but they may take this
view for non-moral reasons.[7] Reasons for accepting the rule of recognition
may be diverse, and it is precisely this diversity that entitles us to treat the
domain of legal reason as partially autonomous from the general body of
practical reasoning.

Games provide a useful analogy. One may play a game for quite diverse
reasons: for amusement; as a source of income; to please a friend; to humiliate
an enemy; to keep a promise. At the same time, games possess a certain internal
complexity: they are structures of rules, and the actions of players are shaped
by strategic considerations in addition to the rules. This combination of
internal complexity with potentially diverse reasons for playing the game is
what leads us to distinguish between reasons obtaining within the game and
reasons for playing the game. For example, I may play a game with a child
because I want to please the child, and not because I want to win a game; but if
I am genuinely to play the game, the moves that I make within the game must
be aimed at winning. If the child perceives that I am not trying to win but to
lose, they may object that I am not *really* playing the game. Similarly, when the
rules require me to make a certain move, I make the move because the rules
require it, and not because I wish to please the child. Nevertheless, my reason
for playing the game in the first place (and so for guiding my conduct by the
rules) may be to please the child.

Hart's theory accommodates the fact that the framework of legal thought,
embodied in the principal legal concepts, has to be understood as normative in
character. But this normative character is captured without its being reduced
to some more familiar form of normativity such as morality or rational prudence. This is *not* because legal normativity is a self-standing body of practical
reason that is independent of both morality and prudence, but because it is a
partially autonomous domain of reasons, internal to a particular type of social
practice, that may be connected with the general body of practical reason in
different ways. In this way, Hart captures our sense that the law is a system of
prescriptions that is distinct from morality, while acknowledging that the law's

---

[7] HLA Hart, *Essays on Bentham* (Oxford: Clarendon Press, 1982) 159.

practical bearing upon our conduct is always contingent upon the moral or prudential reasons supporting it. Judges and citizens may attach prescriptive force to the law for various reasons. Legal theorists can *understand* the law's normative character simply by appreciating the possibility of such diverse attitudes, and seeing how the action-guiding character of law may be related to them. As *citizens* upon whom the law places demands, we need to consider the moral and prudential reasons for compliance or for non-compliance with the law; but as *theorists* seeking to comprehend the law as a distinctive type of social institution, we can set these questions on one side.

Judgment, Legality and the Rule of Recognition

The subtlety and power of Hart's theory should not be underestimated. Nevertheless, I will argue, his theory should be rejected.

Let us begin with a reminder of some settled understandings that we have about law, for they will play a part in the argument which is to follow:

- Judgments (judicial opinions) are addressed amongst others to the litigants and to other citizens, and are intended to explain the justification for the decision.
- In that justification, the status of certain rules as laws plays a key part. Defendants are ordered to pay damages, for example, because they have violated laws, and not just because they have violated rules accepted for whatever reason by the judge.

Surely, an adequate legal theory ought to be able to explain these facts, or ought at least to be consistent with them.

But how are these facts to be explained? What must law be that it can coherently be regarded as offering a justification for the state's use of force? What exactly does 'justification' mean in the context of the judgment? Are we speaking of a *moral* justification? Or are we speaking of some purely 'technical' justification, that consists solely in the subsumability of an action under established rules without any assumption that the application of the rules is morally required or permissible?

Most of the great classical philosophies of law took the justification involved here to be a form of moral justification. In offering an account of the nature of law they were, in effect, answering the question of what law must be, if it is to be capable of morally justifying the use of force. Consequently, much of the history of the philosophy of law has involved rival accounts of the relationship between those two most fertile concepts of the western legal tradition, *ius* and *lex*.

Kant's philosophy of law is in the first place a theory about *ius* (*Recht*), or the ordering background principles and values which form the matrix from which enacted law (*lex*) emerges and from which it derives its legitimacy. Kant takes this system to be the set of principles that embody the possibility of jointly possible freedoms: 'the sum of conditions under which the choice of one can be united with the choice of another in accordance with a universal law of freedom'.[8] He tells us that, although a system of wholly posited laws is possible, 'a natural law would still have to precede it, which would establish the authority of the lawgiver'.[9] Consequently, the principles of *Recht* represent 'the immutable principles for any giving of positive law'.[10] Positive laws can justify coercive force, on this view, when they embody the set of conditions within which freedoms can be jointly realized.

Hobbes, by contrast, wishes to reduce the idea of law to *lex* alone, rejecting the thought that enactments can be law only by virtue of their groundedness in *ius*. To this end, he cunningly exploits the association of *ius* with individual rights, rather than the idea of *ius* as a matrix of juridical values and principles. At the same time, he seizes upon the fact that the then most influential theory of *ius*, that of Grotius, centred upon the idea of a basic right to self-preservation. Whereas for Grotius such a right gave rise to non-overlapping domains of entitlement constituting an ordered body of principles, Hobbes argues that the structure of human interaction is such that a basic right to self-preservation will generate endemic conflict, requiring the enactment of positive law to create boundaries between jointly possible, non-overlapping domains of entitlement. Rather than *lex* being grounded in *ius* therefore, *lex* and *ius* are for Hobbes fundamentally antithetical concepts.[11] The coercive force of law is justified, not by reference to the principles of *ius*, but by the inability of men to overcome the deadly conflict inherent in the idea of *ius*, without the intervention of lawmaking authority.

More recently, philosophers have adopted a variety of perspectives from which it is hard to see how inquiry into the *nature* of something can also be a normative inquiry into justifications. As a result, many legal theorists have sought to detach inquiry into the nature of law from the broader domain of political philosophy, where we might reflect upon justifications for the use of force.[12] They take it for granted that a knowledge of law's content (of the kind

---

[8] Above n 4, 6:230.   [9] Ibid, 6:224, 379.   [10] Ibid, 6:230, 386.

[11] Thomas Hobbes, *Leviathan* (1651) Chapter 24 (various editions).

[12] John Gardner adopts a somewhat different line in his essay 'Legal Positivism: 5½ Myths' (2001) 46 *American Journal of Jurisprudence* 199. Rather than detaching inquiry into law's nature from political philosophy, he claims that legal positivism 'is not a whole theory of law's nature, after all' (210). '[L]egal positivism explains what it is for a law to be legally valid in the thin *lex* sense, such that the question arises of whether it is also legally valid in the thicker *ius* sense, i.e. morally binding

imparted by university law schools) is a form of social scientific knowledge, not a matter of moral wisdom or moral understanding. At the same time, they are aware that propositions of law are action-guiding prescriptions, not descriptions of social facts. This sets the agenda, for it is not immediately obvious how a knowledge of action-guiding prescriptions (as opposed to a knowledge of the fact that certain prescriptions have been issued, or are likely to be acted upon) can be a form of social-scientific knowledge.

The most familiar response to this agenda is Hart's theory of law. For, as we have seen, Hart's aim is to show that the normative character of law need not be construed as a matter of moral bindingness. We can acknowledge the way in which legal concepts are not descriptive of states of affairs, but are bound up with the guidance of conduct by norms, without treating them as intrinsically moral concepts. Judges and citizens might follow the law's prescriptions for various reasons: the normativity that they ascribe to the law can be analysed and understood independently of their reasons for so ascribing normativity.

Hart's solution depends upon the ability of his theory to police a distinction between claims made internally to a system of rules identified by a rule of recognition, and claims made externally to the system. Internal claims apply rules of the sytem and express conclusions about the applicability of those rules, while external claims express factual or moral observations *about* the system or the rules that it contains, without themselves being *applications* of those rules. Hart sees that it is only if such a distinction can be maintained that we can treat the reasons provided *by* the law as partially separable from the moral or prudential reasons that one may have for guiding one's conduct by reference to the law.

As a part of his effort to establish and maintain the relevant distinction, Hart seeks to regiment the types of question that can meaningfully be asked about the rule of recognition itself. About the rule of recognition, we can ask factual questions (is it in fact accepted?) or moral questions (is it a good rule?): but we cannot ask juridical questions. We cannot meaningfully inquire into the rule's legal validity, as it provides the ultimate criterion of legal validity.[13]

---

qua law' (227). It seems to follow that a 'whole theory of law's nature' would address the issue of law's moral bindingness.

Gardner presents his account of legal positivism not as a revision of legal positivism, but as a myth-dispelling correction of popular misunderstandings of the positivist position. Yet the distinction between 'thick' and 'thin' senses of 'legal validity', combined with the idea that a 'whole theory of law's nature' must explain law's moral bindingness, amounts to a position that Hart clearly and explicitly rejects. See, for example, Hart's comments on the very similar theory offered by Finnis, in *Essays in Jurisprudence and Philosophy* (Oxford: Clarendon Press, 1983) at 12. There is equally little doubt that this type of theory would have been rejected by Kelsen.

[13] Above n 6, 107–110.

It is in this way that Hart seeks to block the regress of questions about legality that generates, by way of response, Kelsen's theory of the *Grundnorm*. Kelsen takes the validity of a rule to entail that the rule ought to be obeyed. Thus, when he has traced a hierarchy of derivative norms to their ultimate source in some founding constitutional act or practice, Kelsen asks (in effect) what gives *validity* to the norms resulting from that act or practice. Since the only substantive answer to this question would, Kelsen believes, have to take the form of one or another moral theory of legitimacy (natural law theory), he believes that positivist legal theory must give a purely *formal* answer: validity must simply be assumed as the founding presupposition of legal science, in so far as that science claims to set forth the knowledge of legal norms.

Hart, by contrast, rejects Kelsen's question about the validity of the ultimate constitutional rules as meaningless. 'Validity' for Hart does not entail that the norm in question ought to be obeyed. Propositions about validity simply draw conclusions about the applicability of a basic rule of recognition: valid norms are norms that are derivable from the rule of recognition. For that reason, we cannot meaningfully ask if the rule of recognition itself is legally valid: it is neither valid nor invalid, but provides the ultimate criterion of validity. Thus, Hart tells us that 'no question concerning the validity or invalidity of the generally accepted rule of recognition as distinct from its factual existence can arise'.[14] Such a question makes no more sense than would the question of whether 'the standard metre bar in Paris which is the ultimate test of the correctness of all measurement in metres, is itself correct'.[15]

This general approach of Hart's has further specific consequences. It explains, for example, his characterization of adjudicative decisions in the penumbra of the rule of recognition (or in contexts where that rule is breaking down) as political rather than juridical; and also his associated suggestion that 'when courts settle previously unenvisaged questions concerning the most fundamental constitutional rules, they *get* their authority to decide them accepted after the questions have arisen and the decision has been given', so that '[h]ere all that succeeds is success'.[16]

These are important claims, from any point of view. Yet the thesis on which they are grounded looks very much like a tautology. For Hart has in effect *defined* legal validity in terms of derivability from the rule of recognition, so that it of course follows that the concept cannot be applied to the rule itself. Can such important substantive conclusions be justified by reference to a tautology?

To address the substantive issues involved here, we need to ask whether claims about validity in Hart's sense really exhaust the domain of the juridical.

Ibid, 293.   Ibid, 109.
Ibid, 147–154, at 153. See also JM Eekelaar, 'Principles of Revolutionary Legality' in *Oxford Essays in Jurisprudence: second series*, edited by AWB Simpson (Oxford: Clarendon Press, 1973).

And, to ask this question, we must shift from Hart's concept of 'legal validity' to the broader notion of 'legality', understood as the property of being law.[17] Pursuing this strategy, therefore, we must ask whether one can meaningfully ask questions about the *legality* of the rule of recognition.

Well, it seems to me that one can. Nor do I have in mind the theoretician's question of whether the rule of recognition of a system of law should be thought of as itself a law, or as the non-legal practice on which the law is founded. I am thinking of a much more obvious and practically relevant question, which concerns the status of the system of rules as a whole.

Not all systems of rules derived from a basic rule of recognition are systems of laws. There could be a basic rule of recognition in certain games, for example, where the game is complex and regulated by some official body. But a system of rules might fail to constitute a system of law even though the system provides the basis for governance within a community. A system of governance might possess a rule of recognition, with an associated body of partially autonomous normative reasoning, and yet we might hesitate to describe it as a body of law. Suppose, for example, that the rules stemming from the basic rule of recognition do not purport to guide the conduct of citizens, but simply confer discretionary coercive powers upon various officials, and direct the officials to employ their powers with a view to advancing various objectives. Or suppose that the rules stemming from the rule of recognition set out sufficient conditions for the use of sanctions against citizens, but not necessary conditions, with the result that officials feel free to deploy the state's coercive apparatus against individual citizens whenever they consider that desirable as a way of advancing governmental objectives. Or (if you do not like my examples) take some examples from Fuller: imagine a system where all the rules are kept secret, or all are retrospective, or where the officials never act in accordance with the rules.[18] In systems of this sort, citizens would not guide their conduct by reference to rules but by the prediction of official sanctions.[19] We would, I think, hesitate to describe these systems as systems of law.[20]

Although this should be perfectly obvious, allow me to emphasize that I am not objecting to Hart's theory on the basis that he provides a definition of 'law'

[17] Why not simply ask about the adequacy of Hart's account of 'legal validity'? The answer is, I think, that the term 'validity' is used in a variety of ways by legal theorists but, in its ordinary usage, it tends to be connected with the deliberate exercise of legal powers. Consequently, a focus on the concept of 'legal validity' can create an in-built theoretical bias towards conceptions of law as deliberately enacted in the exercise of legal powers.

[18] Lon Fuller, *The Morality of Law* (revised edition, New Haven, Conn: Yale University Press, 1969) Chapter 2.

[19] Cf. Simmonds, 'Rights at the Cutting Edge', in Matthew Kramer, NE Simmonds and Hillel Steiner, *A Debate Over Rights* (Oxford: Clarendon Press, 1998) 113 at 166.

[20] For the present we can take this to be a claim about our semantic intuitions. In due course we will discover that such understandings are inchoate moral insights rather than mere reflections of settled linguistic usage.

that is over-inclusive in that it would apply to systems that we might ordinarily hesitate to describe as systems of law. At one point in *The Concept of Law*, Hart does provide something that looks like a definition of 'law', but the book as a whole makes it clear that the provision of such a definition is not his objective.[21] In any case, even if his aim was to provide a definition, and even if the definition was more inclusive than ordinary usage, there is no reason why Hart should be constrained by that ordinary usage if he has grounds for regarding his own definition as, on balance, enlightening and clarificatory. In fact, of course, my point has nothing to do with the possible over-inclusiveness of Hart's account of law. Rather my object is to challenge Hart's thesis that questions about the legality of the rule of recognition cannot meaningfully be raised.

But, in expressing a doubt about the status of such systems as law, are we expressing a doubt about the legality of the relevant rules of recognition? What must be remembered here is that we cannot equate the relevant notion of 'legality' with Hart's account of 'legal validity', for Hart treats legal validity as purely a matter of derivability from the rule of recognition, and this makes his exclusion of certain questions concerning the rule of recognition a mere tautology. Since the consequences that Hart derives from that exclusion are of considerable importance, we cannot rest content with this tautology, but need to adopt a framework within which the soundness of Hart's exclusionary thesis can be addressed. Ultimately, of course, the soundness of that thesis must be evaluated as but one part of Hart's theory as a whole, and its merits and its demerits must be judged by reference to the insight that Hart's theory as a whole yields. But in the construction of any such assessment of Hart's theory we must proceed by provisionally detaching individual issues from the set of interlocking theses that Hart presents: otherwise each theory (including Hart's) would become a hermetically sealed position, challengeable only in so far as it contradicts itself. To make progress, therefore, we formulated the issue as one concerning the possibility of questions concerning the 'legality' of the rule of recognition, where 'legality' is construed as being the quality of being law. Admittedly, the deviation from legality, in at least some of the examples I have given, seems more likely to have sprung from the way in which lawmakers and other officials have exercised their powers than from some deficiency in the rule of recognition itself. No matter: we have identified a question concerning the legality (the quality of being law) of the system of rules as a whole (however we describe the question), and this seems to suggest that questions of legality can arise outside the limited domain that is bounded by the rule of recognition.

21 Above n 6, 116–117.

At this point, Hart's supporters will doubtless say that I have confused different questions. For when Hart excludes the possibility of questions about the validity of the rule of recognition, he means to sustain the autonomy of the domain of legal reasons by demonstrating that those reasons cannot exist beyond the bounding outer limit of that domain. His concern is therefore with the action-guiding rules and normative considerations that make up the field of legal reason. But my question about the legality of the rule of recognition forms no part of the normative reasoning guiding action or decision within the legal order as conceived by Hart: it is a conceptual or classificatory question about the status of the system as a whole (including its rule of recognition). The conflation is concealed by the word 'legality', which is ambiguous as between (on the one hand) 'the derivability of one rule from another, or the subsumability of an action under a rule' and (on the other) 'the property of being law'. In the first sense, 'legality' refers to a property that is relevant within the field of legal reason, while in the second broader sense it may not do so; and, in the case of my 'classificatory' question, it does not do so.

At first this seems a sound reply to a very misguided challenge. But in fact it reveals a problem in Hart's theory. For it invites us to regard the normative or justificatory force of the rules as entirely a function of their derivability from the rule of recognition, regardless of their status as law. And this conflicts with one of the settled understandings from which our argument began: the idea that, in the judicial justification for the ordering of sanctions, the status of the relevant rules as law plays a key part.

To see the point, imagine a judge who informs the defendant that he is to be punished because he has violated a rule stemming from the basic rule of recognition that the judge and his colleagues accept. Why should the defendant care about that? Why should anyone regard this, without more, as a justification for the decision? How then can the judge regard it, without more, as a justification for the decision? The intelligibility of the purported justification is thrown still further into doubt if we remember that (according to Hart) the judge may accept the basic rule for purely non-moral reasons, including reasons of self-interest.

What the judge needs to add is the claim that the rule violated was a law. This still provides us with a source of puzzlement, for we find ourselves asking how exactly *legality* can bear upon the justification of force; but this is now the philosophical puzzlement that seeks for a deeper elucidation of our settled moral understandings, rather than the straightforward puzzlement of finding someone's remarks wholly at odds with those understandings. The claim that the rule violated was law, moreover, is not a classificatory or conceptual afterthought forming no part of the justificatory reasoning: it is a central (indeed, *the* central) element in that reasoning.

There is of course *one* sense in which claims about the status of the system of rules as a whole may form no part of the reasoning leading to the decision. If I am sentenced by a judge for breaking some rule, and I suggest that the system to which the rule belongs is not a system of law, the judge may well refuse to consider my argument. For it is that very system that forms the basis of the judge's authority, so that he or she may well feel that the judicial role and oath of office exclude consideration of the argument. But to say this is not to say that the argument is irrelevant in principle. A consideration of the nature of the system as a whole may not form part of the justificatory reasoning that is expressly set out in the judgment: but this is not to say that certain assumptions about the system as a whole (specifically, the assumption that it is a system of law) may not be presupposed by the justification offered in the judgment. If we are to have a theory of law that is compatible with the settled understandings from which my argument began, it cannot present legal justificatory argument as bounded by the rule of recognition. For the status of rules as law plays a key part in the justification, and that status always depends upon *more than* derivability from a basic rule of recognition. It depends upon the approximation of the system of rules to an abstract idea of law.

Justification

Hart's supporters will of course say that they have no need to show that judicial decisions are *justified*. But my response is that they do need to explain how adjudicative legal reasoning could *intelligibly be offered* as a justification, and they need to explain this in a way that is compatible (so far as possible) with our settled understandings. This they have failed to do, and the failure has two aspects that it is important to distinguish, because the second failure is ultimately of greater significance than the first:

(1) It is impossible to understand how any official could think that the acceptance of a rule of recognition by himself and his colleagues (for what might be entirely non-moral reasons) could without more be offered as a justification for the ordering of force against a defendant.

(2) On Hart's account, as reconstructed above, it seems that the justificatory force of the rules is entirely a matter of derivability from the rule of recognition. But derivability from a rule of recognition qualifies the relevant rules as law only if the system as a whole is a legal system. Claims about the status of the system as a whole, however, form (on Hart's account) no part of the justificatory reasoning. Consequently, the status of the rules as law plays no part in the justificatory reasoning, while our settled understandings tell us that such status is critical to the justification.

The first point challenges Hart's account of the partial autonomy of legal reasons, by suggesting that derivability from an accepted rule of recognition could never, on its own, provide a basis for justifying the use of force (in the form of sanctions). Consequently, without more, it could not intelligibly be offered by the judge as a justification for the use of force. Derivability from a rule of recognition will provide a justification for sanctions only if it forms a part of a broader body of reasoning which draws on considerations lying outside the domain of reasoning that is bounded by the rule of recognition.

In response to this argument, it might be said that Hart's theory ascribes only *partial* autonomy to the domain of legal reasons; and this partial autonomy means that, while legal reasons are for certain purposes distinct from the general background of reasons supporting compliance with the law, they can enjoy full practical force only in conjunction with those (moral or prudential) reasons. Legal justification, in other words, is justification *relative to the rules*: it becomes justification in a non-relative sense only when and if the application of the rules is itself justified. The internal complexity of the system of legal rules, combined with the fact that the reasons for following and applying such rules may be quite diverse, warrants our treating the body of rule-relative reasons as a partially autonomous domain of reasons that can, for many purposes, be considered in isolation from the deeper considerations that explain and justify observance of the rules. The justification of decisions *relative to the rules* is, therefore, perfectly intelligible, and it is this form of justification that is involved when the judge simply invokes rules derivable from the rule of recognition, without considering any reasons that go beyond the issue of such derivability.

But this argument, far from offering Hart a line of defence, actually highlights his vulnerability at this point, for it concedes that 'justification-relative-to-the-rules' is always dependent on the justification for following the rules. This point is, in effect, acknowledged by Neil MacCormick's well-known argument about the 'underpinning reasons' for official acceptance of the rule of recognition. MacCormick observes that legal rules and principles are treated as conclusive reasons for decisions, but 'what gives these reasons conclusiveness *as justifications* is the tacit presupposition of the obligatory character of respect for criteria of recognition'. MacCormick goes on to argue that an essential element of the officials' attitude towards the rule of recognition must be 'some conscious commitment to pursuing the political values which are perceived as underpinning it, and to sustaining in concrete form the political principles deemed inherent in the constituted order of the society in question'. He says that this 'is not inconsistent with Hart's thesis'.[22]

---

[22] Neil MacCormick, *Legal Reasoning and Legal Theory* (revised edition, Oxford: Clarendon Press, 1994) 139–140.

Some confusion is introduced into the argument by MacCormick's description of the 'underpinning reasons' as giving 'conclusiveness' to the justifications that are offered by invoking legal rules. In the absence of such underpinning reasons, the purported 'justifications' would be unintelligible, not simply inconclusive; and, even given the existence of such underpinning reasons, the justification is not 'conclusive', for there may always be competing considerations of an extra-legal sort. But let us ignore this complicating factor, which probably represents no more than a slip on MacCormick's part. What remains is an argument that justification relative to the rules is perfectly intelligible in so far as such justification tacitly presupposes an obligation to follow and apply the rule of recognition; and MacCormick makes it clear that such a tacit presupposition involves a commitment on the part of officials to upholding certain political values or principles.

It is of course perfectly true that, if we assume that the officials have moral reasons (of the type adverted to by MacCormick) for accepting the rule of recognition, and we treat the judgment as tacitly relying upon those moral reasons, the judgment's invocation of the rule of recognition becomes intelligible as a justification. But it is surely a mistake to say that this 'is not inconsistent with Hart's thesis', for it acknowledges the presence of a necessary connection between law and morality in a way that is very much at odds with Hart's positivism.[23] In fact, MacCormick's view undercuts our warrant for separating the reasons obtaining *within* the practice of law from the reasons we might have for engaging in that practice in the first place. On MacCormick's account, a full and proper engagement in the practice requires that one has reasons of an appropriate sort for one's engagement: for, without such reasons, one's legal reasoning cannot sincerely and intelligibly be offered as a justification for judicial decision. What if the officials' tacitly presupposed reasons for applying the rule of recognition were non-moral reasons of self-interest (such as a desire to sustain an unjust and exploitative regime that happens to benefit the officials themselves)? MacCormick's argument implicitly concedes that the invocation of the rules as justifications for the use of force would then become unintelligible, or intelligible only as insincerely expressing a moral outlook not in fact adopted by the judges.

Hart makes clear his own rejection of the idea that, if the judgment is to be intelligible as a justification, the judge must accept the rule of recognition for moral reasons:

[T]hough the judge is ... committed to following the rules his view of the moral merits of doing so ... is irrelevant. His view of the merits may be favourable or

---

[23] Needless to say, I reject John Gardner's suggestion that Hart did not intend to deny the existence of such necessary connections. See Gardner, above n 12. Gardner's views on this matter face many difficulties, including those that confront the 'concession' reading of Hart, discussed in Chapter 3 above.

unfavourable, or simply absent, or, without dereliction of his duty as a judge, he may have formed no view of the moral merits.[24]

In any case, and quite apart from the question of whether MacCormick's view is consistent with Hart's theory, my second problem still remains. For officials might accept a rule of recognition for moral reasons of the sort that MacCormick describes, and yet their acceptance of that rule might nevertheless be unrelated to the status of the rule of recognition, and the system to which it gives rise, as a system of law. As we have seen, the presence of a rule of recognition does not in itself guarantee that the system in question is law, nor need the political values accepted by MacCormick's officials have any necessary connection with the nature of law. Their invocation of an individual rule as a justification for the ordering of sanctions would therefore itself be unrelated to the status of that rule as law. Consequently, a Hartian theory amended along the lines MacCormick proposes would still fail to capture the second of the two settled understandings from which my argument began: the understanding that, in the adjudicative justification of sanctions, the status of the relevant rules as law plays a key part.

Could it be argued that the rule-relative justification offered by Hartian officials is perfectly intelligible even without the presupposition of MacCormick's 'underpinning reasons'? Perhaps the Hartian officials are saying, in effect, 'that's just how we do things around here.' They do not appeal to any deeper reasons, but simply to the fact of a shared practice. We might not find this a convincing or attractive justification for the use of force, but (it could be argued) it is perfectly intelligible.[25]

There are indeed contexts where people can quite intelligibly seek to justify their action by saying 'that's just how we do things around here'. But the contexts are such that they reveal a range of moral or prudential considerations tacitly underpinning the appeal to shared practice. For example, in some situations we need to coordinate action in pursuit of a goal and, for that reason, a familiar pattern of coordination might be invoked on the grounds of its settled and familiar nature. Here, the appeal to shared practice is intelligible as a justification in so far as we take the context (of the need for coordination in pursuit of a goal) for granted. A full explanation of the justification, however, would have to go beyond the simple appeal to shared practice in order to set out the relevant justificatory circumstances.

In other contexts, the justification ('it's just how we do things around here') might be addressed to someone who has recently joined the community in

[24] HLA Hart, *Essays on Bentham* (Oxford: Clarendon Press, 1982) 159.
[25] This argument was pressed upon me when I presented parts of this chapter as a *Current Legal Problems* lecture at University College, London. It is for this reason that I consider it here.

question, and the tacit background suggestion would be that such a newcomer should submit to the established ways of the long-standing members of the community. A full explanation of the justification would therefore have to do much more than point to the shared practice: it would have to appeal to the right of the community to govern its own way of life, the need for newcomers to submit to that way of life if it is not to be eroded, and perhaps the idea that the newcomer has consented to a duty of compliance by joining the community in the first place.

In other words, 'that's just how we do things around here' is *not* intelligible as a justification for the use of force if it is truly no more than an appeal to shared practice. In those contexts where it *does* seem to be intelligible, its intelligibility is always derived from a range of further values forming part of the tacit assumptions structuring our understanding of the situation.

Rejecting as he did proposed amendments to his theory, such as those offered by MacCormick, Hart insisted that the judgment does not offer a *moral* justification for the decision. Judges, when they speak of the subject's legal duty, 'may mean to speak in a technically confined way' that is concerned only with what 'may legally be demanded or exacted'.[26] 'Justification' is here understood as entirely a matter of the relationship between the individual decision and the rules being applied, without any presupposition that the application of the rules is itself morally permissible. It is on this basis that Hart would resist the present argument. For he would accept my claim that positivists must be able to explain how adjudicative legal reasoning, when conceived of in terms of Hart's theory, could intelligibly be offered as a justification for the judicial decision; but he would point out that 'justification' here need not mean 'moral justification'. A justification that is 'technically confined' and purely relative to the rules is perfectly intelligible.

The possibility of such a technically confined form of reasoning is itself, of course, exhibited by Hart's demonstration that it is possible to have a partially autonomous form of normative reasoning. But only in a way that is irrelevant to the present issue. Hart's theory shows us that propositions of law can be analysed as action-guiding statements that express conclusions about the applicability of legal rules, and the requirements of compliance with those rules. But the theory also shows us that these propositions can enjoy full practical force as statements of reasons for action only in conjunction with the moral or prudential reasons there may be for guiding one's conduct by the law.

Hart would, of course, respond by saying that officials who follow and apply the rules might well have good reasons for being guided by the law in their decisions, but these reasons need not be moral reasons: they may be non-moral

---

[26] Above n 24, 266.

reasons grounded in self-interest. What Hart seems not fully to appreciate, however, is that, while such non-moral reasons might indeed explain the conduct of the officials in following and applying the law, they would not render intelligible the invocation of the law, by the officials, as a *justification* for the application of sanctions to the citizen.[27]

To consider whether adjudicative legal reasoning might indeed be a 'technically confined' form of reasoning, we need to imagine in concrete detail a practice that could appropriately be thought of as involving a technically confined form of reasoning, without any intention of offering a moral justification. After all, in deciding what import is to be attached to a form of discourse, we must pay close attention to the context in which it is offered.

Consider, for example, the context of a game, since the example of games gave us an enlightening illustration of the idea of partially autonomous domains of reasoning. If there is a dispute within a game, we would expect the participants to resolve the dispute by reference to the rules of the game, at least in those non-penumbral cases where the rules yield a reasonably determinate answer. We would expect any referee or umpire to be able to justify his decision by reference to the rules. If someone asked whether this was a 'moral' justification, we might at first be at a loss for an answer: it is a justification by reference to the rules, not by reference to moral standards at large; but, at the same time, the players having impliedly consented to play the game by the rules, the application of the rules to their dispute seems morally right.

To make further progress with our inquiry, we need to consider a context where rules are applied to parties who have not consented to the application of the rules. Imagine then a practice under which judges must report to higher authority after making a decision. The judges must carefully demonstrate that, in their decision, they applied the relevant body of rules correctly. This would indeed be a 'technically confined' form of reasoning, for it might set on one side all issues about the moral propriety of applying these rules. The concern of the judges would be to justify their decision, not to the parties whose dispute they decided, but to a higher authority that is exclusively concerned to see that the established rules were applied.

We only have to imagine such a practice to see that judicial judgment is not a practice of this sort. A judgment is not a report to higher authority. Nor is it a report to higher authority combined with some clarificatory remarks, for the

---

[27] This is, of course, not at all to agree with Raz's claim that legal duties are a species of moral duty (the claim to which Hart is responding in his statement about adjudicative reasoning as 'technically confined'). Hart may be quite right that propositions of legal duty simply express the demandability of certain actions under the rules, without any assumption that the citizen is under a duty to comply. But this would be so only on the assumption that the application of the rules, with the consequent ordering of sanctions, would be morally justified.

benefit of the public, about how the law will be applied in future cases. It is a setting forth of the justification of the decision, and is addressed to the litigants amongst others. This was one of the settled understandings from which we began, and we have seen no reason to abandon it.

A Better Concept of Law

The judicial judgment is addressed to the litigants amongst others, and is intended to justify the judicial decision. An adequate account of law's nature must be able to make sense of this, and must therefore be able to explain how the arguments characteristically offered in judicial judgments (arguments that attach central importance to the status of certain rules as law) can intelligibly be offered as a justification for a decision that may involve the ordering of coercive force against the citizen. Since the judgment is not a report to higher authority, but is addressed to the litigants (amongst others), the justification cannot consist simply in a demonstration that certain rules accepted by the judges were correctly applied: the judgment must demonstrate or tacitly assume that the application of those rules was itself proper and justifiable from the perspective of values that the litigants ought themselves to accept and endorse. This is not to say that the judge must draw upon values that the litigants *do in fact* accept: for the judge may know full well that the defendant (for example) denies the whole basis of the court's jurisdiction and the law's authority. But the judgment must implicitly or explicitly appeal to moral or political values that can be regarded as binding and normative for the litigants. The judgment cannot, for example, appeal to rules that are acknowledged to have no other basis than the interests of the judges themselves. Moreover, the values invoked must be intrinsically rather than contingently connected with the status of the rules as law, for it would otherwise be hard to explain the centrality that is attached to such status within the judgment. A natural conclusion seems to be that the justificatory force of the rules is a direct consequence of their legality. But how can this be? What must law be that it can justify the use of coercive force?

Hart concentrates his efforts on an attempt to show that legal positivism need not adopt a reductivist position that denies or obscures the normative character of law. He is therefore careful to show that his theory accommodates the character of law as guiding and prescribing conduct, particularly the conduct of the officials who must (if a legal system is to exist) adopt the 'internal point of view' towards the rules of the system. But he is also careful to insist that this 'internal point of view' need not be a moral point of view: judges may guide their conduct by the rules for many different reasons, which may be of a wholly non-moral sort. The judge is not committed, in Hart's view, to any particular view of the moral merits of following the rules. Judges, when they speak of the defendant's legal duty, may be speaking only in a 'technically confined way' where duty is not a matter of what 'ought to be done' but a matter of what may, under the rules, be 'demanded or exacted'.[28]

Hart takes the view that officials might have a great diversity of reasons for following the rule of recognition, for Hart sees this potential diversity as a part of the case for treating legal norms as partially autonomous (in the way that we have explained earlier in this chapter). But this emphasis upon the diverse reasons that officials might have for guiding their conduct by the rules leads our gaze away from a far more significant question, which concerns the assumptions that must underpin any invocation of the rules as a justification for coercive force. I may choose to play a game for many different sorts of reasons, and any of these reasons will be enough to motivate and explain my acceptance of the rules of the game as conduct-guiding standards. But judges do not simply guide their conduct by the rules: they invoke the rules as the basis for justifications addressed to the litigants. The question is, how can we make sense of this?

We saw above that the status of a rule as law plays a key part in the justification offered by the judge. Defendants are not punished for their injustices and immoralities. Nor are they punished for breaking a rule that the judge and his colleagues happen, for various reasons, to accept. They are punished for breaking the law. The status of a rule as law, moreover, can never depend solely upon its derivability from a rule of recognition, but always depends also upon the character (as law) of the system as a whole. Our task now is to construct a concept of law that incorporates these ideas and explains how a rule's status as law can be given a justificatory role within the judgment.

It is important to see the difficulties that face any serious attempt to accommodate the idea that, in the judicial justification for the sanction, the status of certain rules as law plays a key part. If the role of legality (understood as the property of being law) within the judgment is to be understood, we must find some property that law necessarily possesses and which could be regarded as bearing upon the justification of the use of force. For our settled understanding is that the justificatory relevance of a rule springs at least in part from its status as law. Justificatory force is not a matter of derivability from a rule of recognition alone, nor is it simply a function of the rule's just and reasonable content.

For present purposes we need to see how legality can play a central part in the justification of force; but it is not necessary for us to address the question of how *precisely* legality bears upon such justification. There may, for example,

---

[28] Above n 24, 266.

be important differences here between criminal law and private law. The majority of litigated cases at private law seek the enforcement of a debt or an award of compensatory damages. Judgments at private law seek to allocate the losses (or, occasionally, profits) resulting from a specific transaction such as an accident, a trespass, or a breach of contract. Since the whole point of the case is to allocate a loss that has already occurred, the remedial sanction (typically an award of damages) is an integral part of the judgment on liability. In criminal law, by contrast, the judgment on guilt or innocence represents a stage that is in most cases (mandatory sentences apart) separable from the stage of sentencing, where distinct arguments (such as pleas in mitigation) will be offered and evaluated. Here, breach of the law seems to be a necessary precondition of punishment, but is perhaps not a sufficient condition. Even where (as in the judgment at private law) a breach of the law seems to be taken as a conclusive justification for the sanction, this might conceivably be regarded as resting upon background assumptions relating to the degree of justice attained in the system as a whole: perhaps the justification provided by legality is defeasible when there is a substantial departure from justice. In principle, our settled understandings might be explained by the idea that legality is a necessary condition for the justified use of force; or a necessary and sufficient condition; or a necessary and normally sufficient but defeasible condition. No doubt there are other possibilities as well.

As we noted earlier, when writers such as Hobbes and Kant offer claims about the nature of law, they are addressing the question of what law must be if it is to be capable of justifying the use of force. Needless to say, they seek an account of law's nature that captures and casts light upon the most significant aspects of the general phenomena of law, but they construe those phenomena in the light of law's central place in the ordering of sanctions. We must, of course, admit the possibility that law does not in fact *succeed* in justifying the use of coercive force: a theory of law can in principle offer a sound analysis of law's nature while nevertheless reaching the conclusion that law's *claims* to justify force are groundless. But the law's claims must at least be rendered intelligible: we must see what there is about law that could plausibly, even if erroneously, be regarded as a justification for the use of force.

The ascription of such claims to law is an enterprise that is not wholly separable from the task of seeing how the claims might be justified. A theory that treats the essential features of law as including a set of claims that clearly cannot be sustained should be viewed with suspicion on that ground alone, and such a theory has a heavy intellectual burden to discharge before it could justify its theses concerning the nature of law. We are, after all, trying to deepen our understanding of that form of moral association that we call 'the rule of law'. We are not offering an unstructured report of observable phenomena, but are seeking to draw together into a coherent picture all of the various

assumptions and understandings that make up the relevant form of association. If I say that you claim to be the reincarnation of Napoleon, I can justify
my assertion by (for example) producing letters and e-mails in which you say
just that. But, if we ascribe certain 'claims' to the law, the ascription is to be
justified, not by pointing to a discrete fact, but by the way in which such a
claim makes sense of the totality of our settled understandings. If, in fact, the
claims ascribed to the law are not claims that we would generally be prepared
to acknowledge as soundly based and acceptable, this must count (albeit non-
conclusively) against the truth of the ascription.

Raz has argued that the law claims for itself an obligatory force that goes far
beyond anything that our moral reflections would judge to be plausible or sus-
tainable. This thesis forms the fundamental platform from which his theory of
law is constructed,[29] and we might therefore expect it to be capable of bearing
a considerable weight. Yet the ascription of this claim to the law rests upon a
series of interpretative moves that are strikingly inconclusive. For example,
Raz takes the view that, when judges speak of the law as imposing obligations
or conferring rights, they assume that the law is morally binding upon the
citizen: he rejects the idea that notions such as 'legal obligation' and 'legal duty'
might be best understood, not as expressing conclusions about what the duty-
bearer ought to do, but conclusions about what may permissibly be enforced
against him.[30] His reasons for rejecting that view, however, are certainly contestable and seem quite flawed.[31] In deciding whether such a view should be
accepted, we must look to the long-term costs of its acceptance or rejection for
a unified understanding of our form of moral association as a whole. For the
institutions and practices of law are an integral part of that form of moral association, along with our general moral attitudes *towards* the law. The fact that
Raz's view leads to a gulf between what law claims and what we could regard as
justified is a good reason for rejecting that view, if other interpretations are
possible and defensible.

Ruth Higgins has resisted this general line of argument, and endeavoured to
support Raz's position, by suggesting that each element in our analysis should
be treated independently:

We should analyse and interpret our existing social practices as we find them, and not
shape them to foreclose anticipated consequences of analysis. It is a mistake to sacrifice
certain apparent characteristics of law in pursuit of the goal of theoretical tidiness.[32]

---

[29] Raz takes the view that, while law fails to satisfy the moral conditions for the type of authority
that it claims, it must of necessity satisfy the non-moral conditions for that authority if it is to be law
at all. Joseph Raz, *Ethics in the Public Domain* (Oxford: Clarendon Press, 1994) Chapter 9.
[30] Joseph Raz, 'Hart on Moral Rights and Legal Duties' [1984] OJLS 123.
[31] See e.g. Matthew Kramer, *In Defence of Legal Positivism* (Oxford: Oxford University Press,
1999) Chapter 4.
[32] Ruth Higgins, *The Moral Limits of Law* (Oxford: Oxford University Press, 2004) 17.

But we cannot apply a strategy of taking things as we find them to practices that, in the nature of the case, are laden with semiotic complexity and admit of numerous different interpretations. It is precisely the intimate interconnectedness of our social and moral concepts, and of the phenomena that they call into being, that renders the interpretation of practice a difficult intellectual task rather than an exercise in arbitrariness.[33] Even Higgins seems to sense the unsustainability of her piecemeal approach, for she seeks to reduce the apparent tension within the Razian position by pointing out that, even if law's claims to authority are not justified, the law might nevertheless be justified in making (through its officials) those claims: e.g. in certain circumstances I may be justified in claiming medical expertise even though I am not a medical expert.[34] She fails to see, however, that the *sincerity* of law's claim to authority forms an essential and explicit premise of Raz's argument (for it is on this basis that Raz argues that law must, as a conceptual necessity, satisfy the non-moral conditions for possession of authority).[35]

Laws are invoked as a justification for force, and an adequate legal theory must render this practice intelligible. Drawing upon our general understanding of the values and standards composing familiar moral outlooks, we need to see what features there could be, intrinsic to law, that could be regarded (perhaps misguidedly but nevertheless intelligibly) as providing such a justification. If we do not do that, we have not really grasped the idea of law as it is embodied in our practices and judgments.

This idea of the 'intelligibility' of a justification, apart from its actual soundness or truth, may seem puzzling and somewhat suspect. What is intended, however, is an idea that is quite familiar and innocuous. In trying to understand what it is about law that makes its justificatory role intelligible, we simply try to connect the features of law to widely accepted moral values that would generally be considered relevant to the justification of the state's use of force. If necessary, we can establish what would be so considered by consulting the arguments deployed within the tradition of political philosophy: Hobbes, Locke, Rousseau, Kant and Bentham can give us a sense of what our shared moral inheritance regards as at least a potentially relevant justification for the state's coercive force.

Suppose that someone asks how the rules of games can be invoked as justifications for criticizing those who cheat: what makes the rules binding on the players? One possible reply would point to the fact that players generally enter a game voluntarily, and thereby consent to play by the rules of that game. The binding force of the rules is, on this account, the binding force of a promise.

[33] See also my criticisms of Dworkin above, pp 25–31.   [34] Above n 32, 17–18.
[35] Above n 29, 201.

Such a reply would be enlightening even for one who rejects the idea of the binding force of promises, perhaps on the basis of a strict act-utilitarianism, or because he believes that binding promises involve an immoral and invalid attempt to abandon one's autonomy. For such a one, the reply has not justified the claim that the rules are binding on the players, but it has rendered that claim intelligible by relating it to a moral belief (the binding force of promises) that he knows to form part of our moral traditions and general understandings.

As was pointed out in Chapter 1, our acknowledgment of the possibility of moral error in our institutions, traditions and understandings is embodied in the thought that standards of justice and morality are quite independent of practice. But this independence can easily be overestimated or misunderstood, resulting in a sublimation of morality, projecting its basis into a realm of values that is accessible only to one who has escaped from the cave of conventional understandings. When detached from our ordinary understandings the notions of justice and morality can quickly come to seem no more than empty illusions. We are led to the conclusion that they are mere figments of the imagination. To resist this trajectory of thought, we must preserve a sense of the possibility of moral error within a general acknowledgment that our settled understandings are by and large a sound expression of moral competence and moral value. If our moral understanding is to be seen as real, it must be bound up with our grasp of the commonplace world, forming part of the realm of socially sustained knowledge that renders us mutually intelligible. The structures of meaning and value that are involved here are inhabited before they are reflected upon. The task of philosophy is to seek reflective understanding in a manner that is always alert to the possibility of error and the need for revision: its task is not to discover a bedrock moral foundation lying quite beyond established forms of life, and from which existing structures can be criticized in their totality.

In fact, we have already seen that there is an intrinsic connection between law and a value that forms part of our traditional lexicon of moral or political ideas: the value of freedom, understood as independence from the power of another. Freedom in this sense is not a matter of the number or diversity or value of options open to an individual: for we have seen that the slave may have more (and perhaps better) options available to him than a free man. If we unreservedly equate freedom with the number or value of options then we are forced to conclude that the connection between slavery and the lack of freedom is purely contingent. Yet the connection is not contingent: slavery is the very epitome of unfreedom, for however many options the slave might have available to him, those options are fully dependent upon the will of his master. The free man, by contrast, may have few options available, but some at least of those options will be quite independent of the will of anyone else.

This will be true, however, only where the free man is governed by law. If he inhabits a political community governed in any other way, the options that he has available to him will be dependent upon the will of others. In a tyranny, everyone's options are made to depend upon the will of the tyrant. In an acephalous society with equal political power, but without the rule of law, everyone's options are dependent upon the will of everyone else. In a society where village elders handle disputes by encouraging compromise rather than by strictly enforcing rules, everyone's options will be dependent upon the willingness of others to raise and pursue objections that will lead to compromise. In the absence of the rule of law, there can be no area of my conduct where I can act as I choose, without regard to the fact that others may intensely object to what I am doing, relying solely upon the fact that my actions are legally permissible and will receive the protection of the law.

Even if we restrict our account of law's nature to the relatively austere and formal conditions set out in Fuller's eight *desiderata*, the conditions for liberty as independence will necessarily be realized. This is so even though the *extent* of such liberty might not be great, depending as it will upon the content of the law rather than upon its form. If the government restricts its use of violence to circumstances where a rule has been breached (Fuller's requirement of 'congruence between declared rule and official action'), and if the rules are possible to comply with (another of Fuller's requirements), there will of necessity be zones of conduct where more than one option will be permissible. If the government is to maintain a monopoly upon the use of force, as it must if it is to prevent the obstruction of its policies by opponents, there must be laws prohibiting the more obvious forms of interference with conduct, such as assault, and such prohibitions must reliably and effectively be enforced. Thus, wherever the rule of law exists to any extent at all, citizens will enjoy some zones of optional conduct that are protected from the interference of others. These will be domains of liberty that are independent of the will of anyone, but dependent solely upon the law.

Raz has asserted that the general meaning of the word 'law' (as it applies to the laws of physics, and the moral law, in addition to the laws of legal systems) cannot provide the basis for the legal philosopher's inquiry into law's nature.[36] But this is an error on his part. For the general idea of law encompasses the ideas of universality and necessity: a law is a general standard that governs with necessity. The element of necessity cannot, in the context of legal systems, be detached from the availability of coercive enforcement. Although earlier legal theorists such as Bentham, Austin and Kelsen emphasized the centrality of sanctions to law's nature, theorists since Hart have tended to deny any such

---

[36] Above n 29, 180.

centrality. They are more likely to analyse the special force of law as a matter of how legal duties are intended to feature in the practical reasoning of the duty-bearer: the duty-bearer is intended to regard the duty as having 'peremptory force'. This focus is misleading, for it ignores or neglects a most important aspect of legal order: the ability of the right-holder to rely upon the duty-bearer's compliance with his duty. Such reliability can, in the circumstances of the real world, be secured only by the coercive enforcement of the rules. In the absence of such coercive enforcement, rights would fail to secure genuine domains of liberty and independence.

Law represents the only possible set of conditions within which one can live in community with others while enjoying some domain of entitlement that is secure from the power of others. When a government pursues its objectives through the rule of law, it governs consistently with those conditions. To show that a rule is law is to show that it forms part of a system of universality, necessity and independence: that is to say, a system of general rules and principles (universality) that are given peremptory force and are reliably enforced (necessity) as the only way in which political expression can be given to the idea of peremptory force (given the circumstances of the real world). Such a system of reliably enforced rules represents the only conditions within which one can live in political community and nevertheless enjoy a degree of freedom (independence). The existence of such a domain requires that the law be enforced and therefore the value of such a domain justifies the law's enforcement.

5

Ideal and Experience

The Depth of the Ideal

At one point, Fuller tells us that the idea of perfect compliance with the eight *desiderata* 'is not actually a useful target for guiding the impulse towards legality', and that 'the utopia of legality cannot be viewed as a situation in which each *desideratum* of the law's special morality is realized to perfection'.[1] The remark is intended to remind us that, when applied to the circumstances of social and political life, the eight precepts[2] can frequently come into conflict with each other. In such circumstances of conflict, an abstract knowledge of the principles will not help us: we need, perhaps, practical know-how of a kind that cannot be reduced to a body of precepts. A large part of *The Morality of Law* is taken up with a detailed demonstration of the way in which the pursuit of the ideal represented by the eight precepts places cross-cutting demands upon the lawmaker. This is not something of which we could be aware in the abstract: it is the fruit of experience, of coming to understand what the pursuit of the ideal signifies in the context of the real world.

Perhaps Fuller is simply saying that, while the eight precepts represent as full and adequate a statement of the ideal as one can have, the pursuit of that ideal requires a series of insightful responses to handle conflicts between the precepts. But we might also read him as saying something else: perhaps his remark points to the possibility that our experience of the problems internal to the realization of the ideal will lead to an enriched grasp of what the ideal really amounts to, and how it should be understood. Perhaps the possibility of revision is inherent in any statement of a guiding ideal, for we may always deepen our grasp of the ideal by reflecting upon the experience of its pursuit. Fuller's views are too briefly stated for us to feel much confidence in their interpretation, but they make best sense when located within the context of some well-worn Aristotelian themes.

---

[1] Lon Fuller, *The Morality of Law* (revised edition, New Haven, Conn: Yale University Press, 1969) 41, 45.   [2] See above, p 65.

One familiar observation, not limited by any means to the Aristotelian tradition, points out the incapacity of principles or ideals to provide self-sufficient guides which dispense with the need for judgement in their application. As Kant acknowledges, the application of a general category requires judgement, and this is 'a peculiar talent which can be practised only, and cannot be taught'.[3] Aristotelians, however, might well go further, by challenging the very idea that moral judgment typically consists in the application of general principles to particular circumstances. Thus, discussing Aristotelian notions of moral wisdom, Gadamer observes that the very notion of 'applying' a moral principle is here out of place: 'we do not possess moral knowledge in such a way that we already have it and then apply it to specific situations'.[4] Rather, it is the situation as it confronts us that calls our moral knowledge into being. Having acquired habits of sentiment and perception by our education into structured forms of conduct and judgement, within which the neophyte learns from the practice of his seniors and is corrected when he errs, what we have available to us is a mode of perception rather than a set of principles. In particular circumstances, we can discern what is relevant and can see what ought to be done: only later will we attempt to formulate a principle explaining that judgement, and offering us a provisional guide for the future. Guiding moral principles, distilled from our tranquil reflection upon the occasion for decision, 'are valid only as schemata', and must always be given content by the particular circumstances.[5] We discover the limitations of an explicitly formulated principle, and deepen our understanding of the moral value that it imperfectly expresses, through the experience of trying to apply it in the multifarious circumstances of the real world.

An ethical life that centres upon our subscription to abstract moral principles, by contrast, strips our experience of any intrinsically ethical dimension. Our principles are to be scrutinized and judged acceptable or otherwise independently of the situations in which they must be applied. For this reason, as Kant points out, we can know our duty without any great experience of the world.[6] Moral judgement is thought of as the application of a principle to a set of facts, and an understanding of the facts requires descriptive accuracy rather than moral perceptiveness. Indeed, within this outlook, there can be no special form of moral perception: 'only the ordinary world which is seen with ordinary vision', and the principles or values that one chooses to apply to that world.[7]

[3] Immanuel Kant, *Critique of Pure Reason* (1781) A133/B172.

[4] Hans-Georg Gadamer, *Truth and Method* (1960), translation revised by Joel Weinsheimer and Donald G Marshall (2nd revised edition, London: Continuum Books, 2004) 315.

[5] Ibid, 318.

[6] Immanuel Kant, *Groundwork of the Metaphysics of Morals* (1785), translated by Mary J Gregor, *Practical Philosophy: The Cambridge Edition of the Works of Immanuel Kant* (Cambridge: Cambridge University Press, 1996) 4:403.

[7] Iris Murdoch, *The Sovereignty of Good* (London: Routledge, 1971) 35.

Within the context of such an outlook, it becomes hard to see how an inquiry into the nature of an established social institution can be anything other than a descriptive or analytical enterprise. In particular, it is hard to see how an inquiry into the nature of law can hope to deepen our understanding of any moral or political value. The clear division between our subscription to abstract principles and our apprehension of the world to which they must be applied suggests a similar watershed within jurisprudence. It is assumed that, in so far as jurisprudence concerns itself with the nature of an actual historical institution, it cannot be an enterprise of moral reflection; and, in so far as it is engaged in substantive moral reflection, those reflections cannot spring from any concern to understand the nature of an established institution. The fact that historic texts in the philosophy of law appear to merge these two seemingly different enterprises is treated either as a manifestation of earlier confusions now dispelled, or as evidence that earlier debates were conducted under a convention that required 'political and moral ideals' to be put forward 'as versions of the meaning, definition, or function of law'.[8] Abandoning any such mysterious convention, and dispelling the intellectual confusions that were supposed to have sustained the older tradition, jurisprudence now presents itself as divided into two separate enterprises: an 'analytical' and morally neutral enterprise of conceptual clarification; and a 'normative' enterprise, grounded in moral 'intuitions'.

Jurisprudence can only properly be understood in the light of the possibility that moral insight might be derived from historically informed reflection upon our practices and institutions. Yet even a modest understanding of this possibility requires a considerable imaginative effort on our part.

Suppose that one has the task of installing a fitted kitchen. One begins perhaps with a vision of how the new kitchen will look. One has a plan, the various parts of cupboards, surfaces and fittings, and an orderly sequence for assembling and attaching the parts. In the course of the job, no doubt, one will strike problems: perhaps the walls of the kitchen are not quite straight; the floor is not perfectly level; the window-sill is a few centimetres too far to the left, and so on. Consequently, one will need to make adaptations, and such adaptations can require experience, judgement, ingenuity and skill. But one does not regard these adaptations as deepening one's understanding of the vision with which one began. One has merely deepened one's grasp of what it takes to implement an approximation to that vision in the context of this particular room.

Now, by contrast, imagine that you are a naïve and inexperienced judge whose legal education has been limited to the study of the most general precepts

---

[8] Tony Honoré, *Making Law Bind* (Oxford: Clarendon Press, 1987) 32.

of the law. You take as your goal the enforcement of a prohibition on 'cheating' and 'duress' in commercial transactions. You begin, perhaps, in confidence: you feel that you know 'cheating' and 'duress' when you see them, and you are determined to see that cheats and coercers do not succeed in your court. Alas, life turns out to be more complex and ambiguous than you anticipate. After confronting and deciding a very large number of actual cases where cheating or duress is alleged, you can look back on your initial naïvety with amusement. Perhaps the experience will have led you to doubt whether there really is a coherent notion of cheating or of duress that can be taken as identifying an object for legal prohibition. Or perhaps you will have developed a fully satis-factory set of principles and exceptions that serve to give a precise and just definition to the prohibitions in question. At any event, you will feel that you have now learnt something about the original idea with which you set out: you have discovered its real content, or you have discovered its real emptiness. You will not feel that you have simply discovered something about the adap-tations that are necessary to fit your original idea to the circumstances of the real world.

Explaining the views of Aristotle, Gadamer draws a contrast between the craftsman, who employs a technique, and a judge who has the task of applying the law. The craftsman begins with a design and with the rules of his craft. In the course of executing the design, he may be forced to make modifications in order to adapt to particular circumstances: he might not be able to carry out his design as he originally intended. 'But', says Gadamer, 'this resignation does not mean that his knowledge of what he wants is improved.' By contrast with this, our knowledge of the law may be made more perfect by the experience of needing to apply it in a great number of particular circumstances.[9]

The contrast need not and should not be taken as making a point about law specifically. We can, for example, discover more about the real content of a moral ideal by the experience of its pursuit.[10] For a full understanding of any moral or juridical idea always involves a grasp of the conditions for the realiza-tion of that idea, and of the broader form of association that such conditions themselves suggest and require. Whereas the kitchen-fitter has a merely par-ticular end, moral knowledge always tacitly contemplates an entire way of life, and is ultimately concerned with right living in general.[11] To understand a value (and, therefore, to be able to judge whether it truly *is* a value) we must

---

[9] Gadamer, above n 4, 316.

[10] Perhaps something similar is true of aesthetic ideals in art. For this reason we may hesitate over Gadamer's description of a craft: surely, we might say, the craftsman perfects his knowledge of what he seeks in the course of his seeking. This certainly seems to be a plausible description of the work of the potter, for example, who may have no clear conception of the end result he seeks when he begins to work the clay. See RG Collingwood, *The Principles of Art* (Oxford: Clarendon Press, 1938).

[11] Gadamer, above n 4, 318.

have some grasp of the actions and practices that might best embody it, and must appreciate the broader structures of human interaction which such actions and practices might presuppose or engender. If I am truly 'inexperienced in the course of the world', and 'incapable of being prepared for whatever might come to pass in it',[12] I will be ill qualified to grasp the nature of any moral value.

It is this that gives semantic depth to our moral and juridical ideas, ensuring that their content can always outstrip the criteria for their applicability that we might accept at any particular time. The possibility of such semantic depth does not depend upon a Platonic realism about ideas, at least as such a realism is traditionally conceived. We can treat the real nature of a value as deeper than any of our temporary platforms of moral understanding without needing to locate values in a Platonic realm that is accessible only to the philosopher who has escaped from the cave. Semantic depth can instead be a function of the connectedness of all the elements within the concrete form of ethical life that is intrinsic to realization of the value. We might call this the depth of the ideal.

In some traditional readings of Aristotle, the idea of the good life is determinate and capable of being fully understood in advance of its pursuit and attainment. By contrast with this, what Charles Taylor has called the 'expressivism' of Herder and his intellectual heirs emphasizes the extent to which the pursuit and realization of an idea clarifies and makes determinate the idea's content.[13] Taylor sees this 'expressivist' thought as quite alien to the Aristotelian tradition as a whole, but this is an error. According to Aristotelians, one of the features that distinguishes moral knowledge from technical knowledge (the grasp of means in relation to ends) is the absence, within moral knowledge, of a clear priority for our conception of the end over our understanding of the means. Consequently, there can be no anterior certainty concerning the nature of the good life. It is for this reason that Aristotle's explanations of *phronesis* are therefore marked by uncertainty, emphasizing sometimes the end and sometimes the means to the end.[14]

It might be thought that a form of ethical life that gives priority to habituated moral know-how over articulable moral knowledge, and to particular moral perceptions over abstract moral principles, will require from its participants a degree of unreflective immersion and uncritical endorsement that is incompatible with the idea of an open, liberal society. But this is a mistake. For the practice opens itself to transformation through the very forms of moral perception that it creates. When our comprehension of a value is genuine, it

---

[12] Above n 6, 4: 403.

[13] Charles Taylor, *Hegel* (Cambridge: Cambridge University Press, 1975) 13–29.

[14] Gadamer, above n 4, 318. See also FD Miller, *Nature, Justice and Rights in Aristotle's* Politics (Oxford: Clarendon Press, 1995) 10ff.

cannot be an exercise of the distal utopian imagination, but must be grounded directly or indirectly in lived experience. Moral knowledge is therefore always in part a matter of familiarity with certain established modes of conduct, together with an appreciation of the future possibilities that they create or facilitate in practice.[15]

This is not the picture of responsible moral agency that has tended to dominate modern thinking. Rather, we are encouraged to believe that our particular moral perceptions must be interrogated in the light of articulable principles before they can be given any weight in our deliberations: even 'the Holy One of the Gospel' must first be compared with our abstract ideals before we can judge him to be good.[16] When faced by the question of how our knowledge of principles and ideals is to be grounded, however, the majority of modern philosophers find that they can only turn to the search for 'reflective equilibrium' amongst our moral 'intuitions'. Reliance upon our intuitions is inevitable, and to point out its necessity cannot be a mistake: the attempt to generalize beyond our specific moral perceptions by the identification of implicit principles is itself a manifestation of our reflective and articulate moral culture. But it can nevertheless be a mistake implicitly to suggest that our intuitions are appropriately understood in isolation from the practices, communities and moral or juridical histories that have shaped them and given them content. We should not be misled by the prominence of reflective and self-transformative practices within our ethical life: our ethical reflections always begin within a particular fabric of practice and judgement, and depend upon our education into that fabric. In terms of abstract possibilities, such a practice-based moral competence might give priority to the general formulation of values or to the sensitive understanding of particulars; or it might embody a complex interdependence between the two. The intellectual reconstruction of our ethical life must decide between these and other possibilities: it is not a matter that can be resolved by appeal to a dogmatic, metaphysically bifurcated picture of the relationship between facts and values.

The Loss of Moral Experience

It was said above that the inquiry into law's nature can only be understood properly in the light of the possibility that moral insight may be derived from

---

[15] 'The fact is the moral world, both on its external side of the family, society, and the State, and the work of the individual in them, and again, on its internal side of moral feeling and belief. The theory which will account for and justify these facts as a whole is the true moral theory.' FH Bradley, *Ethical Studies* (2nd edition, Oxford: Clarendon Press, 1927) 89. See also RG Collingwood, *An Essay on Philosophical Method* (Oxford: Clarendon Press, 1933) 133: 'the subject-matter of ethical thought must be conceived as something whose essence involves existence'.   [16] Above n 6, 4:408.

historically informed reflection upon our practices and institutions. Yet the philosophical context within which jurisprudence has been pursued has tended increasingly to obscure this very possibility. We can begin to discern the sources of this tendency if we turn to the early modern period which gave to the problems of jurisprudence much of the centrality that they now enjoy.[17]

Let us take, for example, the work of someone who played a key role in the development of modern jurisprudence: Hugo Grotius. Grotius addressed a Europe that had come to be wracked by religious division, and a philosophical scene that was increasingly dominated by scepticism. Furthermore, the multiple overlapping jurisdictions of medieval Europe were being replaced by the emerging state, claiming exclusive territorial jurisdiction. The nature of the moral or juridical relations obtaining between these exclusive zones began to assume a problematic appearance, with many concluding that states could stand to each other only in postures governed by self-interest and power, rather than by right or law. Theories of natural law that explored the moral relations obtaining between such autonomous entities naturally suggested the possibility that the moral relations between individuals within the state could be conceived of in a similar way: theories suited to the newly emergent international order therefore fostered new forms of individualism in political thought more generally.

If a theory of natural law was to offer a plausible account of the relations between states, it could not focus (as had the older Aristotelian form of political thought) upon the realization of a common good: for no such common good seemed to be possible or acknowledged in such a context. Grotius therefore took the decisive step of separating the juridical questions of justice and rights from the broader ethical domain of well-being and the common good (where Aristotle would have located them). For Grotius, therefore, natural law was not an expression of the requirements for human well-being in community: rather, the law of nature springs from a basic right of self-preservation possessed by each individual.

One effect of this sea-change was to obscure the idea that political thought is a deepening reflection upon the conditions for the realization of a complex good, a good that can only be realized in common. Rather, politics is thought to concern a framework of entitlements governing access to goods that are essentially simple and to be enjoyed by individuals who pursue their potentially varied goals independently. What we described above as 'the depth of the ideal' is a characteristic of complex goods, where it is hard for us to envisage in advance what forms of association those goods might imply and require. A certain impoverishment of the moral landscape therefore followed directly upon the division that Grotius introduced.

---

[17] See Simmonds, *Central Issues in Jurisprudence* (2nd edition, London: Sweet & Maxwell, 2002) 6.

This in turn had consequences for the understanding of law's nature. Law came to be thought of as the system of entitlements governing moral relations between self-seeking individuals in pursuit of their own ideas of the good. The modern natural law tradition of Grotius and the legal positivism of Hobbes (while agreeing on a great many issues) diverged most significantly in the way in which they conceived of this system of entitlement. For Grotius, the basic right of self-preservation gave rise to a system of jointly possible rights: positive enactment would be necessary to give full determinacy to this system, and to secure its enforcement, but it had sufficient content to provide the basic framework of thought informing legal interpretation and systematization. For Hobbes, the same right of self-preservation (given some basic features of the necessary structure of human interaction) simply generated a 'war of all against all' that could be terminated and converted into legal order only by the positive imposition of rules based in sovereign authority.

What both of these approaches lack is a full appreciation of how the rule of law secures a good that is only to be realized and enjoyed in common. Liberty as independence from the power of others is a condition that can only be realized by that form of moral association that we call 'the rule of law'. This is not an individual good, access to which is regulated by the law, and the just distribution of which is contingent upon the law's content. It is a common good that is *intrinsic* to law's nature.

In many respects, Grotius retains an Aristotelian outlook; but he makes certain specific departures from Aristotle. This is true, for example, of Grotius's claim that governmental authority is based upon the transfer of powers to government from the governed, rather than upon the government's capacity or tendency to advance the human *telos*.[18] It is true also of his insistence that Aristotelian distributive justice is not 'justice properly and strictly so called', but a matter of 'generosity, compassion and foresight in matters of government'.[19] Yet, at times, Grotius fails to appreciate the extensive significance of his departures from Aristotle, thereby revealing an imperfect grasp of the deep underpinnings of the Aristotelian view.

Grotius endorses Aristotle's view that 'certainty is not to be found in moral questions in the same degree as in mathematical science'.[20] Yet he also tells us that he has withdrawn his mind from every particular fact, 'just as mathematicians treat their figures as abstracted from bodies'.[21] These propositions are, of

---

[18] Hugo Grotius, *De Iure Belli ac Pacis* (1625) translation by FW Kelsey, two volumes (Oxford: Clarendon Press, 1925) 1.3.8.2.   [19] Ibid, 1.1.8.1.

[20] Ibid, 2.23.1.

[21] Ibid, Prolegomena 58.

The relevant passage is as follows:

'If anyone thinks that I have had in view any controversies of our own times, either those which have arisen or those which can be foreseen as likely to arise, he will do me an injustice. With all

course, formally consistent with each other in the sense that Grotius's approach to moral questions might conceivably resemble mathematics in its abstraction from particular facts, while differing from mathematics in its degree of certainty. In any case, the comparison with mathematics might be intended primarily as a rhetorical way of emphasizing Grotius's lack of any intention to intervene in current political disputes (such controversies having led in the recent past to his imprisonment, and to the execution of his benefactor Oldenbarnevelt). What the two propositions reveal, however, is Grotius's failure to grasp the way in which Aristotle's denial of certainty within moral reflection is bound up with a denial of the very possibility of engaging in moral inquiry while 'withdrawing one's mind' from particular facts. Grotius's assumption seems to be that certain moral principles can be discovered and understood in abstraction from particular facts, prior to their application in the moral evaluation of those facts.

This assumption becomes more clearly dominant in the work of Pufendorf. Pufendorf seeks to restrict the significance of Aristotle's remarks on the lack of certainty in moral affairs by confining the validity of those remarks to the realm of prudent concern for individual and collective welfare, distinguishing this from questions of the rectitude of human actions according to natural law. Grotius's own acknowledgment of moral uncertainty is accommodated by Pufendorf's distinction between the abstract clarity of moral concepts and the complex circumstances in which they must be applied.[22] In these respects, Pufendorf's writings represent a shift towards the idea of morality as a distinct and autonomous outlook on the world, separable from other practical concerns (such as the concern for individual prudence and well-being, or for wise governance) and composed of principles or concepts with clear intelligibility in abstraction from their practical applications.

This understanding of morality fitted Pufendorf's view of nature. Nature for Pufendorf was not the teleologically ordered universe of Aristotle, but something closer to the Baconian or Cartesian understanding. Consequently, Pufendorf attacks Grotius's view that certain acts are intrinsically evil, insisting that all acts are morally indifferent before the imposition of a divine law: '[t]hat reason should be able to discover any morality in the actions of a man without reference to a law, is as impossible as for a man born blind to judge between colours'.[23] The step into a recognizably modern intellectual landscape has, at this point, become a good deal shorter: all that is required is that

---

truthfulness I aver that, just as mathematicians treat their figures as abstracted from bodies, so in treating law I have withdrawn my mind from every particular fact.'

[22] Samuel Pufendorf, *De Iure Naturae et Gentium* (edition of 1688), translated by CH and WA Oldfather, two volumes (Oxford: Clarendon Press, 1934) Book 1, Chapter 2.   [23] Ibid, 1.2.6.

a source of normativity in the divine will should be replaced by a source located in human sentiment (Hume and Smith) or in the will of the autonomous agent (Kant).

Like Pufendorf, Kant rejects the location of morality within a broader domain of concern for human well-being, viewing it as wholly distinct from such values. This emphasis upon the irreducible distinctness of the moral point of view is closely tied to an uncompromising insistence upon the soundness and clarity of our moral knowledge; we can know our moral duty without the need for special wisdom of a sort that might be restricted to a few exemplary individuals, and without the need for great experience of the world and its affairs:

I do not, therefore, need any penetrating acuteness to see what I have to do in order that my volition be morally good. Inexperienced in the course of the world, incapable of being prepared for whatever might come to pass in it, I ask myself only: can you also will that your maxim become a universal law?[24]

Having, in his *Critique of Pure Reason*, destroyed the possibility of theoretical knowledge of God, Kant's goal is to reverse the relative priorities of moral and religious knowledge. Rather than our understanding of the binding force of morality being grounded in our knowledge of the divine will, the bases for reasonable faith in God are, Kant holds, to be found in our moral knowledge. This requires an understanding of moral knowledge as not only real and accessible, but also as irreducible to more worldly concerns. The (now widely accepted) idea that there is a distinct domain of moral reasons, perhaps amounting to a moral outlook upon the world, finds its most influential exponent in Kant.

Nevertheless, the Kantian inheritance here contains the seeds of its own vulnerability. For Kant's demonstration that the certainty and availability of our moral knowledge provides us with reasonable grounds for faith and hope depends upon two theses, only one of which is typically acknowledged by those numerous modern philosophers who invoke Kant's name. The first thesis, as we have seen, is that we possess moral knowledge, and that knowledge is not reducible to some worldly concern for prudence or well-being. The second thesis, however, serves to undercut the implication of the first, for it consists in the claim that morality is *not* fully intelligible as a self-standing domain of reasons, but points beyond itself to an unknowable completion.

Most readers will be familiar with Kant's claim, in the *Groundwork of the Metaphysics of Morals*, that the only thing that is unconditionally good is the

---

[24] Above n 6, 4:403.

'good will'.[25] What is less familiar is Kant's acknowledgment that the good will does not represent the *complete* good:

Happiness, taken by itself, is, for our reason, far from being the complete good. Reason does not approve happiness (however inclination may desire it) except in so far as it is united with worthiness to be happy, that is, with moral conduct. Morality, taken by itself, and with it, the mere *worthiness* to be happy, is also far from being the complete good. To make the good complete, he who behaves in such a manner as not to be unworthy of happiness must be able to hope that he will participate in happiness.[26]

Since the good will of morality does not represent the complete good, but only one condition of that good, morality would lack a point if we could not reasonably hope for an afterlife within which happiness will be the reward provided for the just by a 'wise Author and Ruler':

Such a Ruler, together with life in such a world, which we must regard as a future world, reason finds itself constrained to assume; otherwise it would have to regard the moral laws as empty figments of the brain, since without this postulate the necessary consequence which it itself connects with these laws could not follow.[27]

In this way, Kant separates morality from well-being as a worldly concern, while entangling morality with well-being as a spiritual concern. His discussions of the relationship between moral imperatives and the broader concerns of practical wisdom are, in consequence, remarkably impoverished. Thus, he tells us that 'counsels of prudence' are to be distinguished both from 'imperatives of skill' and from the categorical imperative of morality. Moral imperatives are not conditional upon one's goals or desires, whereas 'imperatives of skill' are so conditional. 'Counsels of prudence' are marked out by the indeterminacy of the value that they serve, namely happiness. Principles of prudence therefore cannot be determined with any certainty: the best we can hope for are certain 'empirical counsels, for example, of a regimen, frugality, courtesy, reserve and so forth, which experience teaches are most conducive to well-being on the average'.[28]

While preserving some disfigured remnants of the older Aristotelian view, these remarks of Kant clearly ignore a possibility that the older outlook did not neglect. I refer, of course, to the possibility that the experience of pursuing happiness (or any other value) might contribute, not simply an empirical understanding of how that value is best attained, but an increasingly refined and determinate understanding of the intrinsic *nature* of the value. Indeed, we may even wonder whether, at the heart of Kant's oversight, there might not lie a certain misunderstanding that later became central to Bentham's

---

[25] Above n 6, 4:393. [26] Above n 3, A 813; B 841. [27] Ibid, A 811; B 839.
[28] Above n 6, 4:418.

utilitarianism: namely, the assumption that counsels of prudence are invariably best understood as indicating a causal relationship between a goal (in this case, happiness) and the actions that may foster realization of that goal. This assumption plays a part, for example, in Kant's argument that the attainment of happiness might better have been served had man been a creature of pure instinct rather than reason.[29]

The Aristotelian understanding of politics centres upon a complex good that could only be realized in common. The plurality of forms of justice (distributive and corrective justice) served to articulate distinct facets of this complex good. Within the post-Aristotelian liberal vision, however, justice comes to be viewed as distinct from the realm of well-being, and as regulating access to goods which are essentially simple,[30] individual and competing. Those maxims of prudence that are derivable from experience are therefore conceived of as wholly distinct from the imperatives of justice, and are taken to concern the causal mechanisms whereby the good might be attained, rather than the intrinsic nature of the good itself.

Kant's views of prudence reflect this shift, by overlooking the possibility that the desired goal might not be a simple state, but a complex set of conditions exhibiting a certain structure. Where our goal is complex and structured, the experience of pursuing the goal might enlighten us not simply as to the causal relationships serving to advance the goal, but also as to the structural conditions integral to the goal itself. This may very well be true, for example, of the value of liberty, conceived as something that is intrinsically (rather than contingently) opposed to slavery, and that consists in one's not being in the power of another. For our principal problem in relation to this value is not that of discovering the causal levers by which the goal may be attained, but that of forming a clear conception of what such freedom would involve in the circumstances within which human life is conducted.

Reflexivity and Legal Thought

Resistance to the idea that the concept of law might be an archetypal concept may to some extent spring from the idea that law cannot be a matter of

[29] The argument is one that Kant takes from Herder, to whose 'misology' Kant is responding at this point in his theory. Kant challenges, however, the idea that reason is best judged by its serviceability for happiness, invoking a teleological argument about the purpose of reason in support of this claim. (The role of such teleological arguments within Kant's moral philosophy has perhaps received insufficient study in the literature of Kantian scholarship.) Above n 6, 4:395–396.

[30] Kant regards the idea of happiness as *indeterminate*, but indeterminacy resembles simplicity in so far as we cannot learn more about the nature of the value by reflecting upon our experience. Thus, Kant tells us that even the 'most insightful' being cannot form a determinate concept of what he wills when he wills happiness: above n 6, 4:418.

degree: something either is law or it isn't. Consequently, standards cannot count as law by varying degrees of approximation to an archetype: they are either valid or invalid.

This worry does not trouble us so long as we take the relevant archetype directly to govern, not the ascertainment of law within particular systems, but our judgements concerning which forms of political ordering should or should not be regarded as legal systems. On such an approach, the idea might be that legal reasoning within legal systems proceeds in terms of a basic rule of recognition, such a rule being the basis for the particular form in which the archetype of law is realized in concrete instances. Thus the bivalence of legal validity and invalidity would be preserved by the fact that legal standards within the system are identified, not by reference to the archetype, but by reference to the rule of recognition. The system as a whole, however, would count as a legal system in virtue of its approximation to the archetype, and this is a matter of degree.

It is clear, however, that Fuller himself rejected the notion of the rule of recognition. His view seems to have been that judges are and ought to be guided in adjudication, not by something like a basic rule of recognition, but by the eight precepts or *desiderata* themselves. That is to say, judges in Fuller's theory are to give the decision that would best advance overall attainment of the eight *desiderata*. Fuller regards the eight *desiderata* as constituting a conception of 'law', but (as we saw earlier) he seems to acknowledge the possibility that this conception might be open to further refinement in the light of experience. Perhaps the judicial task is one of fidelity, not to a rule of recognition, but to the idea of law itself; and perhaps our understanding of that idea is deepened by the experience of pursuing it. As Fuller expresses this in the title of one of his books, law is 'in quest of itself'.[31]

But if legal thought is guided in this way by reflection upon the archetype, legal standards must count as law by approximation to the archetype.[32] Does this not undercut the assumed bivalence of legal validity and invalidity? And does that not indicate that (at least when it manifests itself in a reflexive form) the idea of law as an archetype actually fails to make good sense of our settled understandings?

Ronald Dworkin many years ago pointed out that the notion of 'validity' is not one that is comfortably applicable to all of the standards that typically

---

[31] Lon Fuller, *The Law in Quest of Itself* (Chicago: Foundation Press, 1940).

[32] The archetype can perhaps be instantiated in both reflexive and non-reflexive forms. Some systems may instantiate the archetype by a fully reflexive practice wherein judges and citizens identify the law by reflection upon the nature of law itself; other systems may adopt the non-reflexive practice of guidance by a basic convention (rule of recognition). The distinction is ultimately one of degree however. Even the most fully reflexive form of legal thought must rely upon convention to some extent, while Chapter 4 demonstrates that legal thought can never be *wholly* non-reflexive.

make up a legal system.[33] Indeed, it is probably correct to say that, while legal theorists use the term 'validity' in a variety of different ways, lawyers themselves use it only in the context of the exercise of legal powers.[34] The legal theoretical usage thereby creates an unjustified prejudice in favour of theories that can ascribe a simple valid/invalid bivalence to all legal standards. Once we abandon this prejudice, the way is open to seeing how assertions made within doctrinal argument may reasonably claim to be statements of law, even when they go beyond anything that could be justified by direct reference to the authoritatively established rules.

Suppose that judges are guided by reflection upon the nature of law itself. As the set of conditions for the realization of liberty as independence, law represents a complex good and exhibits all the depth of the ideal. Our understanding of its nature is deepened by the experience of its pursuit. Any particular account of the archetype of law is therefore always subject to refinement and revision in the light of experience and deeper understanding.

Perhaps, therefore, in a more refined account of the archetype, the essence of law would not consist simply in the Fullerian characteristics of promulgation, generality, and so forth. It might also include, for example, conditions that would integrate the totality of published enactments more closely into an intelligible and possible way of life which is compatible with the various projects that humans typically wish to pursue. Such integration might require the extrapolation of principles that go beyond the enacted rules, and would ground interpretations of enacted rules without the need to invoke the interpreter's own authority. The forms of doctrinal reasoning and analysis that compose both the treatise and the judgment could perhaps be understood as an attempt to construe legal enactments in terms of such a background, and fit each piece of doctrine into a coherent system of social interaction, practice and understanding. On such an account, the propositions offered in such doctrinal reasoning can legitimately be offered as propositions of law precisely in so far as they move our understanding of each isolated rule or doctrine closer to the archetype of law, when that archetype is more fully understood.

Refining the Archetype

I have argued that the rule of law is intrinsically linked to liberty, understood as one's not being under the power of others. Liberty, understood in this sense, is not a simple state of affairs of which we can immediately form a clear con-

---

[33] Ronald Dworkin, *Taking Rights Seriously* (Cambridge, Mass: Harvard University Press, 1977) Chapter 2.
[34] Simmonds, *The Decline of Juridical Reason* (Manchester: Manchester University Press, 1984) 109–112.

ception, so that only factual questions of implementation are left. Rather, when we consider the circumstances of human life within an organized political community, it becomes hard to see how such liberty can be coherently imagined, let alone actually attained. Reflection upon the history of legal thought and legal institutions may reveal to us possibilities we would not otherwise have anticipated, as well as dangers we would not have foreseen, and false trails that lead into emptiness and are to be avoided. If the fundamental idea of law is the idea of a domain of universality, necessity and independence, we can acquire a sense of what might constitute such a domain within human affairs only by considering some historical realizations of the idea. Yet any such historical realization can in principle be challenged as not representing the best conception of the fundamental idea.

A fundamental question for legal theory concerns the basis of legality. How does a rule acquire the character of law? Not by the simple fact of enactment, we may say: for the enactment of rules can create law only when the enactment was itself authorized by law. Nor by the simple fact of acceptance by some powerful cadre of 'officials': for law is invoked by judges as a justification for their decisions, and judges could not intelligibly invoke the mere fact of their acceptance of a rule (for what might be wholly self-regarding reasons) as a justification for their decision.

One possibility would be to say that the conditions of legality are the conditions of liberty as independence. For the fact that a rule forms one part of a system of rules embodying those conditions would explain many of the features that we tend to associate with legality. Thus it would explain why we tend to associate legality with the subsumability of actions under rules, and the derivability of rules one from another. It would also explain how the legality of a rule can intelligibly form part of a justification for the state's use of force, or for a judicial decision; and it would explain why the precise nature of legality has been continuously contested, so that 'the nature of law' continues to be a major philosophical problem that is not capable of being resolved by simple description of familiar institutions. Perhaps legal thought is at bottom a continuous reflection upon the possibility of realizing (and so fully comprehending) its own guiding ideals.

Fuller arrives at his eight *desiderata* by means of an allegory about Rex, a sovereign who tries but fails to make law. The allegory is presumably intended to identify some of our more settled understandings about what would and would not count as an instance of 'law' or a 'legal system'. For example, a system where there were no rules at all, or where all the rules were kept secret, would not count as law. These settled intuitions, when taken together, can be seen to amount to the archetype of the eight principles. In the main part of his book *The Morality of Law*, Fuller endeavours to show how this archetype reveals the inner coherence of the diverse practices forming a legal system.

Having established a preliminary grasp of the archetype by invoking our settled intuitions (and having seen that human institutions instantiating the archetype are intelligible only as embodiments of a certain moral idea) we can now enrich our understanding of the archetype by bringing our moral understanding to bear upon our experience of actual legal institutions. In the allegory of Rex, Fuller shows us that complete failure in any one of the eight principles will lead to a system that we would not regard as law at all. But it does not really follow from this that the best conception of the archetype is to be found in the eight principles precisely as Fuller formulates them, and without more. Perhaps Fuller's account of the archetype should be regarded as heuristically useful but ultimately deficient: having come to see that law is to be understood by reference to a guiding moral idea, we might conclude that Fuller's understanding of that idea represents only a provisional way-station upon a longer journey towards moral or political wisdom.[35]

One indication that this may be so is to be found in the fact that some instantiations of law seem to depart significantly from Fuller's account of the eight principles, without striking us as marginal instances of law. Take, for example, the notion that the rules must be *published*; and the fact that this requirement sits only somewhat uncomfortably with the most obvious features of the common law: such as the fact that a rule may be articulated for the first time in the very case to which it is applied. Yet, while the common law may strike some theorists as falling well short of their ideal model of legal regulation, many of us will sense that the perception of shortfall here stems from the over-simplistic nature of the theory being espoused, rather than from some genuine deficiency in the common law.[36] Perhaps, therefore, its shortfall from the eight principles indicates not a deficiency in the instantiation so much as a deficiency in Fuller's grasp of the archetype.

In Fuller's case, one cannot fail to be struck by the gap between his insightful discussions of the common law and the basically legislative model of law that informs the eight precepts. Understanding case law is said to be a matter of the 'collaborative articulation of shared purposes', where our grasp of the law is refined and deepened as new problems are thrown up and addressed.[37]

---

[35] Consider in this context Collingwood's account of 'a method repeatedly used throughout the history of philosophy': 'To define a philosophical concept, therefore, it is necessary first to think of that concept as specifying itself in a form so rudimentary that anything less would fail to embody the concept at all. This will be the minimum specification of the concept, the lower end of the scale; and the first phase of the definition will consist in stating this. Later phases will modify this minimum definition by adding new determinations, each implied in what went before, but each introducing into it qualitative changes as well as additions and complications.' *Essay on Philosophical Method*, above n 15, 100–101.

[36] See Simmonds 'The Ethics of Legal Positivism' (1999) 2 *Legal Ethics* 87.

[37] Lon Fuller, 'Human Purpose and Natural Law' (1958) 3 *Natural Law Forum* 68.

This seems to be a long way from the idea of rules that are published in advance.

To be a law, there must be a rule in the sense of a general standard, and the rule must be capable of governing conduct. To be capable of governing conduct, the rule (or the general considerations that may be expressed as a rule) must be *knowable* in advance of the performance of the acts that the rule is to govern. But this need not be a matter of the rule having been published in advance. It is sometimes the case that, once a situation has arisen or a particular course of action is proposed, we have a pretty clear idea of the standards that will be applied to the situation because we have an understanding of the values most relevant to that situation, and the settled expectations that surround it. Such a knowledge may result from a study of existing case law, or it may be a simple matter of our everyday understanding of particular human practices, and widely shared values.[38] But we might not have been able, in advance of any such situation or proposed action, to formulate a complete set of rules governing such situations in a satisfactory way.

When we find express formulations of rules in caselaw, wise and experienced lawyers know that those formulations are to be treated as approximations only, to be read in context and in a full awareness of how they might need to be modified in future cases. Of course, to say that particular rule-formulations might need to be modified is not to say that *the law itself* will thereby be altered. Perhaps our knowledge of the law is never fully articulable as a set of rules, even though we may with confidence state what the law is in its application to a particular case. The position is aptly described by Hart when he tells us that, while 'there is no authoritative or uniquely correct formulation of any rule to be extracted from cases', nevertheless 'there is often very general agreement, when the bearing of a precedent on a later case is in issue, that a given formulation is adequate'.[39] The important point to notice is Hart's careful qualification: agreement on the accuracy of a rule-formulation is relative to the contemplated application of the rule in a particular case ('when the bearing of a precedent on a later case is in issue').

---

[38] What I have described as the symbiotic relationship between law and background understandings is important in this context. See Simmonds, 'Between Positivism and Idealism' (1991) CLJ 308. See also Simmonds, 'Why Conventionalism Does Not Collapse Into Pragmatism' (1990) CLJ 63 at 74–75; Simmonds, 'The Possibility of Private Law' in John Tasioulas (ed) *Law, Values and Social Practices* (Aldershot: Dartmouth, 1997).

[39] HLA Hart, *The Concept of Law* (2nd edition, Oxford: Clarendon Press, 1994) 134. Unfortunately, Hart goes on to cloud the issue by describing the judicial narrowing or widening of such formulations (to meet the problems posed in future cases) as 'creative or legislative activity' that narrows or widens the rule. One is left confused as to whether the legal rule is an entity that is only partially, and in a context-relative way, captured by a particular formulation, so that later formulations seek to state the law more fully rather than changing it; or whether Hart identifies the legal rules with the particular rule-formulations, and regards courts as regularly exercising a power to alter the legal rules.

Some legal positivists explain these features of caselaw by saying that the judges have legal powers to alter the law. But, quite apart from the other difficulties that this approach faces,[40] the interstitial modification of rule-formulations is so pervasive in caselaw that anomalies would flow from an analysis that treated such modifications as alterations of the law itself. The principal difficulty is, of course, that the rule-as-modified is applied in the very case that gave rise to the modification, so that all such cases would have to be regarded as most serious departures from the rule of law. If our task is to understand that form of moral association that we call 'the rule of law', and that we take to be realized and embodied to some considerable extent in our settled institutions, the notion of 'law' that is involved cannot be construed exclusively in terms of a fundamentally legislative model.

We might also consider revising Fuller's eight *desiderata* by the addition of a requirement that the rules should be *enforced*. This idea reflects our intuition that a law should carry a kind of necessity. Laws do not simply provide us with reasons for acting in a certain way: we think of them as possessing a kind of *peremptory force*. It is not entirely clear, however, what peremptory force could be in the context of individual practical reasoning. Raz has endeavoured to elucidate the idea by invoking his notion of an exclusionary reason: a law has peremptory force in so far as we regard it not only as a reason for action but also as a reason for disregarding other, potentially conflicting, reasons. But this fails to capture our sense that the idea of law is fully realized only when we feel that we can rely upon the compliance of others, and this we cannot do in the absence of coercive enforcement of the rules. To be governed by law is to live within the assurance that others will comply with their legal duties. As theorists such as Hobbes and Bentham saw clearly, the structure of human interaction is such that this assurance can be given only if the law is backed by effective sanctions. Within the practices of law, therefore, the idea of peremptory force is given reality in so far as laws will be *enforced*, if necessary by violence.[41]

The picture of law that we seem to find articulated in the eight precepts is law as a body of enacted rules. Yet this fails to capture an aspect of law that we mentioned in the opening chapter: that is, the character of law as something that is never fully reducible to a great assemblage of enacted rules, but is always a system awaiting construction from those materials. Lawyers can know all of the published rules and yet still disagree about what the law is (and not simply disagree about how the rules should be applied to particular cases). How is this feature of law to be explained within a theory that takes Fuller's eight precepts as its starting point?

[40] See above n 17, 146–149.   [41] See Simmonds, above n 17, 261–267.

A theorist such as Hart would no doubt respond by denying that law is in any sense an ideal system that is always awaiting construction. Hart would see any such idea as grounded in illusion: a projection of the idea of governance by rules beyond the limits that are intrinsic to it, given the open texture of language. What response to the problem might be offered by Fuller?

Let us think a little more about the moral significance of the Fullerian archetype. Its moral significance is to be found in the fact that, where the law satisfies the eight principles, it will consist of intelligible and followable rules; and, where the law consists of followable rules, citizens will enjoy certain areas of optional conduct. These areas of conduct will receive some protection from interference (probably in the form of general prohibitions on trespass and assault) and their existence will be independent of the will of any person, being dependent solely upon the content of the law.

The intelligibility and followability of a rule, however, is a matter of degree. A high degree of compliance with the eight principles guarantees that the rules will be published, prospective, intelligible, free from contradiction, not impossible to comply with, and so forth. Yet a body of rules might satisfy all of these conditions while still being impracticably *difficult* to comply with. Suppose that the rules place various demands on citizens all of which are individually satisfiable, and the totality of which are jointly satisfiable in the sense that they do not directly conflict, let alone contradict one another; yet the rules do not add up to an intelligible and viable way of life which is compatible with the various projects that humans wish to pursue (enjoying some degree of material comfort, establishing close personal relations, pursuing work that may be of a potentially satisfying nature). Although technically possible to comply with, such rules would almost certainly encounter extensive non-compliance. Either vast resources would need to be expended upon relentless enforcement, or a substantial gap would develop between the law in the books, and the law as actually enforced.

Somewhat similarly, we may at one level be able to understand what a rule means simply in virtue of our grasp of the language in which it is written. But if we are to have a real understanding of what it requires of us, so that we can guide our conduct by it, we must be able to grasp the values or objectives that the rule serves, and to see how the rule fits intelligibly into some possible pattern of life.[42] For reasons of both followability and intelligibility, therefore, the law will need to have a certain fit with existing forms of life, habits of conduct, settled expectations and shared moral sentiments.

---

[42] See above n 38. See also Gerald J Postema, 'Philosophy of the Common Law' in *The Oxford Handbook of Jurisprudence and Philosophy of Law*, edited by Jules Coleman and Scott Shapiro, (Oxford: Oxford University Press, 2002) 588 at 613–614.

Doctrinal Scholarship

Jurisprudence has concentrated a good deal of attention upon adjudicative reasoning, but has devoted much less thought to the practices of legal doctrinal scholarship. This is unfortunate for a number of reasons. The doctrinal writer does not take as his central task the resolution of a specific dispute, but the systematization of a whole area of law. Consequently, features of legal thought bearing upon or constituting the systematic, principled aspect of law tend to be much more visible and conspicuous in the scholarly text than they might be in the judgment. Law's character as a body of standards exhibiting deep systematic properties is both puzzling and important: it is by no means obvious why we should find it natural to assume that law exhibits the properties of a system, what those properties might be, or how their significance should be construed. The doctrinal scholar does not claim to possess any formal, rule-based, authority: in this respect, the propositions in the treatise differ from those in a judgment. One consequence of this is that questions concerning the nature and objectivity of law are raised more starkly in the context of doctrinal writing than in the context of adjudication. To reflect upon the nature of doctrinal writing one must therefore address directly and in conjunction the law's objectivity and its systematic character.

Doctrinal writing is of great importance for the liberal polity. The body of doctrinal scholarship appears to testify to the existence of a sophisticated and coherent system of principles providing a distinctive framework within which disputes may be addressed. The suggestion seems to be that, when planted within the intellectual traditions of legal scholarship, the bare texts of statutory provisions and judicial pronouncements will blossom into a rich tracery of entitlements and juridical standards. Doctrinal writings provide a broader context that helps to underpin and appears to justify judicial choices within the area of penumbral uncertainty. Yet we may upon reflection have the troubling sense that all of this appears to be achieved only by stepping beyond the limits of what the scholar claims to be doing: that is, offering an exposition of the existing law.

Suppose that we adopt Hart's view that rules have both a 'core of settled meaning' and an area of 'penumbral uncertainty'. The area of penumbral uncertainty might seem relatively untroubling when we contemplate its implications for our account of adjudication. For, in addition to rules of recognition that identify the law's content, there is also a need for rules of adjudication that authorize persons to give binding decisions concerning the applicability of rules. When judges decide penumbral cases, therefore, their decisions do not lack legitimacy, for the legitimacy of those decisions is derived from rules of adjudication even when it may not be derived from the rule of recognition; and, if penumbral uncertainty is unavoidable, and the reasons given for the resolution of the penumbral case are good reasons, there may seem to be little here that is troubling. Certainly this will be so if the great bulk of human situations (by which we do *not* mean the bulk of litigated cases, still less reported cases) fall within the 'core of settled meaning' of the rules.

Nor will we be unduly troubled by the suggestion that, if problematic cases actually fall within areas of penumbral uncertainty and therefore do not have outcomes prescribed by law, the judicial citation of laws and legal principles in such cases is somehow bogus. When a penumbral case is judicially resolved, the law is supplemented by the addition of a specific rule where none formerly existed.[43] Prior to the decision in *Bully v. Brat* we did not know if the word 'vehicle' in the Municipal Park (Prohibition of Vehicles) Regulations applied to a kiddy-car or not; now we know that it does. There was a gap; now it has been filled. In deciding how best to fill such a gap, the judge naturally has to pay close attention to the system of rules into which his new creation will be introduced. He does not wish to introduce a rule that will conflict with other rules, or defeat the values or policies that they serve: nor does he wish to create a set of requirements on conduct that will be unduly or insufficiently demanding.

When we switch the focus to doctrinal writing, however, the problem assumes a less tractable guise. The doctrinal writer offers certain propositions as statements of the existing law. Typically, some of these statements concern the proper resolution of penumbral cases, either specifically, or as a general implication of a broader interpretation being proposed. Yet the doctrinal writer has no formal, rule-based authority on which such proposals can be grounded. If his statements go beyond what is warranted by the core of settled meaning of the legal rules, how can they be justified? More specifically (for the scholar may have good reasons for his favoured interpretations), how can they be justified as propositions of the existing law?

Hart's discussion of the penumbra of uncertainty is intended to identify a feature that will necessarily be exhibited by any system of rules. But the idea of penumbral uncertainty does not provide an entirely apt way of dealing with the types of example cited by Dworkin,[44] for Hart sees penumbral uncertainty as arising from the 'open texture' of language, while Dworkin's examples do not seem to turn upon any linguistic indeterminacies. When positivists have not gone down the route of 'inclusive' legal positivism,[45] therefore, they have

---

[43] I am thinking here of a system that includes a doctrine of precedent. In the absence of such a doctrine, judicial resolution of a penumbral case may add to the law only by creating a rule binding upon the specific parties to the litigation (*res judicata*).   [44] Above n 32, Chapter 2.

[45] See Wil Waluchow, *Inclusive Legal Positivism* (Oxford: Clarendon Press, 1994).

endeavoured to respond to Dworkin's critique by arguing that judges (at least in common law systems) have the power to alter legal rules, and the 'principles' made much of by Dworkin are in reality and for the most part extra-legal considerations that are invoked as reasons governing the exercise of such powers. We saw above that this view is hard to reconcile with the idea that the pre-existing law is binding on the judges, for it proves to be impossible convincingly to spell out the conditions limiting such a judicial power to alter the rules in a way that is compatible with the familiar features of adjudicative reasoning and that also goes beyond the ordinary constraints of propriety governing judicial decisions in general. Furthermore, the account compels us to view a good deal of familiar adjudicative activity as a most serious departure from the rule of law in the form of retrospective rule-making. Since the rule-as-modified is applied to the very case that prompts its modification, case law would on this account frequently involve (and would always contemplate the possibility of) retrospectivity.

Hart's positivism is motivated by a desire to demystify the institutions of law.[46] In particular, Hart wants to resist any tendency to sublimate the idea of law by projecting it into an ideal realm beyond the mundane facts of judicial and legislative practice. He sees the idealistic appearance of law as a kind of illusion to which we fall victim when we project the notion of governance by rules beyond the limits that are properly integral to it. It may indeed seem at first that law is not to be identified with the body of enacted rules and decisions: rather that law is an ideal system to be constructed partly from these raw materials. But we should resist and reject such an impression. Once we grasp the fact of the open texture of language, we will see that rules always have an unavoidable degree of indeterminacy; and, once we see that rules can bind while nevertheless being subject to the possibility of future modification by the judge, we will see that judicial activity is not always best construed as an attempt to state the law more accurately. Regardless of how they present their decisions, judges are often resolving indeterminacies on the basis of extra-legal considerations, or modifying the rules in the light of circumstances. The insistence that law is an ideal system only partially and inadequately expressed by the articulated rules merely obscures these simple realities.

Suppose that we are persuaded by Hart's view. Rather than projecting the idea of law into abstraction, we prefer to treat judges as resolving indeterminacies in the law, and modifying the existing rules when they consider such modification to be desirable. We are prepared to treat judges as having the necessary legal powers; and (for some undisclosed reason) we are untroubled by the thought that our analysis reveals judges to be departing from the rule of law (by altering the rules with retrospective effect) on a daily basis. Even if we

---

[46] HLA Hart, *Essays on Bentham* (Oxford: Clarendon Press, 1982) Chapter 1.

consider this theoretical ascription of legislative power to the judges to be convincing, it can have no application to the forms of argument employed by doctrinal scholars. They possess no law-making authority of any sort, yet they nevertheless offer, as accurate statements of law, propositions that go beyond the explicit rules established by legislative authority or judicial acceptance.

Before we conclude that the forms of doctrinal scholarship must be radically revised to reflect our 'demystified' account of law, we should perhaps first ask ourselves what conception of law might underpin the practices of doctrinal scholarship. What justifies the scholar's claim to be putting forward an accurate statement of the law even though his statements go beyond anything that could be found in the formal authorities?

Some theorists seem to reject the idea that legal theory should attach importance to the conception of law underpinning doctrinal legal scholarship. Raz, for example, suggests at one point that this gets things back to front: we should *first* decide on law's nature and *then* we will be in a position to understand the form that a science of law (such as the doctrinal study of law claims to be) must take.[47] But this view rests on the assumption that legal scholarship is the study of a wholly independent object. As we saw in Chapter 1, law is not a straightforwardly observable phenomenon: rather, the idea of law provides a focal point that draws together a large number of settled understandings structuring social practice. The philosophical problem of law's nature springs from the fact that these understandings do not fit together in easy and obvious ways. Practices of doctrinal scholarship play an important part in this complex assemblage of practices and understandings. We need, so far as possible, to make coherent sense of the practices of doctrinal scholarship as an integral part of our effort to elucidate our concept of law.

We have now done enough to see that the claims of doctrinal scholarship fit very well with the account of law as a moral idea. The forms of doctrinal reasoning and analysis that compose both the treatise and the judgment can be understood as an attempt to fit each discrete rule into a coherent system of social interaction, practice and understanding. The propositions offered in such contexts can legitimately be offered as propositions of law precisely in so far as they move our understanding of each isolated rule or doctrine closer to the archetype of law, when that archetype is more fully understood.[48]

---

[47] Joseph Raz, *Ethics in the Public Domain* (Oxford: Clarendon Press, 1994) 186.

[48] This step beyond the purely formal conditions of universality and promulgation is one that may perhaps be found in Kant's *Doctrine of Right*, a work that has exerted considerable influence upon the history of doctrinal scholarship, but that is still very imperfectly understood. Kant defines *Recht* as 'the sum of the conditions under which the choice of one can coexist with the choice of the other according to a universal law of freedom'. Immanuel Kant, *Metaphysics of Morals* (1797), translated by Mary J Gregor, *Practical Philosophy: The Cambridge Edition of the Works of Immanuel*

Some legal positivists resist the idea that a standard can count as part of the law in virtue of its coherence with other legal standards. When arguments of doctrinal coherence are offered in support of a proposition of law, they should be treated as arguments for changing the law by the introduction of a proposed new rule, rather than as arguments aimed at establishing that the rule already represents the law. For, it is argued, if 'coherence' involves something more than bare intelligibility (if it involves something like mutual support-iveness or subsumability under a limited number of general principles, for example) the law is not necessarily coherent.[49]

The argument seems a poor one. It is true that lack of coherence with the rest of the law does not preclude an enacted rule from being legally valid. In that sense the law is not necessarily coherent. But nothing follows from this about the possible role of coherence in positively establishing that a given rule *is* part of the law. The concept of 'coherence' is one that can be unpacked in many different ways, and any role for coherence amongst the truth-conditions for propositions of law would necessitate a more precise conception of the kind of coherence that is in question. But from the fact that coherence need not be a necessary condition of legal validity we obviously cannot infer that it cannot be a sufficient condition.

Kant (Cambridge: Cambridge University Press, 1996) 6:230. As Thomas Pogge points out, 'a universal law makes it possible for persons' choices to coexist only if it is effective' so that the full range of conditions for efficacy must be included in the 'sum of conditions' mentioned in the definition: Thomas Pogge, 'Is Kant's *Rechtslehre* a Comprehensive Liberalism?' in Mark Timmons (ed) *Kant's Metaphysics of Morals: Interpretative Essays* (Oxford: Oxford University Press, 2002) 138.

⁴⁹ Andreì Marmor, *Positive Law and Objective Values* (Oxford: Clarendon Press, 2001) 69.

6

Legality as a Value

On the face of things, justice and legality look very different. When we consider the *legality* of a rule or an act, we seem in the first place to be concerned with its derivability from some established law. Legality, then, appears to be a matter of an institutional system's compliance with its own standards. Justice, on the other hand, is an independent standard against which all human institutions must be measured. The difference seems on the face of things quite sufficient to ensure that from time to time justice and legality will conflict, and to suggest that the two notions should be kept quite separate in our deliberations.

Our initial impressions receive confirmation in a large body of legal positivist writing that is aimed at firmly asserting and deepening the contrast between justice and legality. The theoretical conclusions echo our initial impressions to the extent of presenting justice and legality as distinct. But they also depart from our naïve pre-theoretical outlook in one respect. For, prior to studying works of legal theory, we may well be inclined to think of governance by law as itself a lofty moral ideal, and the legality of an action as important for that reason. Many legal positivists, however, take a different view. Some of them claim that even wicked regimes, with no concern for moral values, have good reason to comply to a substantial extent with the requirements of the rule of law, and they take this to reveal the character of law as a morally neutral instrument rather than the embodiment of an intrinsically moral idea.[1] On this view, the legality of an action might sometimes have a bearing upon its moral permissibility or desirability, but, when this is so, it will be so for purely contingent reasons: legality (we are told) is devoid of intrinsic moral significance. Others claim that, when we speak of 'the rule of law' as a value, the notion of 'law' that we have in mind is quite distinct from that which finds expression in the general framework of legal thought, and which jurisprudence is primarily concerned to explicate. They conclude that 'the rule of law' is a purely negative virtue, in so far as it protects us only from harms that are themselves the products of law.[2]

---

[1] See Matthew Kramer, 'On the Moral Status of the Rule of Law' (2004) 63 CLJ 65.
[2] Joseph Raz, *The Authority of Law* (Oxford: Clarendon Press, 1979) Chapter 11.

The first step towards a better understanding is taken when we come to see that legality cannot simply be a matter of the derivability of one rule from another, or the subsumability of an action under a rule. Such derivability or subsumability represents legality only when the rule invoked as a source of validation is itself a law. The legality of that validating rule (its status as a law) cannot always be derived from a superior rule, for this would involve an infinite regress. Nor can the regress be blocked by the idea of derivability from a rule of recognition that is simply accepted by the judges rather than validated by a higher derivation. For a rule of recognition accepted by the judges can confer legality only if it is itself the rule of recognition of a system of law. The problem manifests itself most clearly when we consider the role that legality plays in the adjudicative judgment. Judges justify their decisions by invoking the law. Their judgments could not intelligibly be offered as justifications if they were construed as simply invoking a rule that the judges happen to accept, for reasons that might be reasons of self-interest. The status of the rules as law is not a purely taxonomic issue addressed by the legal theorist: it is central to the intended justificatory force of the judgment. What then qualifies a rule as law? And how does the property of being law confer upon a rule a special justificatory force?

Modern analytical legal positivism views this way of posing the problem as a fertile source of confusion, rather than (as I suggest) a 'first step towards better understanding'. According to positivists, the nature of law and legality cannot be understood so long as we search for a single set of criteria that both confers upon a rule the quality of being law and gives to that rule its justificatory force. Nor can we understand law's nature if we fail to distinguish between the general features characterizing legal systems, and the system-specific criteria in terms of which individual laws within such systems are identified. To make progress in jurisprudence, we must carefully disentangle three different sets of criteria governing slightly different questions.

(1) In the first place are the general characteristics that will be exhibited by any non-marginal instance of a legal system. A structured account of these characteristics provides an answer to the question 'what is law?' as it might be asked by one who is concerned to identify the core features of a distinctive type of human institution. In Hart's theory these characteristics include the acceptance of a 'rule of recognition' by officials, and general but not universal compliance by the populace with the rules stemming from that rule of recognition.

(2) Second, there are the criteria, specific to each legal system, that determine whether or not a rule is a valid law within that system. An account of these criteria will set out the 'rule of recognition' of the system. Such an account

will not answer the general question 'what is law?', but the different question 'what is *the* law within this particular system?'

(3) Third, there are the various moral considerations bearing upon the question of whether the law is just, and whether its enforcement in this or that situation is morally justifiable.

Positivists suggest that, by separating different questions in this way, we can dissipate the sense of mystery that surrounds the nature of law. For that sense of mystery springs in large part from our inability to find a single satisfactory answer to the question 'what is law?' when it is asked at large and without an awareness of the distinct issues that it can be taken to raise.

Hart's legal theory introduces a regimentation of questions along the lines set out above. This is not done explicitly and at the outset of Hart's inquiry: rather, the regimentation is introduced gradually, as an implicit consequence of his argument. This revision in our understanding of the questions is in fact the major contribution of Hart's jurisprudence. One misunderstands Hart if one takes the questions for granted and sees his contribution as consisting in the answers that he offers, for the way in which the questions are tacitly framed itself depends upon the soundness of the answers. Take, for example, the idea that we must distinguish the question 'what is law?', as a general question about law's nature, from the question 'what is *the* law (within this particular jurisdiction)?' This distinction is now sometimes taken to be obvious, and anyone who denies it is taken to be simply confused. But in fact the distinction itself *assumes* the truth of Hart's theory of the rule of recognition. If doctrinal legal thought is typically guided by a basic rule of recognition, then the question 'what is *the* law?' is quite distinct from, and independent of, the question 'what is law?' But if, on the other hand, doctrinal legal thought is reflexively guided by reflection upon the nature of law as such, then the answer to the former question depends upon the answer to the latter question.

Prior to Hart's work, jurisprudence had long given the impression of being trapped by questions that invited only a limited range of possible answers, all of which seemed to be unacceptable. Legal theorists sought to derive the validity of individual legal rules from an ultimate source of legal validity in the nature of law itself, and many of them assumed that this source of validity would also provide a basis for the law's justificatory force. In this way they found themselves confronted by a road that some felt must terminate in a metaphysically unacceptable 'incarnation' of value within reality, if it does not lead into an infinite regress.[3] Many theorists sought to overcome the problem by adopting a reductionist analysis that stripped law of its normative character. But Hart

---

[3] Alf Ross, *Towards a Realistic Jurisprudence* (Copenhagen: Munksgaard, 1946) 11, 20.

made the deficiencies of such analyses very clear, while suggesting that a theory could preserve law's normativity without any need to ground law in moral values. This was to be done by distinguishing those confined and technical justifications that obtain *within* the system of legal norms from the general moral or prudential reasons that one might have for guiding one's conduct by law in the first place. The solution depended upon the theory of the rule of recognition, and the associated separation of three distinct issues.

I have already explained, in Chapter 4, my reasons for thinking that this approach to the problem of law's nature ultimately fails. For, in the end, it cannot explain how laws can intelligibly be invoked by judges as a justification for the imposition of sanctions, and how it can be precisely the status of a rule as law that plays a key part in that justification. Judges order sanctions against defendants, and justify this by setting out the relevant laws. They do not justify the imposition of sanctions by pointing out that the defendant has violated a rule that the judges happen to accept. Nor do they justify the sanction by pointing out that the rule violated was a just rule. Nor do they tell us that, given all of the circumstances, the enforcement of the rule is morally justified. Instead, they point out that the rule violated was a law. This is not an irrelevant classificatory footnote to the judgment, but its foundation: the judge does not conclude that enforcing the rule is the right thing to do (given its derivability from the rule of recognition, or its justice, or a host of other considerations) and then add that, as it happens, the rule is a law. It is the fact that the rule is law that provides the basis for the justification of the decision. The conception of law implicit within this practice is one wherein the legality of a rule is fundamental to its justificatory force.

The central justificatory place assigned to law within the judicial judgment is impossible to capture within a theory like Hart's. It was a clear appreciation of law's justificatory role that fuelled the older forms of jurisprudential analysis. Hart's analysis tries to dissolve the problem by a strategy of disentanglement. By distinguishing different questions we can create an intellectual landscape within which it becomes impossible even to formulate the problem of law's nature as a deep philosophical issue, for we can no longer ask any question along the lines of 'what must law be, that it can justify the use of force?' Instead, we must ask such questions as 'what are the distinctive features of the social structures that we describe as legal systems?'; or 'what is the content of the rule of recognition within this particular system?'; or 'is the enforcement of this law, in these circumstances, just and morally permissible?' None of these questions seems to be truly philosophical in character. The first question appears to call for careful description combined with some classificatory decisions; the second question is simply a descriptive issue about the rules accepted in a particular system; and the third is a moral question that derives its substance from particular circumstances and cannot be answered in abstraction as a general philosophical issue. Once these distinct questions are answered, Hart seems to say, no other questions remain to sustain our puzzlement.

The widespread and long-lasting influence of Hart's theory in a sense demonstrates its success. But its success did not consist in the genuine dissolution of a bogus problem. Rather, Hart succeeded in obscuring, and leading people to forget, the deep and intractable problem that had always been at the heart of philosophical reflection upon law. Hart's theory chimed with the spirit of an age that was keen to reveal the big traditional problems of philosophy as unreal: the philosopher's task was above all 'to show the fly the way out of the fly bottle'.[4] Having lost sight of its fundamental question, positivist jurisprudence was firmly set on a path that was to lead it towards ever greater sterility.

Hart, however, was too perceptive a scholar to be entirely comfortable with his own dissolution of the problem of law's nature. Those with little sensitivity to the world's complexity, and none of the patient submissiveness that is required by any attempt to capture that complexity, find it easy to maintain a strikingly clear and consistent view. But Hart was not one of these natural dogmatists. Accordingly we find signs of intellectual discomfort appearing here and there in his work whenever the nature of legality, and its status as a value, comes up for debate. It is worth examining some of the manifestations of that discomfort.

Consider, for example, Hart's criticisms of Gustav Radbruch. Radbruch had argued that grossly unjust enactments ought not to be regarded as laws. Hart's reply accused Radbruch of a form of 'romantic optimism' that implicitly denied the possibility of fundamental value conflicts. Hart was reflecting upon situations where the courts had to decide whether to punish a defendant for acts that were permissible under the enactments in force at the time when the relevant acts were performed.[5] He concluded that these cases involved a fundamental clash of values: on the one hand was the desirability, as a matter of justice, in seeing that the defendants were punished for their wicked acts;[6] on the other hand was the fact that any such punishment would violate principles of legality that restrict legitimate punishment to circumstances where a prospective legal rule has been breached. Hart rejected Radbruch's approach because 'there is an insincerity in any formulation of our problem which

---

[4] Ludwig Wittgenstein, *Philosophical Investigations*, translated by GEM Anscombe (2nd edition, Oxford: Blackwell, 1958) para 309.

[5] This is how Hart construed the relevant cases: we may set on one side the question of whether his understanding of them was accurate.

[6] Hart says that 'one can sympathize with and endorse the view that' the defendants should be punished: HLA Hart, *Essays in Jurisprudence and Philosophy* (Oxford: Clarendon Press, 1983) 76.

allows us to describe the treatment of the dilemma as if it were the disposition of an ordinary case'.[7]

The relationship between Hart's criticisms of Radbruch, and his legal positivism more generally, is considerably more complex and ambiguous than one might at first think. Hart objects to Radbruch's position on the basis that it obscures a conflict of value that arises when legal systems must consider the possibility of punishing people for wicked acts that were permitted by the enactments in force at the time. If this situation involves a conflict of value, what are the relevant values? Would we not have to say that they are the demands of retributive justice (or, perhaps, sound penal policy) on the one side, and legality on the other? And does this recognition of legality as a value not conflict with the positivist insistence that law as such is not a value?

Various responses might be offered to this problem, and they reflect alternatives that we have already encountered. There are times, for example, when Hart seems inclined to distinguish between the nature of law and the 'principles of legality'. Thus, at one point, he speaks of 'the requirements of justice which lawyers term principles of legality'.[8] This suggests a picture of certain principles of justice that, amongst other things, prohibit the punishment of individuals who have violated no published prospective law. Such principles could be thought of as integral to the concept of 'legality' or 'the rule of law', but not integral to the concept of law itself. We have already encountered this type of position in the arguments of Raz that were examined in Chapter 2. Hart's argument against Radbruch would then be read as saying that a positivist concept of law is to be preferred on the grounds that it can clearly bring out the value conflicts that arise when principles of legality conflict with the principle of retributive justice.

In the end it is hard to sustain such a position, however. For it invites us to regard the principles of legality as quite *distinct* from the concept of law, while nevertheless treating those principles as having a decisive bearing upon our analysis of that concept. If we assume that principles of legality are quite distinct from the nature of law as such, the reality of the value conflict would be most appropriately brought out by a revision or clarification of our understanding of the relevant principles, rather than by the adoption of a positivist account of law's nature. Treating the principles of legality as quite distinct from the concept of law, we could if we wished endorse Radbruch's suggestion that grossly unjust rules are not really law, while nevertheless insisting that, for the purposes of the principles of legality, the morally relevant feature is the publication of a rule, or the widespread belief that it is law, rather than our

---

eventual conclusion as to its legal status. Whatever one may think of such proposals, it seems reasonable to conclude that, if our intellectual object is to outline the true nature of a particular value conflict, careful moral reflection upon the relevant values is more appropriate than prescriptions for the analysis of a concept that is claimed to be quite distinct from those values.

At other points, Hart seems to adopt a different line. In a passage that I quoted earlier in the book, he describes and endorses the views of writers such as Bentham when they hold that 'the activity of controlling men by rules and the principles designed to maximize its efficiency are not valued ... for their own sake .... They are valued so far only as they contribute to human happiness or other substantive moral aims of the law.'[9] Since these remarks are directed against Fuller, they seem to suggest that the 'principles of legality' with which Fuller is concerned are in reality but principles designed to maximize the efficiency of controlling men by rules, the value of which is always contingent upon the goals that such governance by rules is intended to serve. Yet how are these observations to be squared with Hart's description (quoted above) of the principles of legality as 'requirements of justice'?[10]

Hart's uncertainty about the status of legality reflects a deeper uncertainty. When he criticizes Gustav Radbruch, Hart adopts both the outlook and the language of Isaiah Berlin's pluralism. In considering the denial of legal validity to a duly enacted statute, on the ground that the statute was grossly unjust, he tells us that such a denial of validity would 'cloak the true nature of the problems with which we are faced and will encourage the romantic optimism that all the values we cherish ultimately will fit into a single system, that no one of them has to be sacrificed or compromised to accommodate another'.[11]

On the other hand, when he engages in combat with Fuller, Hart seems to reject this fox-like pluralism, and to adopt the position of the hedgehog. Thus we saw earlier that Hart points to the compatibility with iniquity of Fuller's eight precepts as a reason for rejecting Fuller's claim that the eight precepts represent an 'inner morality of law'.[12] But this argument rests on the assumption that there cannot be distinct institutional or personal moral virtues, or that all moral virtues ultimately require each other so that particular virtues cannot be possessed in isolation. That represents a very distinct and contentious moral view, and one that is at odds with Berlin's pluralism.

---

[9] Above n 6, 357. See also above, p 72.

[10] Bentham's denial of intrinsic moral force to legality formed a part of his more general utilitarian philosophy. But, from the viewpoint of utilitarianism, traditionally recognized 'requirements of justice' are themselves of purely instrumental significance: valuable only in so far as they serve to maximize welfare. Hart detaches Bentham's analysis of law from his utilitarianism, and seeks to offer a positivist theory that does not depend upon any such wider moral philosophy. We see here one of the tensions that flow from that endeavour.   [11] Above n 6, 77.

[12] Above n 8, 207.

Hart therefore vacillates between incompatible positions on more than one level. At times he is tempted by the thought that the 'principles of legality', or of 'the rule of law', are indeed expressive of a moral value, but that those principles and values are distinct from the concept of law. At other times, he seems to suggest that the relevant principles are in themselves morally neutral, deriving any value that they might contingently possess from the particular circumstances and the uses to which the law is put. At times he enthusiastically endorses Berlin's pluralism; while at other times he sees compatibility with evil as negating moral virtue, thereby appearing to assume that all genuine virtues must be at least mutually compatible and perhaps more intimately bound up one with another.

These uncertainties indicate an inability to rest content with any of the standard positions that have tended to dominate political philosophy and jurisprudence in recent times. Hart hesitates between treating legality as a value that is independent of our practice, and treating it as a morally neutral feature of our practice. He hesitates between seeing values as distinct and competing and seeing them as mutually entailing or at least mutually compatible.

If we are to move beyond such unsatisfactory shifts, we must consider other possibilities. Perhaps values stand in a more complex relationship, both to our practices and to each other, than we are inclined to imagine. Perhaps our practices express values that they fail fully to realize, so that we can understand the practice only by its approximation to, and orientation towards, the value. Perhaps certain values (complex political goods, such as that aspect of freedom that consists in independence from the power of others) can be fully understood only by reflection upon their embodiment in practice. Since practices can exist and possess an identity only within broader patterns of ethical life, they may embody values that are to a large extent distinct yet nevertheless bound together in complex ways. Perhaps, for this reason, some values can compete yet can fully be realized only in conjunction.

Pluralism and Moral Knowledge

Suppose we retain the hope that our collective life may be structured by, and grounded in, reasoned dialogue rather than conflict and the assertion of will. We will then also hope that, at least in relation to our core political values, pluralism may be false. For, if pluralism is true of those values, politics must at some point be a matter of ungrounded choice between equally fundamental and incommensurable values. Berlin's own position emphasizes this fact, but also serves to obscure it. While Berlin was quick to accuse others of romantic optimism, his own thought embodies an optimism that is both striking and implausible. For Berlin took the view that pluralism could provide an appropriate justification for a form of liberalism in which the political community would sustain a great plurality of values, and leave choices so far as possible to individuals. Even if we consider such a political vision to be coherent,[13] however, it is doubtful if the vision can really be derived from the pluralism that Berlin invoked as its underpinning. Liberal democracy might exclude the possibility of realizing certain values that we might believe to be genuine and admirable (the values realized by the Homeric hero, perhaps); yet if, as Berlin holds, such values are incommensurable with those of liberal democracy, we cannot say that the gains of liberal democracy outweigh the cost. Given the non-availability of some calculus of gains and losses, it is hard to see how politics can be anything other than a matter of ungrounded choice. Liberal democracy may be one option, but plebiscitary democracy is another, as is choice by an authoritarian leader.

Driven by the hope that we may establish or sustain a politics of reasoned dialogue, we might search for ways in which our main political values can be connected one to another by rational reflection. This is the aspiration of the hedgehog. But if all our best efforts fail, we may be forced to adopt the outlook of the fox. We can call this 'the pluralism of defeat'. To adopt pluralist conclusions in this way is a very different matter from invoking pluralism at the outset, as a general metaphysical thesis. The pluralism of defeat reflects the (perhaps temporary) failure of our attempts to be hedgehogs, and therefore embodies a permanent openness to the possibility of deeper understanding. But there can also be more general interpretations of pluralism that reject the hedgehog's hopes and aspirations from the outset, viewing these as signs of intellectual confusion or even moral weakness and self-delusion.

The more resolute and unyielding forms of pluralism are sometimes presented as linked to the rejection of moral realism of a traditional Platonic sort. In the absence of mind-independent moral realities, value is thought to be an imposition of the will upon an ethically inert nature. In Max Weber's elusive but influential version of this position, pluralism is seen as an aspect of our 'fate' within modernity. Modern life has caused the greatest values to be stripped from public life, retreating into the now private realm of religion, or of personal relations. Confronted in the public domain only by the clash of subjective opinions, and faced with the need to choose, we find that 'only a prophet or a saviour' can give compelling answers. Such a prophet will not reveal to us an independent truth, but rather will take upon himself the responsibility for ungrounded choice. In the absence of genuine prophecy, one

---

[13] To name only one problem, values must inform the decision on how far it is 'possible' to leave choices to individuals.

must 'bear the fate of the times like a man'.[14] Within modernity, therefore, value's dependence upon the will is not exhausted by some founding moment of value-creation, but pervades the whole of our ethical life: the plurality of value ensures that we confront at every turn the ultimate responsibility of choice. Berlin's view is of course different, in so far as he ascribes to values an 'objective' status. But we find in Berlin's work also much that shares with Weber a grim celebration of the need for choice in the full acknowledgment of moral costs, and a portrait of the responsible moral agent as the person who can face this situation without a desire to hide in comforting obscurities.

The enterprise of conceptual analysis, as it appears in the context of modern political and jurisprudential thought, is not uncommonly bound up with background commitments of precisely this sort. We are invited to adopt a certain regimentation of our value concepts, and the fact that the regimentation presents those values as wholly distinct is very commonly seen as a point in its favour. If we reflect upon the concept of 'liberty', for example, we will be urged to avoid construing that notion in ways that would render it applicable to values that are describable in other ways: lack of freedom should not be confused with poverty; nor with inequality; nor lack of power. The approach is presented as one of simple intellectual hygiene. Those who resist its entreaties to cleanliness are seen as bent on obfuscation, or as simply unable to think clearly.

Yet it should be obvious that this enterprise rests upon a particular and contentious understanding of our moral life. It is assumed that we already possess, in advance of philosophical inquiry, a reasonably adequate grasp of the relevant values: this is why an impoverished diet of hypothetical examples is thought to be quite sufficient to activate the 'moral intuitions' in which the philosopher is interested. We fall into error largely as a result of the temptation to romantic monism, or through having absorbed without due scepticism the monistic constructions of the great dreamers of the past. By way of remedy, we are offered a clarificatory regimen for our basic evaluative concepts. The assumption seems to be that values, being an imposition of the will, are already in some sense transparent to our understanding. Swayed by a long-standing unwillingness to face our responsibilities for choice, past humanity may have bequeathed to us ways of thinking that serve to obscure the plurality and distinctness of those values. But the study of that doubtful inheritance is seen as a purely historical enterprise, quite distinct from the effort to clarify and systematize values, of which we have an ahistorical and intuitive grasp. From this point of view, hedgehogs are slow, lumbering creatures inhabiting a dreamworld

---

[14] Max Weber, 'Science as a Vocation' in *From Max Weber: Essays in Sociology*, translated and edited by HH Gerth and C Wright Mills (London: Routledge, 1948) 153, 155.

of comforting self-deception in which they seek to escape from the responsibilities that confront us all.

Perhaps, however, the hedgehog is not dreaming. He is simply less anxious than the fox to be constantly demonstrating that he is wide-awake. Indeed, from the hedgehog's perspective, the fox seems to be largely absorbed in a solipsistic fantasy. For the fox seems remarkably confident of his ability to grasp the real nature of our fundamental values, and to dismiss the beliefs of others as merely confused. The fox is transfixed by a static image of himself as courageously and responsibly facing up to harsh realities, a self-image which is always confirmed and never dented by the efforts of others to articulate a different view. The hedgehog, by contrast, sees only a collective endeavour, through dialogue, better to comprehend structures of value that ultimately link us one to another and render us mutually intelligible. The fox finds confusion and obfuscation where the hedgehog sees only an appropriate submissiveness to the fact that no aspect of the world is immediately transparent to our understanding (even our own will is not transparent to us, let alone values that are a collective rather than individual product). Even if we reject moral realism, the rejection gives us no reason for construing our ethical life as devoid of scope for the deepening of wisdom, as already fully accessible to a clear understanding, or as grounded in radical choice.[15] Before seeking to regiment the array of evaluative ideas bequeathed to him by tradition, the hedgehog is prepared quietly to reflect upon those ideas to see what they might teach. Foxes might decide, on the basis of some general metaphysical thesis, that our shared moral and political life is but a series of ungrounded choices, and might then proceed to delineate our concepts of liberty, legality and justice in a way that guarantees that this voluntarist conception of politics becomes unavoidable. But the hedgehog is more likely to wonder whether this regimentation might not simply serve to obliterate all those subtle pathways of significance that can link one value to another, and so provide a basis for reasoned dialogue rather than voluntaristic decision.

The outlook of the fox is not really separable from the idea that philosophy can and should concern itself with 'conceptual clarification' rather than substantive moral reflection. This is not simply because the fox will regard substantive moral issues as ultimately boiling down to a matter of ungrounded

---

[15] It is possible that there is no mind-independent moral reality, and that fundamental values have no basis other than our own practices and understandings. But it does not follow from such a rejection of realism that moral questions confront us (individually or collectively) with a need for ungrounded *choice*. Any such *choice* could necessitate massive changes in everything else that we value and believe, and the possibility of such change is not genuinely open to us. Moreover, in so far as our identities are constructed dialogically in the context of our practices of ethical orientation and debate, it is not clear who are the 'selves' who will be doing the choosing.

choice: for the pluralist position can admit plenty of room for moral deliberation before that moment of ungrounded choice is reached. Rather, the connection springs from a certain implicit attitude towards the fluid development and transmutation of concepts within dialogue. The enterprise of conceptual analysis makes best sense if we believe that our concepts are structured by implicit criteria that the philosopher can unearth, articulate, and perhaps regiment. Consider, by contrast with this, the following observation of Wittgenstein's:

> We are unable clearly to circumscribe the concepts we use; not because we don't know their real definition, but because there is no real 'definition' to them. To suppose that there *must* be would be like supposing that whenever children play with a ball they play a game according to strict rules.[16]

When the enterprise of 'conceptual analysis' is applied to political values such as freedom, justice and legality, we might think of it as resting upon a lack of trust in the free development of dialogue. By adopting some simple and clear definition of 'freedom', for example, we seek to render the idea rigid and invulnerable to the twists and turns it can receive in ordinary human discourse.[17] Yet those twists and turns can embody our historical experience of the conditions that are involved in the realization of such complex political values. Viewed by the fox as a source of corruption and confusion, they can in fact represent our openness to the depth of the ideal, and to the possible ways in which one value might be connected to another.

Resources may be available to the hedgehog in the form of structures of meaning that are inhabited before we come to examine them reflectively. Those structures are explored in dialogue with others, and may be indicated by the history of our practices. To attain a reflective understanding of them, we need to adopt a mood of submissiveness that cannot be combined with a disposition prematurely to impose one's categorizations upon a refractory subject matter. The state of quiet reflection that is appropriate in such contexts can easily be mistaken for sleep by those who have come to believe that only they are fully awake.

We must therefore exhibit due scepticism towards the scepticism of the foxes, and must consider the possibility that rational reflection can reveal complex relationships of mutual support between seemingly distinct values, while also resisting the temptation to regard all sound values as realizable without significant moral cost. What one may then find is that neither foxes nor hedgehogs have the position quite right, for there are various complex ways in which values can be interdependent yet nevertheless capable of conflict.

---

[16] Ludwig Wittgenstein, *The Blue and Brown Books* (Oxford: Blackwell, 1975) 25.
[17] See Joel Weinsheimer, *Gadamer's Hermeneutics* (New Haven, Conn: Yale University Press, 1985) 1.

Conflict and Moral Knowledge

While we may hope to find reasoned pathways that link our values one to another, and so may rescue us from a bleak dependence upon ungrounded choice, we should not pretend that those pathways are readily available or can be achieved simply by definitional *fiat*. The tendency to think of philosophy as an enterprise of conceptual clarification, quite distinct from any informed reflection upon actual experience and institutional history, has tended to encourage the solipsistic tendencies of foxes; but it has also encouraged the hedgehogs to find definitional short cuts that do little to advance our understanding. In this spirit, some theorists might be inclined to argue that an unjust enactment can never be legally valid, so that justice and legality can never truly conflict. Or that true freedom consists in doing only that which would be permitted in a society where resources are distributed equally, so that liberty and equality can never truly conflict.[18] But such approaches generally fail to convince. For the suggestion seems very vulnerable to precisely the type of critique that a pluralist might offer: by insisting that justice and legality (or liberty and equality) cannot conflict, we simply impoverish our moral landscape by denying one or other of the two distinct values. On the one hand we might insist that enacted rules should be regarded as law only when we judge them to be just: but this invites judges and citizens to act on their convictions about justice without regard to the enacted rules, or to attach importance to the enacted rules only on matters that would otherwise be morally indifferent. In this way the position fails to capture and explain the distinct moral importance that we feel attaches to the observance of law. On the other hand, the position might invite us to regard all enacted rules as just in virtue of the fact of their enactment. But in this way it would obscure the role of justice as a basis for independent criticism of the law's content. The suggestion that only *grossly* unjust enactments fail to constitute laws overcomes these difficulties by leaving some room for conflict between justice and legality, but tends to be offered more as a pragmatic strategy of adjudication than as a deep elucidation of the nature of law.

The pluralist is anxious to draw our attention to the potential moral costs of our decisions. In this respect, the pluralist resembles the utilitarian who sees moral decision as a type of cost/benefit analysis. The pluralist differs from the utilitarian principally in denying the existence of (and sometimes celebrating the absence of) any common scale of measurement for the costs

---

[18] See Ronald Dworkin, *Sovereign Virtue* (Cambridge, Mass: Harvard University Press, 2000) Chapter 3; Ian Carter, *A Measure of Freedom* (Oxford: Oxford University Press, 1999) 72.

and benefits.[19] But the pluralist nevertheless tends to share an instrumental conception of moral understanding, where our knowledge of the goal can clearly be separated from our grasp of the means. Our values are thought to be intelligible in abstraction from the circumstances within which they might be realized, and it is assumed that they are capable of being accurately and exhaustively described at that abstract level. Indeed, a tenacious attachment to relatively simple and abstract understandings of our central values is often regarded by the pluralist as a virtue: a hard-headed and undeceived determination to face up to the reality of value conflict, refusing to allow such conflict to be obscured by the development of complex and qualified understandings of value.

However, as we have had cause to emphasize earlier in this book, moral knowledge is distinguished from technical knowledge precisely in the absence of any clear priority, within moral knowledge, for our understanding of the goal over our understanding of the means whereby the goal is to be advanced. Like the judge or the artist, we discover more about the nature and content of our goal through the experience of pursuing it. Unlike the kitchen fitter, we do not simply discover some facts about the modifications that must be made if an approximation to our goal is to be practically implemented. In deepening our understanding of the conditions within which a complex good can be realized, we deepen our understanding of the content of that ideal. In advance of such reflection, and of the historical experience that must inform it, we should not assume that values are wholly independent of each other, even if this seems to be suggested by their abstract descriptions and by the possibility of a degree of conflict between them. For it can still be the case that the full realization of the set of conditions for one such good requires or includes the full realization of the conditions for some other, seemingly distinct good.

The Becoming of Law

One way of reading Hart might see him as supporting positivism by reference to an account of the human condition. Given certain general facts about human nature and the general circumstances of human life (the argument

---

[19] This statement of the difference will serve for present purposes, although strictly speaking it is inaccurate. Contrary to the suggestion of theorists such as Finnis, the absence of a common scale for goods does not render the injunction to maximize the goods meaningless. Consequently, any form of incommensurability that is strong enough to rule out utilitarianism must involve more than the absence of a common scale of measurement. See Simmonds, *Central Issues in Jurisprudence* (2nd edition, London: Sweet & Maxwell, 2002) 106–108. See also Ruth Chang (ed), *Incommensurability, Incomparability and Practical Reason* (Cambridge, Mass: Harvard University Press, 1997); Boaz Ben-Amitai, 'The Incommensurability of Values Thesis and its Failure as a Criticism of Utilitarianism' (2006) 19 *Canadian Journal of Law and Jurisprudence* 357.

runs) we need shared rules if we are to survive; but, in a society of any complexity, we can have shared rules only if we have publicly ascertainable rules, identified by reference to a basic rule of recognition. Consequently, we can conclude that the provision of such publicly ascertainable rules is the most important feature of the general phenomenon of law. An analysis of law's nature should emphasize and give priority to law's most important feature, and Hart's positivism is the result.

If this is the basis of Hart's positivism it is highly contestable. For complex societies can, in certain (historically and globally not uncommon) circumstances, manage very well without any basic rule of recognition that would render the primary rules ascertainable by formal criteria. They can tolerate a considerable degree of uncertainty about the precise content of those primary rules, and can respond to disputes concerning their requirements and applicability in ways that do not depend upon the authoritative definition of the rules. For example, where the mode of production is based on relatively stable traditional practices, a society may deal with uncertainty in its rules not by trying to render the rules more certain and ascertainable, but by responding to disputes about the rules in a manner that is aimed at compromise rather than precise rule enforcement. In such societies, accepted social rules ('primary rules' in Hart's account) can form the general background for the conduct of life, without there being a high degree of certainty about the precise content of such rules. Typically, members of the community will find it hard to distinguish between binding rules and settled patterns of conduct: the rules will be implicit in the way of life, rather than being discrete objects of reflection. Settled practice will assume a normative character to the extent that it becomes the framework for communal trust and mutual reliance. When disputes arise, rival claims may well be made about what precisely is required by the customary rules of the community: but the resolution of such disagreements about the rules is likely to take second place to the settling of the dispute itself. Disagreement about the applicability of customary rules is likely to be regarded as a relatively superficial phenomenon: the mere tip of an iceberg of hostility and mistrust between the disputing parties. If (as will be common in such societies) the existing relationship between the parties is enduring and multifaceted,[20] and no substitute relationships are easily available, the main objective of the community will be to encourage the disputants to patch up their

---

[20] X and Y may be neighbours, but also related by kinship, while the agricultural practices of the community may involve a high degree of mutual dependence: X has always pastured his cattle on Y's land for part of each year; Y's cattle cross X's land daily to drink from the river; X and Y have always assisted each other in the harvesting of their different crops, and so forth. Max Gluckman labels relationships of this sort 'multiplex': see *Judicial Process among the Barotse* (2nd edition, Manchester: Manchester University Press, 1967) 19.

quarrel and preserve the relationship.[21] In this context, an attempt to give more precise definition to the customary rules may seem an irrelevant distraction from the real problem.

My point is not, of course, to suggest that such a community ought to be thought of as possessing 'law' even though it does not possess a rule of recognition. I think it debatable whether it is helpful to speak of 'law' in such communities;[22] and, in spite of Hart's unguarded claim that the invention of a secondary rule of recognition is a step from the pre-legal to the legal world,[23] I do not take him to be committed to a denial of the claim that law can exist in such communities. My point, rather, is that the provision of a set of publicly ascertainable rules identifiable by some general rule of recognition is not necessary for survival, even in quite complex societies: for societies can respond to disputes in ways other than strict norm-definition and enforcement.

Indeed, we should perhaps conclude that a society that responds to uncertainty in its rules by developing a secondary rule of recognition may by that very choice reveal a commitment to values that go well beyond Hart's minimal goal of survival. For, to the extent that a community handles disputes by compromise rather than by strict rule-definition and enforcement, it confers upon people no inviolable sphere of entitlement. Such an inviolable sphere can be assured only by the strict enforcement of rules. If the invention of a rule of recognition *can* be regarded as a step from the pre-legal to the legal world, this is perhaps because the invention embodies a new insight: the understanding that it is only by creating a domain of universality and necessity within human affairs that values of freedom and independence can effectively be realized.

Such talk of 'invention' in the development of basic social institutions is, of course, a convenient but potentially misleading way of describing a much more complex process. It is potentially misleading in so far as it smacks of the general outlook that Hayek calls 'constructivist rationalism': an outlook that regards institutions as serving human purposes only because they were deliberately invented and established to serve those purposes.[24] In fact, many social institutions are the systematic but unintended outcome of a great diversity of intentional actions aimed at other objectives. In the case of the development of law, we confront a complex dialectic between such systematic but unintended outcomes on the one hand, and intellectual reflection upon the significance of such outcomes on the other. Understanding this dialectic is essential

---

[21] For where else can Y's cattle drink? And who will help with the harvest if the bond of trust between X and Y is irrevocably broken?

[22] See Simon Roberts, *Order and Dispute* (Harmondsworth: Penguin Books, 1979).

[23] Above n 6, 94.

[24] FA Hayek, *Law, Legislation and Liberty* volume 1 (London: Routledge, 1973).

if we are to understand the long-standing philosophical debate concerning law's nature. A brief exercise in imaginary history will clarify the point.

Suppose that our community has always been governed by primary rules alone, and has responded to disputes by encouraging compromise. Although you occupy no official position in the community (there are no secondary rules of adjudication), you are a widely respected individual who is regarded as both wise and fair. Several of the more intractable disputes that have cropped up in recent years have involved our customary rules on the pasturing and watering of cattle. You take the view that, while these disagreements about the rules were indeed only superficial manifestations of much deeper problems of bad blood and lack of trust between the parties, a certain lack of clarity in the rules did contribute to the problem, and provided opportunities for an underlying lack of trust to erupt in more serious conflict. You therefore begin to urge upon your neighbours a more precise understanding of the relevant rules, citing precedents from the community's history. Your persuasion works, and a clearer definition of the rules comes to be accepted. The exercise in rule-definition is judged successful, as the number of cattle-pasturing disputes is significantly reduced. Similar experiments are undertaken in relation to other vague and potentially troublesome customary rules.

Now three things start to happen:

(1) In the past, the community had no clear sense of the rules as discrete objects for reflection, detachable from the ordinary course of social life: there was settled practice, and there was communal trust and mutual reliance, but the 'rules' were rarely discussed as such. But now, as a result of the attempt to give clearer definition to the relevant standards, the rules have become discrete objects for scrutiny, detachable from the ordinary course of everday life and of reliance on one's neighbours. People discuss the rival merits of alternative understandings of the rules, and in some contexts a distinction might emerge between what certain parties have always done (on the one hand) and what is actually required by the rules (on the other).

(2) Once the rules have, in this way, become discrete objects for reflection, certain members of the community come to be noted for their capacity to remember the rules, and for the sensitivity of language and flexibility of thought that enables them to formulate the rules with precision and determine their relevance and applicability.

(3) A shift occurs away from pure compromise as a response to disputes. In the great bulk of cases, compromise is still the favoured option, for all of the reasons favouring compromise (such as the multiplex character of relationships) still obtain. But when a customary rule has been accepted as having a

fairly precisely defined ambit, and where one of the disputants has clearly violated the rule as so understood, there is an increasingly common tendency to deal with the dispute by penalizing the rule-breaker and vindicating the rectitude of the other disputant's position.

At this point, the ethical life of the community has changed in a way that invites reflection. For the new emphasis upon clear rules is likely to have had effects that go far beyond the reduction in disputes that was its original objective. In the first place, it may have given great power to those members of the community who have come to be acknowledged as repositories for the knowledge of the rules, and may in this way have disrupted the greater equality of power that was a feature of the older forms of dispute settlement. Yet, at the same time, the new emphasis upon rules may have revealed possibilities for value that were not previously discernible on the ethical horizon. I refer to the thought that the clear definition and strict enforcement of rules creates domains of inviolable liberty that could not exist under the regime of irreducibly vague rules and compromised disputes. Not only that, but the *existence* of these domains of liberty is seen not to be dependent upon the goodwill of one's neighbours, but upon the accepted rules of the community.

The crystallization of rules as discrete objects for reflection and recollection now takes on a new significance, as a guarantor of that form of independence that only the governance of law can realize. It is possible that the growing appreciation of this fact will generate a systematic activity of trying to articulate, record and refine the accepted rules. The activity of doctrinal scholarship has its roots here, in the attempt to articulate as discrete rules the pattern of expectations and practices that have made up the customary life of a community. There may also be an effort to integrate the provision of formal legal procedures and remedies with the background of customary understandings within which they operate. At some much later stage a distinct set of criteria for the 'validity' of legal rules might emerge (a 'rule of recognition'). But, far from being the step that marks off the legal from the pre-legal world, the development of such criteria tends to be an expedient aimed at addressing deficiencies in what is already fully recognizable as a legal order. Juristic expositions of the law aim to stabilize customary understandings, and rules of recognition aim to stabilize those juristic expositions in response to problems posed by growing diversity and dissent. Just as a strict doctrine of precedent was a late development within the common law, so Laws of Citation were a late development within Roman legal science.[25] The step from the pre-legal to

---

[25] AWB Simpson, 'Common Law and Legal Theory' in Simpson (ed), *Oxford Essays in Jurisprudence*, second series (Oxford: Clarendon Press, 1973); Fritz Schulz, *A History of Roman Legal Science* (Oxford: Clarendon Press, 1946) 278–299.

the legal world is to be found, not so much in the introduction of a specific institution such as the rule of recognition, but in the growing appreciation that, by creating a domain of universality and necessity within human affairs, we may realize forms of freedom and independence that would not otherwise be conceivable.

Communities that handle disputes mainly by compromise rather than by strict rule-enforcement are likely to be communities that emphasize the values of mutual trust and supportiveness, rather than the values of self-assertion, individuality, and independence. The change from one type of ethical life to another does not occur overnight, or as a result of some single institutional change. But a single institutional change can nevertheless be a seed that, given appropriate soil and conditions, can germinate and grow so that the resulting flora transform the landscape.

The community that we have imagined does not have a central government that aims to implement a set of policy objectives by means of deliberate regulation and organized force. Once such a government is present, however, the ethical significance of being governed by clear and ascertainable rules takes on a new importance. Regardless of the particular content of the government's policy agenda, it will have good reason to publish rules and enforce them as a way of advancing its goals. But it will also have good reason to use force against individuals who oppose or obstruct its aims, even where they have violated no rules. This is quite regardless of whether the government's objectives are moral and benign or selfish and wicked (for even benign governments encounter opposition, and the use of extra-legal violence against such opponents can be a powerful tool).[26] It is in this context, therefore, that the moral value of governance by law becomes most obvious; for, in the absence of some concern for that moral value, governments would have no reason for governing by law (i.e. for restricting their use of force to circumstances where a rule has been breached).

It is unclear whether Hart would wish to ground his legal positivism in any general theoretical claims about the need for publicly ascertainable rules. Although all the elements of such an argument are present in *The Concept of Law*, they seem to be scattered throughout the book, rather than developed as a continuous flow of argument. Hart's intention may well be to invoke these considerations as an additional support that lends added significance and value to legal positivism, while rejecting any claim that legal positivism must depend for its truth or acceptability upon such a general anthropological argument.

At the same time, questions concerning the rational grounds for acceptance of a basic rule of recognition do need to be addressed within the context of

---

[26] See above, pp 85–88.

jurisprudential inquiry into law's nature. Hart emphasizes the importance for legal theory of the 'internal point of view', and claims that this point of view need not be a moral attitude of any sort. Officials, he tells us, can accept and apply a system of law for entirely non-moral prudential reasons. In this, he may well be correct. But, unfortunately for his argument, all of the contexts in which officials can accept and follow such a system for non-moral reasons are parasitic upon moral considerations, or are dependent upon the system already existing.[27] Given the existence of a system of law, the officials of a wicked regime may well find that they can enact and enforce laws that advance their wicked goals. But this does not demonstrate that the establishment of a system of law where none exists would itself help to advance their wicked goals. A system of law involves certain commitments, in particular a commitment to use force only against those who have violated the rules, and such commitments would not be serviceable for wicked goals, for (contrary to the claims of some positivists)[28] such restrictions on the use of violence would not serve to increase the efficiency of the regime's pursuit of its goals, but would rather impede that pursuit. Wicked regimes may maintain existing legal systems, but when they do this they do it in order to exploit the moral value that is widely associated with government by law, or simply because the strategic behaviour of the individuals composing the regime makes it impossible to capture the gains that would flow from a wholesale abandonment of legality.[29]

Furthermore, as we saw in Chapter 4, it is insufficient to explain how judges might be *guided by* the rule of recognition, for judges must *justify* their decisions. The mere fact that the decision is derivable from a rule of recognition accepted by the officials could not intelligibly be offered to the litigants as a reason that *justifies* the decision. For this reason, we should not think of legality as simply a matter of derivability from a basic rule of recognition. For such derivability will confer legality only if the system, of which the rule of recognition forms part, is itself a system of law. The features that qualify a system as legal in character (features provisionally identified in Fuller's eight *desiderata*) necessarily entail the provision of domains of optional conduct that are independent of the will of others. It is the provision of such domains of conduct that forms the value of legality, and provides the basis for the legal judgment's justificatory force.

In fact, the rule of recognition can only ever form an abbreviated statement of the way in which the value of legality bears upon the judge's duty. The judge's duty is not fully reducible to a duty to follow a basic rule of recognition, but a much broader duty of fidelity to law. To determine the precise

---

[27] See above, p 61.   [28] Kramer, above n 1.   [29] See above, p 61.

scope and content of this duty, a judge must reflect upon the idea of law, in the light of our collective historical experience of attempts to realize that idea. The idea of law is the idea of a domain of universality and necessity within human affairs, making it possible to enjoy a degree of freedom and independence from the power of others, in the context of life within a political community. But the precise content of the set of conditions for realization of the idea of law is a matter for debate, and the resulting debate forms the core of jurisprudential inquiry. Is the idea of law most fully realized when judges adhere as closely as possible to the literal meaning of the published rules? Or does the notion of 'literal meaning' here set up an illusory idea of determinate acontextual meanings, when all meanings are contextual and purpose-dependent? To what extent does the idea of law imply a content going beyond the requirements of Fuller's eight precepts?

It is not the aim of this book to address such questions as these. Rather, the aim has been to reveal their significance, so that we may understand something of the relationship between jurisprudential reflection and substantive legal argument. In the closing pages of the book, I will confine myself to a few observations only, in the hope that this may draw out some of the lessons to be learnt, and the approaches to be explored.

Fidelity to Law

If we think of law as a finite body of rules stemming from a basic rule of recognition, we must consider adjudicative legal reasoning to be only in part a matter of the application of law. For, when applied to the circumstances of the world, the rules will generate penumbral cases and such cases must be decided by reference to criteria that form no part of the system of rules. But, if we think of legal thought as guided by a basic fidelity to the idea of law, the guiding idea will be capable of exerting its influence even beyond the 'core of settled meaning' of the rules. For we have seen that the idea of law possesses a degree of semantic depth in so far as it represents a moral ideal our understanding of which can be enriched by experience, particularly the experience of pursuing the ideal. We may begin with a thin and provisional grasp of what the set of conditions might be within which, in a political community, we could enjoy a degree of independence from the power of others; but that understanding is one that can been deepened by reflection.

We saw, for example, various ways in which Fuller's eight precepts might be refined. The refinements proposed included a requirement that compliance with the body of rules should be reasonably compatible with a viable way of life; and, since the intelligibility of a rule is a matter of degree, the archetype of full intelligibility should require some consonance between the system of rules and the settled moral understandings of the population governed by those rules. These refinements help us to grasp the conception of law that seems to underpin legal doctrinal scholarship. For, within the body of doctrinal scholarship, propositions will be offered as accurate statements of law even though they go beyond anything that is to be found in the authoritatively established rules. Indeed, it is central to the practices of doctrinal scholarship that the legal scholar claims to be able to establish the correct meaning of the established rules, and to be able to discern more general categories, principles and organizing ideas that are implicit in the established rules.

If we think of law as a body of rules identified by their source of enactment, it is hard to see how the claims of doctrinal scholarship could possibly be justified in the terms in which they present themselves: they must be reconstrued as (for example) embodying proposals about how the courts might exercise various powers to modify or supplement the existing law. We have already found good reason to conclude that the idea of 'law' is the idea of a domain of universality and necessity within human affairs, providing a degree of independence from the power of others. A system of rules identified by their source might form an important element in the realization of such an ideal. But we learn more about the nature of ideals by the experience of pursuing them. The emergence and stabilization of practices of doctrinal scholarship forms a part (fully intelligible to moral reflection) of the history of attempts to realize the ideal of law, and should therefore be treated as bearing upon, or clarifying, the nature of the idea of law. It is therefore an error to argue that we must *first* arrive at a clear conception of law's nature, and *then* adapt our forms of legal scholarship so that they are reflective of that nature.[30] For our experience of the practices of legal scholarship should itself provide an enlightening key to the nature of law.

Joseph Raz distinguishes between 'law' and 'the rule of law.' He takes 'the rule of law' to be an ideal with which law is expected to comply, albeit an ideal that protects us only from harms that are themselves the products of law. It is possible for him to adopt this view only because he believes that the concept of 'law' employed in the phrase 'the rule of law' is distinct from the general concept of law studied by legal theory, and with which lawyers are generally concerned. In the former (lay, or non-technical) sense, 'law' is a matter of general rules; while in the latter (technical, lawyers') sense, 'law' encompasses any prescription that is derivable from the rule of recognition. We saw in Chapter 2 that Raz's argument rests upon a certain confusion, and we saw in Chapter 4 that legality cannot be just a matter of derivability from a basic rule of

---

[30] Joseph Raz, *Ethics in the Public Domain* (Oxford: Clarendon Press, 1994) 186.

recognition; for, if it was a simple matter of derivability, the legality of a rule would be incapable of offering any intelligible justification for a judicial decision.[31] Judges justify their decisions by reference to the law; and, if the status of a rule as law is to provide a justification for a decision in this way, that status cannot be simply a matter of the rule's derivability from a basic criterion of recognition accepted by the officials. To provide a justification, the rule must be derivable from a system that exhibits certain properties that go beyond the acceptance of criteria of recognition. Those properties will mark the system as one that approximates to the ideal of the rule of law; and they will be logically tied to the notion of freedom as independence from the power of others.

There is, therefore, no sense of 'law' in which law can be detached from the value that we call 'the rule of law', or in which legality is reduced to a simple matter of derivability from a rule of recognition. For, if it were so detached or reduced, legality (the status of a rule as law) would be incapable of intelligibly being offered as a justification for a judicial decision. What follows from this is that judicial invocations of the law, in the context of justifications for decisions, must be construed as ultimately appealing to the ideal (of the rule of law) from which they derive their justificatory force. But we have already seen that the ideal of the rule of law involves conditions that have a relevance going beyond the core of settled meaning of clearly ascertainable rules, and pointing towards appropriate ways of resolving penumbral cases.

Hart seeks to dispel the idea that the existing law is something other than the extant statutes and decisions. In particular, he wishes to dispel the thought that the law is an ideal system of principles or entitlements that is only partially captured by those discrete legal provisions. But his theory is unable to account for the way in which the status of a rule as law is invoked as a justification for judicial decisions; and, once we have started to move towards a theory of law that can accommodate this justificatory force, we are already on a path that leads us beyond the settled rules and towards an understanding of the sense in which law is always an ideal to be constructed, rather than a finite body of materials.

This relationship to the ideal is central to legal thought, although rarely acknowledged within contemporary legal theory. Take, for example, the question of coherence and consistency within the law. If we think of legal validity as solely a matter of derivability from a basic rule of recognition, nothing in

---

[31] Raz presumably would not dispute this latter point (which, in Chapter 4, is aimed at Hart rather than Raz) as he takes the view that judges can only treat the law as imposing duties and conferring rights in so far as they (sincerely or insincerely) regard it as morally binding upon the citizen. But Raz offers no way of deriving this morally binding force from the status of a rule as law, and indeed views such a derivation as impossible: the morally binding force of a law is, for Raz, always a matter of contingency, dependent upon the law's relationship to values other than legality.

the notion of legal validity will guarantee that a legal system will not contain laws imposing conflicting duties. That is to say, a valid law might be enacted requiring one to perform a certain action X, and another valid law might be enacted prohibiting one from performing that very action. Or a law might be enacted requiring one to do X, and another law might be enacted requiring one to do Y, and the circumstances might be such that doing X precludes any possibility of doing Y. Most legal systems include principles (such as the principle that a later law derogates from an earlier one; or that a more specific rule derogates from a more general one) that have the effect of eliminating such conflicts, but the status of such principles is a matter for debate. If they are simply contingent features of particular systems, they do not affect the point that conflicting duties imposed by equally valid laws are logically possible; whereas, if they are somehow integral to the concept of legal validity itself, the notion of legal validity cannot be identified with derivability from a rule of recognition without more.

Once we see that a form of governance constitutes a legal system only by its approximation to a particular moral ideal (the ideal that we call 'the rule of law'), we are able to see a way of surmounting such theoretical difficulties. For it is true that nothing in the concept of law or legal validity guarantees that there will not be conflicting duties: we may well encounter a system within which such conflicting duties exist, and we would not for that reason withhold from it the label 'law'. But to the extent that the system contained no way of resolving or eliminating the conflict, we would see it as a departure from the ideal of legality, an ideal that provides the justificatory force attaching to a rule's derivability from the rule of recognition. Rules that aim to eliminate conflict from the system, such as the rule that later enactments derogate from earlier ones, are therefore in one sense contingent, but in another sense they are necessary features of the idea of law. It is certainly conceivable that we might encounter a legal system that had no such rules, or a very imperfect set of such rules, with the consequence that the system could generate, and be unable to resolve, conflicting duties. In that sense, conflict-resolving rules are contingent features of a legal order. But to the extent that a system lacks such conflict-resolving rules and thereby generates conflicting duties, it departs from the ideal of legality. Since particular systems of rules count as instances of law in virtue of their approximation to that ideal, the possession of conflict-resolving rules can be said to be a conceptual feature of law. Legal theorists have generally tended to assume that the concept of law is to be understood as a class-concept, structured by a set of characteristics that are possessed equally by all non-marginal instances of law. As a consequence of this assumption, they have been puzzled by the status of conflict-resolving rules, which cannot comfortably be classified as either necessary or contingent so long as we are assuming that 'law' is a class concept. Once we see the true relationship between the practices of law and the ideal of legality, however, the situation becomes much clearer.

This is not the only illustration of a tangled jurisprudential debate that can be clarified by analysis along the lines proposed in this book. Take, for example, some current debates regarding the nature of legal rights. One historically very influential understanding of rights found its most famous expression in Kant's *Doctrine of Right*, and came to exert a powerful influence upon later juristic scholarship. This Kantian view (as I shall call it) ascribes to rights what I have elsewhere called 'internal complexity' and 'peremptory force'.[32] Rights possess internal complexity in so far as possession of a right entails a number of distinct juridical consequences. Thus, on the Kantian view, possession of a right entails both the permissibility of a certain action on the part of the right holder, and the inviolability of that action, in the sense that others are under a duty not to interfere with the action. Possession of a right may also entail certain powers of waiver and alienation, and immunities against loss of the right independently of one's choice.

Rights possess 'peremptory force' in so far as they are taken conclusively to settle the issues that they govern: thus, a right is not merely a weighty reason for saying that the right-holder's action is permissible, but is conclusive of that permissibility. The peremptory force of rights is given effective expression by the practice of coercively enforcing rights: thus, rights are (in Kant's view) connected with authorizations to employ coercion.[33]

The principal insight of Hohfeld's theory lay in its appreciation that internal complexity and peremptory force could not be joint attributes of any concept of rights capable of fitting the complexities of a modern legal system. Hohfeld tacitly assumes that peremptory force is the more vital and distinctive of the two characteristics of legal rights. From a viewpoint that is in this respect wedded to the importance of peremptory force, he concludes that what has been taken for the internal complexity of rights is in fact the ambiguity of the word 'right'. In other words, we do not have a single concept with distinct juridical consequences, but several different concepts which happen to be referred to by the same word. Thus, rights do not entail both the permissibility and the inviolability of the right-holder's action: it is rather the case that in one sense ('privilege' or 'liberty') rights entail the permissibility of an action, while in another quite distinct sense ('claim-right') they entail a duty incumbent upon some other person, and owed to the right-holder.[34]

[32] Simmonds, above n 19, Chapter 8.

[33] Immanuel Kant, *Metaphysics of Morals* (1797), translated by Mary J Gregor, *Practical Philosophy: The Cambridge Edition of the Works of Immanuel Kant* (Cambridge: Cambridge University Press, 1996) 6:231.

[34] WN Hohfeld, *Fundamental Legal Conceptions as Applied in Judicial Reasoning* (New Haven, Conn: Yale University Press, 1923).

The Kantian notion of a right as possessing internal complexity formed an important element in the intellectual underpinnings of systematic doctrinal scholarship. For, in the Kantian account, rights formed complex nodal points around which the various discrete legal rules and doctrines could be organized. Within the Hohfeldian view, this promise of inherent systematicity is shattered. Rights can no longer be treated as fertile general ideas from which a host of juridical consequences (in the form of powers, immunities, permissibilities and duties) can be inferred. The inference from one type of right to another is in reality a choice, made on grounds of social policy or considerations of justice. The judge cannot, for example, infer the impermissibility of X's interference with Y's action simply by invoking Y's established legal right to act as he did: the question to be decided by the judge is whether Y's entitlement to act should be protected by a duty of non-interference on X, and if so what types of interference should be prohibited.

In recent times, many legal theorists have opposed the Hohfeldian view. They have pointed out that the various complex juridical consequences of a right need not be linked by a relationship of entailment, but by a looser and more defeasible form of connection. In this way, they believe, Hohfeld's challenge to the complex notion of a right can be deflected: for Hohfeld assumes that his analysis fragments the discourse of rights in so far as it demonstrates that relationships of entailment are unsustainable. But that fragmentation can be avoided by associating the various elements of complex rights on a different basis. Thus it is argued that a right does not *entail* the existence of duties and permissibilities, powers and immunities, but it provides a defeasible and non-conclusive reason for recognizing or conferring such juridical protections. The principal difficulty with this anti-Hohfeldian view is that it preserves a notion of internal complexity only by tacitly abandoning the peremptory force of rights. For rights no longer entail duties or permissibilities: they become merely powerful but non-conclusive reasons for recognizing such.[35]

The idea of a right's internal complexity serves the ideal of legality by creating possibilities for greater system within legal doctrine. To the extent that internal complexity obtains, it becomes possible to view specific juridical consequences as stemming from legal provisions that are already fully endorsed and familiar, rather than viewing those consequences as requiring a fresh act of legislative choice on extra-legal policy grounds. But this advance in terms of

---

[35] It may be thought that here I am ignoring one of the key elements in the position: namely, the idea that rights are exclusionary reasons. This is not so, however, for an exclusionary reason is not at all the same thing as a conclusive reason. Reasons for action that are protected by exclusionary reasons nevertheless have to be balanced against those categories of reason that have not been excluded by the exclusionary reason. Raz may redefine 'peremptory' to mean 'exclusionary', but this does not alter the substance of the issue. I have criticized Raz's position at greater length elsewhere: above n 19, 283–304.

legality is purchased only at the price of a corresponding setback: for internal complexity can be achieved only by an abandonment of the right's peremptory force. We see here a clear illustration of a feature emphasized by Fuller: when applied to the circumstances of the real world, the various facets of the rule of law can cut across each other and present both lawmaker and legal theorist with intractable problems.

Once again, the situation is clarified when we take account of the relationship between our juridical practices and the ideal that they partially embody and express. The idea of law is the idea of a domain of universality and necessity in human affairs, providing a degree of independence from the power of others. Such a domain requires the enforcement of rules and of the rights that those rules confer. Hence, the peremptory force of rights is an important feature of legality. If a system begins to treat rights as merely weighty considerations that have to be balanced against other factors, it departs to that extent from the idea of law and the value of legality. But legality is also advanced when the rules become more clearly intelligible and followable, and when the room for variable interpretative judgement in adjudication is reduced. These advances in legality are best achieved to the extent that the discrete rules and entitlements of the legal order can be integrated into a systematic structure, particularly one that resonates to some considerable extent with background moral understandings. To the extent that such systematic integration exists, it will become appropriate to think of rights as entities possessing numerous juridical consequences. Internal complexity and peremptory force are conjoined when the idea of law is fully realized, although in the unsatisfactory circumstances of the sub-lunar world, the two requirements tend to pull apart. In that sense, the 'idea' of a right may involve both internal complexity and peremptory force, while our actual rights can possess one or the other, but will not necessarily possess both.

Justice and Fidelity to Law

One final illustration of the importance of this relationship to the ideal can be offered, although it raises such large issues that our examination can be no more than a sketch. I refer to the relationship between justice and legality.

Let us return for a moment to the understanding of law's nature that is found in Fuller's account of the eight *desiderata*. If this was a fully adequate understanding of law's nature, law would consist of a finite body of published rules. As Hart points out, any such body of rules will contain penumbral uncertainties, and cases falling within the area of penumbral uncertainty will not receive a determinate resolution within the system of rules. Such cases will necessitate a step outside the system of rules, if they are to be resolved.

The judge's duty is one of fidelity to law, and this is never fully reducible to a duty to follow a basic rule of recognition. For the fact that a rule is derivable from a rule of recognition cannot intelligibly be offered as a justification for a judicial decision unless the judge can claim that the system containing that rule is a system of law. If we assume that the law consists of a finite body of rules, we are committed to the idea that there are penumbral cases that are not resolved by the rules. How then does the judge's duty bear upon the decision of those cases?

In the first place we should notice that no default strategy will work: in other words, the judge's duty in the penumbral case cannot be anything like a duty always to decide in favour of the defendant, on the grounds that the law is unclear.[36] Nor could it be a duty to decide such cases by the toss of a coin; or to decide such cases by pushing the law-books on one side and making a social policy decision without regard to the existing rules (or taking account of those rules only in so far as their existence bears on the desirability and effectiveness of this or that policy). The reason is very simple: there is no discernible boundary between the core case and the penumbral case, the distinction between the two being a continuous one. A default strategy involves a discontinuous strategy of adjudication: the judge is required to decide core cases one way (by applying the rules) and penumbral cases a different way (by giving judgment for the defendant; by tossing a coin; by making a social policy decision). But a discontinuous strategy of adjudication cannot be mapped onto a continuous distinction.

It would not help to say that the default strategy of deciding cases in favour of the defendant should be adopted only in situations where it is *perfectly clear* that the case is a penumbral case. For the principle on which the judge was then acting would require him or her to distinguish between cases where the situation is *clearly* penumbral and cases where the situation is not-so-clearly, or only possibly, penumbral. And this distinction is no clearer than the one between core cases and penumbral cases. In an individual case, it might indeed be crystal clear that the case is a penumbral situation about which reasonable people may disagree. What must be remembered, however, is that (if judges are to observe fidelity to law) they must act on the basis of articulable principles, and the principle which would need to be invoked in order to justify a default decision in the defendant's favour, even in the context of a clearly penumbral case, would be too uncertain to be workable.

---

[36] For the suggestion that such a strategy is the appropriate way to implement a concern for 'fair warning' and the protection of expectations, see Ronald Dworkin, *Law's Empire* (London: Fontana, 1986) 142. For further criticism of Dworkin's argument, see Simmonds 'Why Conventionalism Does Not Collapse into Pragmatism' [1990] CLJ 63.

Judges often have to make do with vaguely formulated principles, of course. But the adoption of a general default rule for penumbral cases (or for 'clearly penumbral' cases) would place an irreducibly vague concept at the heart of adjudication in such a way that it would potentially affect the whole of the law. Fidelity to law requires an effort to reduce such uncertainties whenever reasonably possible, and it therefore precludes adoption of a default strategy.

In the penumbral case, the best the judge can do (from the viewpoint of legality) is to decide the case justly. For justice consists of objective principles that apply to all cases with equality and impartiality (to doubt this is to say that there is no justice, only beliefs about justice). In the absence of a clearly applicable legal rule, the closest that the judge can come to respecting the value of independence from the will of another is to be guided by his understanding of the value of justice.

To say that judges should decide cases justly may seem to be a yawn-inducing platitude. But it must be remembered that my claim is that such a decision is required by the value of *fidelity to law*, and not simply by the general duty (incumbent upon everyone) to act justly.

The real importance of this duty to decide penumbral cases justly, however, lies in its pervasive implications. For we have already seen that a discontinuous strategy of adjudication in relation to penumbral cases is impossible: one cannot map a discontinuous strategy onto a continuous distinction, so the judge should not adopt a principle requiring core cases to be decided in one way, and penumbral cases to be decided differently. Consequently, the judicial concern for justice (a concern that is rooted in the duty of fidelity to law) cannot be limited to penumbral cases. Justice must be relevant to every case. The judges must, so to speak, read the law as a body of texts concerning justice.

When we read Plato's *Republic*, we read it on the understanding that it is a book about justice. Understanding Plato is not a technical exercise in the application of semantic rules, or hermeneutical guidelines. We interpret what Plato is saying partly by drawing upon our own understanding of the object to which he is referring. We are, as it were, alongside Plato thinking about justice in dialogue with him. To possess a degree of moral understanding is to have acquired habits of perception and a grasp of value that is inhabited before it is reflected upon. When we confront a text about justice, we read it, not as a description of a strange landscape that we have never encountered, but as an attempt to articulate that which is already, in some sense and to some extent, understood.

Now clearly, this interpretative posture will be easier to adopt in some contexts than in others. Very bad books, based on little real understanding, can be very hard to understand: indeed, we might conclude that there is not much about them to be understood. Deliberation about how the gaps and uncertainties in such books are to be filled will not, in all probability, prove to be profitable. Similarly, legal systems offer us less interpretative guidance the further they depart from the requirements of justice. The more remote from justice that a body of law may be, the greater the scope that it will leave for the exercise of ungrounded choice by the judge who must interpret its provisions. Since legality is the set of conditions within which we can be independent of the power of others, and since subjection to the choices of the judge is a clear subjection to the power of another, significant departure from justice tends to breed departure from legality.

What this suggests is that, while justice and legality are distinct and can compete with each other, legality can only fully be achieved where justice is achieved also. For only when the law is just will the judge's 'justice-guided' interpretations be a smooth and natural fit for the law.

But not only can legality only be fully achieved where justice is also achieved, but the reverse also holds: justice cannot be fully realized without legality. For the judge's decision is just only if it can be shown that the sanctions inflicted upon the defendant contain nothing arbitrary: every feature of the treatment of any litigant must be shown to stem from some general consideration that applies impartially to everyone. It should never be possible, for example, for the defendant to say that, so far as the reasons given extend, the sanction might with equal justification have been inflicted upon some different person instead; nor should it be possible to say that a different sanction might have been equally justified. Yet considerations of justice contain a degree of indeterminacy that entails the frequent possibility of making precisely such observations. That indeterminacy can be overcome by having established rules of law that implement some specific scheme for the realization of justice. When this is so, although general considerations of justice-apart-from-law might contain large indeterminacies on the question of who should suffer, or what they should suffer, the indeterminacy should have been overcome by the specific legal rules. Legal rules therefore frequently provide the bridge between general considerations of justice and the particular decision of the case.

Legality and justice are distinct concepts and values, and are capable of competing with each other. But each of the two values can be fully realized only in conjunction with the other. Outside the context of law, the idea of justice can seem empty and arbitrary: even if invoking justice is not like banging on the table to reinforce a demand,[37] it still seems to leave plenty of room for individual variation of opinion. Detached from its background in justice, the law will be a set of rules permeated by penumbral situations where the will of the judge must be decisive. Only in the union of legality and justice is either idea fully realizable.

---

[37] Alf Ross, *On Law and Justice* (London: Stevens, 1958) 274.

Index